50% OFF CNA Test Prep Course!

Dear Customer,

We consider it an honor and a privilege that you chose our CNA Study Guide. As a way of showing our appreciation and to help us better serve you, we have partnered with Mometrix Test Preparation to offer you **50% off their online CNA Prep Course.** Many Certified Nursing Assistant courses are needlessly expensive and don't deliver enough value. With their course, you get access to the best CNA prep material, and you only pay half price.

Mometrix has structured their online course to perfectly complement your printed study guide. The CNA Test Prep Course contains **in-depth lessons** that cover all the most important topics, over **400 practice questions** to ensure you feel prepared, more than **320 flashcards** for studying on the go, and over **10 instructional videos**.

Online CNA Prep Course

Topics Covered:

Physical Care Skills

- o Body mechanics
- o Infection Control
- o Emergencies
- o Restorative Skills

Psychosocial Care Skills

- o Maslow's Hierarchy of Needs
- o Age-Related Needs and Abuse
- o Spiritual and Cultural Needs

Role of the Nurse Aide

- o Client Rights
- o Legal Behavior
- o Ethical Behavior
- o Communication

And More!

Course Features:

CNA Study Guide

- o Get access to content from the best reviewed study guide available.

Track Your Progress

- o Their customized course allows you to check off content you have studied or feel confident with.

6 Full-Length Practice Tests

- o With 400+ practice questions and lesson reviews, you can test yourself again and again to build confidence.

CNA Flashcards

- o Their course includes a flashcard mode consisting of over 300 content cards to help you study.

To receive this discount, visit them at www.mometrix.com/university/cna or simply scan this QR code with your smartphone. At the checkout page, enter the discount code: **TPBCNA50**

If you have any questions or concerns, please contact them at universityhelp@mometrix.com.

SCAN HERE

Test Prep Books in partnership with **Mometrix** TEST PREPARATION

FREE Test Taking Tips Video/DVD Offer

To better serve you, we created videos covering test taking tips that we want to give you for FREE. **These videos cover world-class tips that will help you succeed on your test.**

We just ask that you send us feedback about this product. Please let us know what you thought about it—whether good, bad, or indifferent.

To get your **FREE videos**, you can use the QR code below or email freevideos@studyguideteam.com with "Free Videos" in the subject line and the following information in the body of the email:

  a. The title of your product
  b. Your product rating on a scale of 1-5, with 5 being the highest
  c. Your feedback about the product

If you have any questions or concerns, please don't hesitate to contact us at info@studyguideteam.com.

Thank you!

CNA Study Guide 2023-2024

4 Practice Tests and Certified Nursing Assistant Exam Prep Book [6th Edition]

Joshua Rueda

Written and edited by TPB Publishing.

TPB Publishing is not associated with or endorsed by any official testing organization. TPB Publishing is a publisher of unofficial educational products. All test and organization names are trademarks of their respective owners. Content in this book is included for utilitarian purposes only and does not constitute an endorsement by TPB Publishing of any particular point of view.

Interested in buying more than 10 copies of our product? Contact us about bulk discounts: bulkorders@studyguideteam.com

ISBN 13: 9781637754337
ISBN 10: 1637754337

Table of Contents

Welcome

Dear Reader,

Welcome to your new Test Prep Books study guide! We are pleased that you chose us to help you prepare for your exam. There are many study options to choose from, and we appreciate you choosing us. Studying can be a daunting task, but we have designed a smart, effective study guide to help prepare you for what lies ahead.

Whether you're a parent helping your child learn and grow, a high school student working hard to get into your dream college, or a nursing student studying for a complex exam, we want to help give you the tools you need to succeed. We hope this study guide gives you the skills and the confidence to thrive, and we can't thank you enough for allowing us to be part of your journey.

In an effort to continue to improve our products, we welcome feedback from our customers. We look forward to hearing from you. Suggestions, success stories, and criticisms can all be communicated by emailing us at info@studyguideteam.com.

Sincerely,
Test Prep Books Team

FREE Videos/DVD OFFER

Doing well on your exam requires both knowing the test content and understanding how to use that knowledge to do well on the test. We offer completely FREE test taking tip videos. **These videos cover world-class tips that you can use to succeed on your test.**

To get your **FREE videos**, you can use the QR code below or email freevideos@studyguideteam.com with "Free Videos" in the subject line and the following information in the body of the email:

      a. The title of your product
      b. Your product rating on a scale of 1-5, with 5 being the highest
      c. Your feedback about the product

If you have any questions or concerns, please don't hesitate to contact us at info@studyguideteam.com.

1

Quick Overview

As you draw closer to taking your exam, effective preparation becomes more and more important. Thankfully, you have this study guide to help you get ready. Use this guide to help keep your studying on track and refer to it often.

This study guide contains several key sections that will help you be successful on your exam. The guide contains tips for what you should do the night before and the day of the test. Also included are test-taking tips. Knowing the right information is not always enough. Many well-prepared test takers struggle with exams. These tips will help equip you to accurately read, assess, and answer test questions.

A large part of the guide is devoted to showing you what content to expect on the exam and to helping you better understand that content. In this guide are practice test questions so that you can see how well you have grasped the content. Then, answer explanations are provided so that you can understand why you missed certain questions.

Don't try to cram the night before you take your exam. This is not a wise strategy for a few reasons. First, your retention of the information will be low. Your time would be better used by reviewing information you already know rather than trying to learn a lot of new information. Second, you will likely become stressed as you try to gain a large amount of knowledge in a short amount of time. Third, you will be depriving yourself of sleep. So be sure to go to bed at a reasonable time the night before. Being well-rested helps you focus and remain calm.

Be sure to eat a substantial breakfast the morning of the exam. If you are taking the exam in the afternoon, be sure to have a good lunch as well. Being hungry is distracting and can make it difficult to focus. You have hopefully spent lots of time preparing for the exam. Don't let an empty stomach get in the way of success!

When travelling to the testing center, leave earlier than needed. That way, you have a buffer in case you experience any delays. This will help you remain calm and will keep you from missing your appointment time at the testing center.

Be sure to pace yourself during the exam. Don't try to rush through the exam. There is no need to risk performing poorly on the exam just so you can leave the testing center early. Allow yourself to use all of the allotted time if needed.

Remain positive while taking the exam even if you feel like you are performing poorly. Thinking about the content you should have mastered will not help you perform better on the exam.

Once the exam is complete, take some time to relax. Even if you feel that you need to take the exam again, you will be well served by some down time before you begin studying again. It's often easier to convince yourself to study if you know that it will come with a reward!

Test-Taking Strategies

1. Predicting the Answer

When you feel confident in your preparation for a multiple-choice test, try predicting the answer before reading the answer choices. This is especially useful on questions that test objective factual knowledge. By predicting the answer before reading the available choices, you eliminate the possibility that you will be distracted or led astray by an incorrect answer choice. You will feel more confident in your selection if you read the question, predict the answer, and then find your prediction among the answer choices. After using this strategy, be sure to still read all of the answer choices carefully and completely. If you feel unprepared, you should not attempt to predict the answers. This would be a waste of time and an opportunity for your mind to wander in the wrong direction.

2. Reading the Whole Question

Too often, test takers scan a multiple-choice question, recognize a few familiar words, and immediately jump to the answer choices. Test authors are aware of this common impatience, and they will sometimes prey upon it. For instance, a test author might subtly turn the question into a negative, or he or she might redirect the focus of the question right at the end. The only way to avoid falling into these traps is to read the entirety of the question carefully before reading the answer choices.

3. Looking for Wrong Answers

Long and complicated multiple-choice questions can be intimidating. One way to simplify a difficult multiple-choice question is to eliminate all of the answer choices that are clearly wrong. In most sets of answers, there will be at least one selection that can be dismissed right away. If the test is administered on paper, the test taker could draw a line through it to indicate that it may be ignored; otherwise, the test taker will have to perform this operation mentally or on scratch paper. In either case, once the obviously incorrect answers have been eliminated, the remaining choices may be considered. Sometimes identifying the clearly wrong answers will give the test taker some information about the correct answer. For instance, if one of the remaining answer choices is a direct opposite of one of the eliminated answer choices, it may well be the correct answer. The opposite of obviously wrong is obviously right! Of course, this is not always the case. Some answers are obviously incorrect simply because they are irrelevant to the question being asked. Still, identifying and eliminating some incorrect answer choices is a good way to simplify a multiple-choice question.

4. Don't Overanalyze

Anxious test takers often overanalyze questions. When you are nervous, your brain will often run wild, causing you to make associations and discover clues that don't actually exist. If you feel that this may be a problem for you, do whatever you can to slow down during the test. Try taking a deep breath or counting to ten. As you read and consider the question, restrict yourself to the particular words used by the author. Avoid thought tangents about what the author *really* meant, or what he or she was *trying* to say. The only things that matter on a multiple-choice test are the words that are actually in the question. You must avoid reading too much into a multiple-choice question, or supposing that the writer meant something other than what he or she wrote.

3

5. No Need for Panic

It is wise to learn as many strategies as possible before taking a multiple-choice test, but it is likely that you will come across a few questions for which you simply don't know the answer. In this situation, avoid panicking. Because most multiple-choice tests include dozens of questions, the relative value of a single wrong answer is small. As much as possible, you should compartmentalize each question on a multiple-choice test. In other words, you should not allow your feelings about one question to affect your success on the others. When you find a question that you either don't understand or don't know how to answer, just take a deep breath and do your best. Read the entire question slowly and carefully. Try rephrasing the question a couple of different ways. Then, read all of the answer choices carefully. After eliminating obviously wrong answers, make a selection and move on to the next question.

6. Confusing Answer Choices

When working on a difficult multiple-choice question, there may be a tendency to focus on the answer choices that are the easiest to understand. Many people, whether consciously or not, gravitate to the answer choices that require the least concentration, knowledge, and memory. This is a mistake. When you come across an answer choice that is confusing, you should give it extra attention. A question might be confusing because you do not know the subject matter to which it refers. If this is the case, don't eliminate the answer before you have affirmatively settled on another. When you come across an answer choice of this type, set it aside as you look at the remaining choices. If you can confidently assert that one of the other choices is correct, you can leave the confusing answer aside. Otherwise, you will need to take a moment to try to better understand the confusing answer choice. Rephrasing is one way to tease out the sense of a confusing answer choice.

7. Your First Instinct

Many people struggle with multiple-choice tests because they overthink the questions. If you have studied sufficiently for the test, you should be prepared to trust your first instinct once you have carefully and completely read the question and all of the answer choices. There is a great deal of research suggesting that the mind can come to the correct conclusion very quickly once it has obtained all of the relevant information. At times, it may seem to you as if your intuition is working faster even than your reasoning mind. This may in fact be true. The knowledge you obtain while studying may be retrieved from your subconscious before you have a chance to work out the associations that support it. Verify your instinct by working out the reasons that it should be trusted.

8. Key Words

Many test takers struggle with multiple-choice questions because they have poor reading comprehension skills. Quickly reading and understanding a multiple-choice question requires a mixture of skill and experience. To help with this, try jotting down a few key words and phrases on a piece of scrap paper. Doing this concentrates the process of reading and forces the mind to weigh the relative importance of the question's parts. In selecting words and phrases to write down, the test taker thinks about the question more deeply and carefully. This is especially true for multiple-choice questions that are preceded by a long prompt.

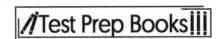

9. Subtle Negatives

One of the oldest tricks in the multiple-choice test writer's book is to subtly reverse the meaning of a question with a word like *not* or *except*. If you are not paying attention to each word in the question, you can easily be led astray by this trick. For instance, a common question format is, "Which of the following is…?" Obviously, if the question instead is, "Which of the following is not…?," then the answer will be quite different. Even worse, the test makers are aware of the potential for this mistake and will include one answer choice that would be correct if the question were not negated or reversed. A test taker who misses the reversal will find what he or she believes to be a correct answer and will be so confident that he or she will fail to reread the question and discover the original error. The only way to avoid this is to practice a wide variety of multiple-choice questions and to pay close attention to each and every word.

10. Reading Every Answer Choice

It may seem obvious, but you should always read every one of the answer choices! Too many test takers fall into the habit of scanning the question and assuming that they understand the question because they recognize a few key words. From there, they pick the first answer choice that answers the question they believe they have read. Test takers who read all of the answer choices might discover that one of the latter answer choices is actually *more* correct. Moreover, reading all of the answer choices can remind you of facts related to the question that can help you arrive at the correct answer. Sometimes, a misstatement or incorrect detail in one of the latter answer choices will trigger your memory of the subject and will enable you to find the right answer. Failing to read all of the answer choices is like not reading all of the items on a restaurant menu: you might miss out on the perfect choice.

11. Spot the Hedges

One of the keys to success on multiple-choice tests is paying close attention to every word. This is never truer than with words like almost, most, some, and sometimes. These words are called "hedges" because they indicate that a statement is not totally true or not true in every place and time. An absolute statement will contain no hedges, but in many subjects, the answers are not always straightforward or absolute. There are always exceptions to the rules in these subjects. For this reason, you should favor those multiple-choice questions that contain hedging language. The presence of qualifying words indicates that the author is taking special care with their words, which is certainly important when composing the right answer. After all, there are many ways to be wrong, but there is only one way to be right! For this reason, it is wise to avoid answers that are absolute when taking a multiple-choice test. An absolute answer is one that says things are either all one way or all another. They often include words like *every*, *always*, *best*, and *never*. If you are taking a multiple-choice test in a subject that doesn't lend itself to absolute answers, be on your guard if you see any of these words.

12. Long Answers

In many subject areas, the answers are not simple. As already mentioned, the right answer often requires hedges. Another common feature of the answers to a complex or subjective question are qualifying clauses, which are groups of words that subtly modify the meaning of the sentence. If the question or answer choice describes a rule to which there are exceptions or the subject matter is complicated, ambiguous, or confusing, the correct answer will require many words in order to be expressed clearly and accurately. In essence, you should not be deterred by answer choices that seem

5

excessively long. Oftentimes, the author of the text will not be able to write the correct answer without offering some qualifications and modifications. Your job is to read the answer choices thoroughly and completely and to select the one that most accurately and precisely answers the question.

13. Restating to Understand

Sometimes, a question on a multiple-choice test is difficult not because of what it asks but because of how it is written. If this is the case, restate the question or answer choice in different words. This process serves a couple of important purposes. First, it forces you to concentrate on the core of the question. In order to rephrase the question accurately, you have to understand it well. Rephrasing the question will concentrate your mind on the key words and ideas. Second, it will present the information to your mind in a fresh way. This process may trigger your memory and render some useful scrap of information picked up while studying.

14. True Statements

Sometimes an answer choice will be true in itself, but it does not answer the question. This is one of the main reasons why it is essential to read the question carefully and completely before proceeding to the answer choices. Too often, test takers skip ahead to the answer choices and look for true statements. Having found one of these, they are content to select it without reference to the question above. Obviously, this provides an easy way for test makers to play tricks. The savvy test taker will always read the entire question before turning to the answer choices. Then, having settled on a correct answer choice, he or she will refer to the original question and ensure that the selected answer is relevant. The mistake of choosing a correct-but-irrelevant answer choice is especially common on questions related to specific pieces of objective knowledge. A prepared test taker will have a wealth of factual knowledge at their disposal and should not be careless in its application.

15. No Patterns

One of the more dangerous ideas that circulates about multiple-choice tests is that the correct answers tend to fall into patterns. These erroneous ideas range from a belief that B and C are the most common right answers, to the idea that an unprepared test-taker should answer "A-B-A-C-A-D-A-B-A." It cannot be emphasized enough that pattern-seeking of this type is exactly the WRONG way to approach a multiple-choice test. To begin with, it is highly unlikely that the test maker will plot the correct answers according to some predetermined pattern. The questions are scrambled and delivered in a random order. Furthermore, even if the test maker was following a pattern in the assignation of correct answers, there is no reason why the test taker would know which pattern he or she was using. Any attempt to discern a pattern in the answer choices is a waste of time and a distraction from the real work of taking the test. A test taker would be much better served by extra preparation before the test than by reliance on a pattern in the answers.

Introduction to the CNA Exam

Function of the Test

All prospective nursing assistants in the United States must pass a proficiency exam to measure clinical skills prior to certification. Some states refer to a nursing assistant as a Certified Nursing Aide, but titles vary from state to state. Although there is no one official test—each state is allowed to establish their own guidelines for certification—many states use core criteria and similar exams. Over twenty states use the National Nurse Aid Assessment Program (NNAAP) competency exam, including California, Colorado, Georgia, North Carolina, Pennsylvania, Virginia, and Washington. Other states such as Arizona, Tennessee, Oregon, and Ohio use Diversified Technologies as their certification vendor, and Florida, Michigan, and New York use a system provided by Prometric.

The exam is comprised of two parts: a written or oral section, and a skills validation segment. The oral section is available in both English and Spanish. Candidates must attain passing scores on both parts of the test before their name can be added to the state nursing assistant registry. The state registry serves as a guarantee for employers that a potential job candidate has met the federal and state requirements for hiring.

Test Administration

Since every state's nursing assistant program is different, nursing assistant exam testing centers, fees, and special rules related to students with disabilities vary from state to state. The test is offered at a variety of locations, including nursing homes, hospitals, community colleges, and American Red Cross facilities.

Candidates typically have up to two years and three attempts after completion of training to pass both parts of the exam. If a candidate fails one portion of the test, then only that section needs to be retaken; an additional fee applies to retake the exam or portion of the exam. A candidate who fails a third time within the two-year timeframe must go back to nursing school to repeat training.

Test Format

Because there is not one standard nursing assistant exam, the structure of each test may vary slightly from one state to another. However, the overall content is very similar. The written exam is typically comprised of a series of multiple-choice questions. Candidates are tested on topics such as medical safety, infection control, patient care, mental health, personal care, communication, patient charting, disease process, older adult growth, basic nursing skills, and the role and duties of a nursing assistant. For the skills section, candidates need to show how well they perform the required clinical responsibilities of a certified nursing assistant. Most tests require the completion of three to six various tasks on a simulated patient. Many test facilities ask candidates to bring a friend or family member to act as a stand-in for the patient.

The number of questions and time allowed for the exam also varies from state to state, but candidates usually have up to two hours to complete the written section of the test, which contains an average of sixty questions. Some states require candidates to complete this portion before starting the skills portion of the test. Most tests contain ten random questions that are not scored, and therefore not

7

included on the final score report. The time frame for the skills section is usually between twenty and thirty minutes.

Scoring

Minimum passing scores for the Nursing Assistant Competency Exam vary by state. Typically, a score of 80 percent or higher is required to pass, although 70 or 75 percent is considered a passing grade in certain states. Although a percentage system is occasionally used to grade the skills portion of the exam, it is usually assessed using a pass or fail methodology.

Study Prep Plan for the CNA Exam

1 **Schedule -** Use one of our study schedules below or come up with one of your own.

2 **Relax -** Test anxiety can hurt even the best students. There are many ways to reduce stress. Find the one that works best for you.

3 **Execute -** Once you have a good plan in place, be sure to stick to it.

One Week Study Schedule		
Day 1	Role of the Nursing Assistant
Day 2	Promotion of Safety
Day 3	Promotion of Function and Health of...
Day 4	Providing Specialized Care for Residents...
Day 5	Practice Tests #1 & #2
Day 6	Practice Tests #3 & #4
Day 7	Take Your Exam!

Two Week Study Schedule			
Day 1	Role of the Nursing Assistant	Day 8	Providing Specialized Care for Residents...
Day 2	Promotion of Safety	Day 9	Psychological Problems
Day 3	Safety Devices	Day 10	Practice Test #1
Day 4	Emergencies	Day 11	Practice Test #2
Day 5	Promotion of Function and Health of Residents	Day 12	Practice Test #3
Day 6	Basic Nursing Care Provided by...	Day 13	Practice Test #4
Day 7	Acute Emergency Situations	Day 14	Take Your Exam!

One Month Study Schedule							
Day 1	Personal Responsibility	Day 11	Effects of Immobility	Day 21	Practice Test #1
Day 2	Promotion and Protection of...	Day 12	Practice Questions	Day 22	Answer Explanations #1
Day 3	Nurse Aide as a Member of the Health Care Team	Day 13	Basic Nursing Care Provided by the Nursing Assistant	Day 23	Practice Test #2
Day 4	Promotion of Safety	Day 14	Acute Emergency Situations	Day 24	Answer Explanations #2
Day 5	Safety and Comfort	Day 15	Vomiting	Day 25	Practice Test #3
Day 6	Safety Devices	Day 16	Sudden Onset of Confusion or Agitation	Day 26	Answer Explanations #3
Day 7	Emergencies	Day 17	Providing Specialized Care for Residents...	Day 27	Practice Test #4
Day 8	Evacuation Procedures	Day 18	Psychological Problems	Day 28	Answer Explanations #4
Day 9	Promotion of Function and Health of Residents	Day 19	Care of the Dying Resident and Post-Mortem Care	Day 29	Rest Day!
Day 10	Health Maintenance/ Restoration	Day 20	Rest Day!	Day 30	Take Your Exam!

Build your own prep plan by visiting:

testprepbooks.com/prep

Role of the Nursing Assistant

Personal Responsibility

Nursing assistants are vital members of a health care team. The nursing assistant is required to act professionally, take their role seriously, and give respectful care within their scope of practice. The following is a discussion of the legal aspects of this role, as well as rights of the residents, how to take care of oneself, and how to communicate effectively with residents and other members of the health care team.

Reporting Requirements

The nursing assistant is an additional set of eyes and ears that monitors a resident's care along with the rest of the health care team. As such, it is the duty of the nursing assistant to report pertinent information to the correct person or entity. Information to be reported includes data, such as abnormal vital signs, changes in a resident's condition, such as unusual behavior, and any suspicion of abuse or neglect. Any violation of ethical resident care must be reported to the appropriate entity.

Chain of Command

When reporting information, it is important that the nursing assistant reports to the correct person. There is a **chain of command** within most health care facilities and in each different health care team that must be followed. When the chain of command is followed, issues are reported to the person in the position to best handle the situation and are resolved more quickly as a result.

The **nursing assistant** reports resident information, such as abnormal vital signs, to the nurse in charge of the patient in question. The nursing assistant may share residents with several different **nurses** and needs to report pertinent data to the correct nurse. The nurse can then assess and intervene as necessary.

Issues between the nursing assistant and the nurse may be reported to the **charge nurse**. The charge nurse is in charge of all the nurses on duty for a particular shift. Charge nurses will likely be in charge of assigning residents to nurses and nursing assistants. If there is an issue with a resident assignment, the charge nurse can amend it.

Above the charge nurse is the **nurse manager** of the unit. Any issue that remains unresolved by the charge nurse can be reported to the nurse manager. If an issue has been brought to the charge nurse, but still needs to be escalated further, it can go to the nurse manager or higher. The nurse manager oversees the functioning of the unit, resident outcomes, and employee performance. Additionally, they provide guidance and discipline when needed.

Depending on the size of the organization, there may be a **nurse director** over several units and/or a **chief nursing officer** (CNO) overseeing the facility's nursing staff. Both are above the nurse manager in the chain of command. They oversee big-picture operations within the facility. They may come to resident care areas to talk about projects for improving care, ask questions of the nursing assistants and nurses, and get a feel for how the work environment is operating.

11

Legal Reporting Obligations

Reporting resident information and work issues in a timely manner and using the correct route on the chain of command are a legal obligation of the nursing assistant. Not reporting important information could result in serious ramifications and punitive action for the nursing assistant, up to loss of employment and/or revocation of certification. When important information goes unreported, it can result in resident harm or unresolved conflicts that turn into bigger problems to deal with later on. Addressing resident issues and resolving conflicts all start with accurate and timely reporting.

Elements in Reporting

A basic definition of a **report** is the relaying of information that one has observed or heard. When this report is given to an authority figure who can intervene, it will contain different elements, such as resident name, situation, time of event, and circumstances surrounding the event.

As one shift ends and another begins, there is a **handoff report** that is given from the off-going team to the oncoming team. The nursing assistant who has completed the shift will tell the nursing assistant beginning the next shift all pertinent information related to each individual resident. Another type of reporting is the exchange of smaller pieces of information between members of the health care team that occurs throughout a shift.

In the handoff report, the nursing assistant should strategically relay information in a simple, concise manner that is easily understood by the oncoming nursing assistant. It can be easy to get carried away with reporting and include every little detail of the day, opinions about residents or other coworkers, and stories of particular conversations or interactions that occurred during the shift. These superfluous details should be limited, and the report should be kept to the essential items only.

Some organizations employ the **SBAR method** to help guide communication. SBAR is an acronym for situation, background, assessment, and recommendation. An SBAR report starts with the situation: why is this communication necessary? The background is a brief explanation of the circumstances leading up to the situation. The assessment is what the reporter thinks the issue is, and the recommendation is what the reporter needs in order to correct the situation.

Legalities Related to Documentation

In addition to reporting resident information, the documenting of resident information and interventions performed is also important. A resident's chart is a legal record of observations about the resident and any care given for the resident. Most facilities use an electronic health record, which the nursing assistant will generally be trained to use as a part of new employee orientation. Documentation may include time of observation, time task was performed, what was done, how it was done, and reaction to intervention.

There are various charting systems used to document resident data by resident care facilities. Documentation requirements will be dictated by facility policy and regulatory guidelines. Two methods are used: charting by exception and comprehensive charting.

Charting by Exception

Charting by exception means that besides recording of vital signs, only abnormal findings are documented. This charting method is somewhat controversial as so much information about the resident is usually left out. It is sometimes argued that this is the safer way to chart, as only what is deviant from normal is noted, and thus, there is less room for documentation errors. The normal is

12

deviant from normal is noted, and thus, there is less room for documentation errors. The normal is assumed, unless otherwise noted. This method also saves time, as less information needs to be documented, leaving more time for resident care.

Comprehensive Charting

Some facilities prefer a **comprehensive method** of documentation, charting everything about the resident—normal and abnormal—in a very thorough manner. This way, when the resident's chart must be reviewed, especially in the case of a safety incident (e.g., a pressure sore develops or a resident falls), all details surrounding the event should be present in the medical record. This method works as long as everything is actually documented, although it can be quite time-consuming and take away from resident care time.

Documentation provides a defense for health care workers and residents in the case of resident incidents to show what was done for the resident. There is an adage that says, "If it wasn't charted, it didn't happen." The nursing assistant needs to be mindful that the medical record is a legal document— a complete, thorough, and accurate documentation of care, according to facility policy.

Common Health Care Terminology and Abbreviations

Upon entering the health care field, the nursing assistant will learn that there is a special language spoken by those working within it. This language contains abbreviations and special terms used to communicate resident information. A lot of medical terminology is based on the Latin language, with which many modern English speakers may not be familiar.

Part of the nursing assistant's training will include health care terminology. As with any language, the more one is absorbed in a culture that speaks it, the more one will be able to understand and speak it. The following is a list of common health care terminology and abbreviations that the nursing assistant may encounter:

- **AC:** before meals
- **AKA:** above the knee amputation
- Anuric: not producing any urine
- **BID:** twice a day
- **BKA:** below the knee amputation
- BP: blood pressure
- C/O: complains of
- **COPD:** chronic obstructive pulmonary disease
- **CVA:** cerebrovascular accident (stroke)
- DM I or II: diabetes mellitus I or II
- DNR: do not resuscitate
- Fx: fracture of a bone
- H&P: history and physical
- H/O: history of
- HTN: hypertension (high blood pressure)
- mL: milliliters
- N/V: nausea, vomiting
- NPO: nothing by mouth
- PO: by mouth

13

- PRN: as needed
- Q2H: every two hours
- Q4H: every four hours
- QAM: every morning
- R/O: rule out
- SO**B**: shortness of breath
- SQ: subcutaneous
- T: temperature
- TI**D**: three times a day
- UTI: urinary tract infection
- VSS: vital signs stable
- Wt: weight

This list is a small sample of the broad expanse of terms and abbreviations commonly used in the health care field. The nursing assistant need not feel intimidated by this new language, however, as it is learned as one is immersed in the health care environment.

Factors Affecting Routine Versus Urgent Reporting

The nursing assistant must make a distinction between **routine** and **urgent** findings. If a piece of resident information is routine, reporting it may be delayed; if it is urgent it needs to be reported to the nurse right away. The nursing assistant may need to delay reporting certain bits of information due to a busy resident care schedule filled with call lights, scheduled tasks, and resident and family demands on time. Many units now have mobile phones for staff to carry and use to make calls or send text messages about resident care to coworkers, aiding quick communication.

Abnormal vital signs or changes in behavior signaling a worsening in condition—such as confusion or agitation and any other changes that appear to be affecting or have the potential to affect resident safety—need to be reported and acted upon immediately. If the resident does not appear to be in any danger, reporting may be delayed for a time. The nurse aid must practice extreme caution when delaying reporting information and always put the safety and wellbeing of the resident first.

Promotion of Personal Health and Safety

The nursing assistant is not only responsible for taking care of the resident, but their own health as well. If the nursing assistant is not healthy, then they may not have the proper focus or adequate energy to provide care for the resident.

Principles of Body Mechanics

One way the nursing assistant can take care of themselves is to employ proper body mechanics. The job of the nursing assistant is often highly physical in nature, with much time being spent on turning residents in bed, transferring them from the bed to the chair or bedside commode, and assisting with **ambulating** (walking) residents to the bathroom or around the unit. Moving another person, especially one with limited ability to assist, can be extremely difficult and taxing on the body.

Depending on the facility in which the nursing assistant works, different equipment will be available to assist with moving residents. Becoming acquainted with how and when to use this equipment will be

14

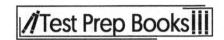

part of the nursing assistant's training in that facility. The nursing assistant should use this equipment whenever possible, even if it takes a little more time to do so.

Basic **safe lifting techniques** include lifting with one's legs, not one's back, avoiding twisting and awkward positions when lifting and moving the resident, and keeping the back upright as much as possible to avoid straining. The individual should make sure to keep their feet as balanced as possible and not rush lifting or moving a resident. The nursing assistant should ask for help from other nursing assistants or nurses whenever needed to avoid injury.

Injury Prevention

A member of the health care team who is not careful could easily become injured, potentially resulting in physical harm, missed days of work, lost wages, and medical bills. Nursing assistants are at high risk for injury due to the amount of lifting they do during a shift. Using the appropriate lifting techniques can help prevent an injury to the back and strains or sprains to the joints of the body. The nursing assistant should employ assistive devices such as gait belts and mechanical lifting devices whenever possible. It is important to ask for help whenever necessary to prevent injury. The following depicts eight steps to use when lifting a heavy object:

- 1. Plan for lift and test the load
- 2. Ask someone for help
- 3. Get a firm footing
- 4. Bend your knees
- 5. Tighten stomach muscles
- 6. Lift with legs
- 7. Keep the load close to you
- 8. Keep your back straight

Self-Care

The job of a nursing assistant is physically, mentally, and emotionally stressful. The strain of moving and lifting residents, along with going from room to room constantly answering the needs of the residents for a long shift, can be physically exhausting. One must organize one's time, prioritize tasks, answer questions, and have countless conversations with the health care team and residents and their families, all of which can take a mental toll. Dealing with residents who are sick, in pain, suffering, and, in some cases, facing death, can drain a nursing assistant's emotional reserves, which can quickly lead to burnout if left unaddressed. Being aware of this potential for overall fatigue is the first step to managing stress and maintaining one's own health.

It is important that a nursing assistant knows how to cope with the effects of stress positively. **Negative coping mechanisms** include unhealthy eating habits and binging behavior, abusing substances such as alcohol and drugs, acting recklessly with one's own safety, and becoming abusive in personal relationships.

Positive coping mechanisms include finding an activity to engage in to unwind and relieve stress in a healthy way. Activities such as daily exercise, spending quality time with friends and family, cooking, yoga, biking, and hiking are all ways to deal with the stress of a demanding job in a healthy way.

The nursing assistant should be careful not to work too many hours as well. It can be tempting to take on extra shifts continually to earn extra money for gifts, vacations, or simply to pay the bills and support

a family. These extra shifts and long hours can put a nursing assistant in a danger zone if they are using up too much mental, physical, and/or emotional energy. It is better to be well rested and have adequate mental and physical energy for a shift than to put the resident and oneself at risk for harm.

Being properly nourished, getting adequate exercise, and maintaining healthy sleep habits will all positively contribute to a nursing assistant's health. The nursing assistant's health is vital to helping their residents regain or maintain their own health and, thus, should be made a high priority. If one needs help learning healthy eating habits, meal planning, how to get involved in an exercise program or routine, or other methods of managing stress, many facilities have programs to help guide employees toward better health. There are a plethora of available online resources aimed at improving one's health as well.

Promotion and Protection of Resident Rights

Each resident has certain rights that must be respected. When residents are admitted to a facility, they are put in a position of vulnerability. This special position of power held by the health care provider should never be abused to violate the rights of the resident. Caring for a resident is an honor, and certain rules of conduct should be followed. The following will be a discussion of resident's rights, violations, and consequences of violations, as well as appropriate avenues of reporting.

Resident Rights

The resident has the right to have health information kept private, and only shared with those who are given permission to view it. The **Health Insurance Portability and Accountability Act (HIPAA)** was passed by Congress in 1996 to protect health information. The term HIPAA is often used to reference resident privacy. There are many different ways a resident's personal health information can be shared: verbally, digitally, over the phone or fax, or through written messages.

The nursing assistant plays an important role in keeping a resident's health information private. Sharing personal details—such as a resident's name, condition, and medical history—in an inappropriate way violates the person's right to privacy. For example, telling a friend who does not work in the facility that the nursing assistant took care of the friend's aunt, without the aunt's consent or knowledge, is considered a violation of privacy. Another way a nursing assistant could violate a resident's privacy is to access the medical record when they are not actually caring for that particular resident. For example, if a celebrity has been admitted to a different unit, and the nursing assistant—curious to find out the details—accesses the celebrity's electronic health record, then they are in violation of HIPAA. Those who violate HIPAA and are caught could lose their jobs, among other punitive actions.

Along with protecting the resident's health information, the nursing assistant must be respectful of the resident's privacy in general. Knocking on the resident's door before entering the room, keeping the door shut to the busy corridor outside the room, and not asking unnecessary personal questions are all ways the nursing assistant can extend common courtesy to the resident. The nature of the nursing assistant's relationship with the resident is already quite personal in nature (e.g., the nursing assistant is giving the resident baths, helping him or her go to the bathroom, etc.), so there is no need to exploit that relationship.

The resident has the right of **self-determination**, which means that he or she has the right to make decisions regarding their own health care. Residents are members of the health care team along with the doctors, nurses, and nursing assistants. What the nursing assistant may think is the right course of

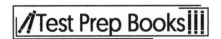

action for a resident may not align with what the resident thinks is right, and that is to be respected. The health care team forms the plan of care and educates the resident as to what a plan entails, but it is the resident who makes the final decision to accept or reject a plan. If the resident is not capable of making their own decisions, the **power of attorney**—usually a close family member such as a wife, husband, or adult child—has the power to make health care decisions for the resident.

Along with self-determination, the residents also have the freedom to express themselves and their opinions. Simply being admitted to a facility does not take away their freedom of speech. Residents may have opinions about all aspects of their care, and they have every right to express these feelings. The nursing assistant needs to be respectful, listen, and try to help when there is a problem that can be solved. Issues voiced by residents can always be escalated by the nursing assistant, using the appropriate chain of command.

Each resident has the right to fair treatment. This means that no resident should be treated any better or worse than another resident for any reason, such as a racial bias or unfair prejudice based on the nursing assistant's personal opinions and beliefs. Giving one resident preferential treatment over another is a violation of the resident's rights, and the nursing assistant will be subject to disciplinary action if they are discovered to be treating residents poorly.

No resident should ever be abused or neglected. This should go without saying, but it is a resident right that is perhaps the most important. Abuse can be physical, emotional, sexual, mental, or financial. Neglect is when the resident's needs are being ignored, usually resulting in resident harm.

Residents who receive care from medical professionals, whether in a medical facility or in the resident's living environment, are legally entitled to safe experiences that promote the quality of the patient's overall health and life. Abuse and neglect in these contexts are criminal offenses. In addition to receiving competent medical care from licensed and credentialed workers, residents are also entitled to be treated with respect and compassion, to participate socially, and to have experiences that are free from prejudice and discrimination. When residents enter a care facility, these rights should be documented and shared with the patient so that an adequate expectation regarding the nursing experience is established between both the provider and the patient.

Responsibility for Recognizing and Reporting Violations

If the nursing assistant suspects abuse or neglect, they are mandatorily required to report it to the appropriate entity. The charge nurse and/or nurse manager should be notified, so the appropriate action can be taken to right the situation. There are also hotlines that can be called, such as the National Center on Elder Abuse (1-800-677-1116).

Resident Abuse

Resident abuse is a broad term that can encompass various types of harm that are inflicted upon a patient. These can include physical events, emotional or mental manipulation, and financial exploitation. While abuse may occur intentionally with malicious care providers, it can also occur unintentionally due to organizational factors such as staffing issues, lack of capital resources, and inadequate training. Residents are a vulnerable patient population, as they are often dependent on their caregivers to meet one or more basic needs. Family members or staff can and should report abuse. In the short term, emergency services can be called to provide immediate care to an abused patient, but in the long term, a facility suspected of abuse should be investigated through regulatory avenues at the state and federal level. Risk factors for resident abuse include patient demographics (for example, women and mentally ill

patients are statistically more likely to experience abuse), low staffing, high turnover rates, or limited check-ins with residents. Preventative measures focus on ensuring a high-quality care facility is chosen in the first place. A high-quality care facility allows current residents and families to share their experiences with prospective residents, has happy staff and low turnover and burnout rates, and is reputable and highly rated by regulatory bodies.

There are different types of abuse. **Physical abuse** involves injuries to the body from punching, kicking, etc. If the nursing assistant notes various bruises or cuts in various stages of healing without explanation, it may be a sign of physical abuse.

Additional signs of physical abuse include unexplained bruising, recurring illness, visible hygiene issues, broken bones, and visible changes in the patient's appearance, such as weight loss, dry and flaky skin, dry lips (a sign of dehydration), or noticeable bedsores. Physical abuse may occur from neglect, where a patient does not receive the full spectrum of care that they need.

Sexual abuse is when sexual contact is made without the consent of one party, including rape, coercion into doing sexual acts, and fondling of genitalia. The nursing assistant should look for unexplained bruising of or bleeding around the perineal area, new difficulty sitting or walking, or increased agitation/aggression as potential signs of sexual abuse.

New diagnoses of sexually transmitted infections are another sign that a resident is potentially experiencing sexual abuse. Additionally, residents may have noticeably awkward or inappropriate interactions with specific staff or family members. Residents may act too familiarly or may seem highly uncomfortable and anxious around people that have behaved inappropriately with them.

Emotional or **mental abuses** are not quite as obvious as physical abuse as the damage inflicted is internal or hidden. Emotional and mental abuses are usually caused by verbal assaults. The abuser may belittle and criticize the victim to the point that the victim feels worthless, insecure, and afraid. If the nursing assistant senses an uncomfortable relationship between an informal caregiver or family member and the resident, this should be monitored, investigated, and reported if abuse is suspected.

Since emotional and mental abuse can be difficult to immediately identify, it has the potential to cause significant long-term harm. Residents may have difficulty identifying their own emotions and thoughts to explain them to a caretaker. Residents may also be distrustful of all caretakers and refuse to share their feelings. Residents may show new signs of mood disorders, low self-esteem, aggression, and self-harm. These symptoms should serve as indicators for potential abuse.

Financial abuse is a type of abuse in which the abuser limits the victim's access to money and financial information, sometimes stealing directly from the victim without the victim's knowledge. Being the caregiver of an older person grants a person special access to personal documents and financial resources; this privilege can be abused. If the nursing assistant suspects that checks and other financial means meant for the resident are being rerouted and misused by a caregiver, this abuse should be reported right away.

Signs of financial abuse can include a new power of attorney, pieces of mail indicating that new lines of credit have been opened, or limited involvement from the resident in their own financial affairs. Residents who receive care may not have the mental or physical capacity to be fully involved in managing their finances but withholding all relevant information from the resident can be an indicator of financial exploitation.

managing their finances but withholding all relevant information from the resident can be an indicator of financial exploitation.

Diversity in the Workplace

Depending on the facility, a nursing assistant will potentially work with a diverse group of fellow health care workers as well as a diverse resident demographic. People from all different cultural, racial, religious, sexual, and economic backgrounds converge in health care, and the nursing assistant must know how to work within such an environment.

When working with a diverse population and with diverse peers, respectful behavior is the best strategy. The nursing assistant will encounter belief systems different from their own, manifested in what people wear, what they eat, how they behave, and lifestyle choices they make. The nursing assistant's initial reaction may be one of shock when they learn certain details about other cultures. It is healthy to be aware of these reactions and examine them and their origins. The best response is to educate oneself to cultivate a deeper appreciation for these different cultures, rather than making judgments or being dismissive.

A diverse workplace, serving a diverse population of residents, can be an enriching environment in which the individuals working together are greater than the sum of their parts. There is no reason why differences in beliefs, lifestyles, and cultures should hinder the work of caring for the sick. The nursing assistant steps into this world, becomes a part of it, and can take away a better understanding and broader perspective of the people of this planet.

Grievance and Dispute Resolution Techniques

There may be times during a nursing assistant's career where they have a grievance against the entity for which they are working or have a dispute with a peer or resident. This is another instance where the chain of command should be followed. Usually the nurse manager is the one to go to with issues that cannot be resolved by the charge nurses. The nurse manager can act as a mediator and meet with the two disputing parties and try to reach a resolution. It is in the best interest of the nursing assistant and all involved to remain professional during times of conflict, avoid personal attacks, and keep the issue private so as to not disrupt resident care.

Resident Personal Property

Each facility will have specific policies protecting the property of residents. When residents enter the facility, they are entrusting the staff to take care of certain items, such as clothing, family photos, and other treasured objects. The nursing assistant must follow facility policy regarding such items and take special care not to lose or damage them. Many residents will have designated spots in their rooms, such as closets and/or lock boxes, where items can be kept safe from theft and damage. Residents should be encouraged to keep valuables at home whenever possible.

Time Management and Work Prioritization

One of the most important skills a nursing assistant must master in the busy health care environment is that of time management and prioritization of tasks. The work day is filled with tasks, scheduled activities, unexpected time conflicts, and constant interruptions.

As best as the nursing assistant can, they should have a way of planning the day. Some find it best to have some sort of written system to take notes and jot down vitals in between charting periods. Meal times can be the busiest times of day, so it should be accounted for in planning.

Countless interruptions will occur throughout the day, such as a call light going off when the nursing assistant was planning to start a bath or a resident needing assistance to the bathroom when the nursing assistant was planning on taking a break. It is vital that the nurse prioritizes tasks and makes sure the most important tasks get done in a timely manner. It is easy to put off tasks for later that really should be done immediately, but that sort of procrastination can have adverse results. The day will be busy; that is a given. Developing one's time management and prioritization skills will help the day go a lot more smoothly.

Workplace Standards: Ethical and Unethical Behaviors

In any work environment, there are certain standards of professionalism that must be met. The nursing assistant's conduct, way of dress, and even conduct outside of work is subject to these high standards. As caregivers of those in need, this special honor comes with a duty to behave professionally and with propriety.

The nursing assistant must always behave in an ethical manner. Violating any of the discussed resident rights, such as privacy, the right to speak opinions, and the right to make health care decisions, will subject the nursing assistant to disciplinary action. Any abusive or neglectful behavior by the nursing assistant, as well as stealing or damaging resident property, will also put the nursing assistant at risk for punitive action.

In addition to workplace behavior, the nursing assistant has a responsibility to maintain a certain manner of decorum outside of work as well. Some states have regulations about how health care workers conduct themselves on social media. Any posts or photos on these websites that badly reflect on an organization, hint at resident abuse or slander, or portray the nursing assistant in a light that is below the standards of the organization may be subject to disciplinary action. Certain crimes and misdemeanors, such as driving while intoxicated, may also subject a nursing assistant to disciplinary action.

As a caregiver, the nursing assistant holds a place of honor in society. It is important that their conduct in and out of the workplace is exemplary of what a caring, compassionate individual should be.

Nurse Aide Registry

Each state has a **registry** in which each nursing assistant must register. Employers access this registry to verify eligibility for employment as a nursing assistant. The registry generally includes information about nursing assistant training and competency, criminal background check status, and any administrative findings of resident abuse, neglect, or misappropriation of property. Some states will not allow a nursing assistant to work after being convicted of certain crimes or may require additional documentation to complete a waiver or appeal prior to employment.

Certification Maintenance Procedures

The nursing assistant will be required to keep their certification and competencies current according to their state and employer. Every year to two years, depending on the state, the nursing assistant will

need to renew their certification. This usually entails a fee, as well as showing proof of a certain number of continuing education credits. These can usually be obtained through the facility in which one works or online. Competencies, such as **cardiopulmonary resuscitation (CPR)**, must be renewed according to facility policy, usually every two years.

Legal Ramifications of Abuse, Neglect, and/or Misappropriation of Property

The nursing assistant must be aware that there are serious legal consequences if they are found to be abusing, neglecting, or committing theft against a resident. Loss of job, revocation of certification, and even penalties within the criminal justice system are all potentialities the nursing assistant may face should they risk illegal and unethical behavior with a resident.

Employer's Responsibilities Prior to Hiring

Before a nursing assistant is hired into a facility or entity, the potential employer will go through a process to verify the nursing assistant's eligibility for hire. The employer will check the state registry of public health workers—which includes a criminal background check—to make sure the nursing assistant does not have a criminal history that would prevent employment. If the nursing assistant has a history, the employer will check to see that a waiver is in place that allows the aide to work. The employer will also look at and potentially contact references from previous places of employment to get an idea of the employee's character and work ethic.

Nurse Aide as a Member of the Health Care Team

The nursing assistant is an essential member of the health care team, providing invaluable care to individuals in need, as well as being an additional set of eyes and ears to monitor the resident's condition.

To become a nursing assistant, most states require at least seventy-five hours of training—including classroom instruction and clinical hours—verification of certain skills, and the passing of the state board of certification examination. In addition to initial certification, most states require the nursing assistant to provide proof of at least twelve hours of continuing education each year to maintain certification. The facility with which the nursing assistant is employed will often provide ways to complete these continuing education hours; otherwise, the nursing assistant should contact their supervisor for help completing continuing education hours.

Job Responsibilities of the Nurse Aide

The nursing assistant is an invaluable assistant to the nurse, overseeing the most basic elements of care. This care primarily entails helping the resident with **activities of daily living (ADLs)**. Activities that the nursing assistant will assist with include feeding, bathing, ambulating the resident, transferring the resident from bed to chair and back, turning and repositioning the resident in bed, keeping the room stocked with necessary supplies and linens, taking vital signs and reporting them to the nurse, and helping the resident with elimination. Another important function of the nursing assistant is to closely monitor the resident for any changes in condition or behavior and to report these changes to the nurse in a timely manner.

The nursing assistant must practice within their scope of practice and level of certification. The nursing assistant may not perform sterile procedures, insert or remove tubes or intravenous accesses (IVs) from the resident's body, administer medication, or take doctor's orders. Some facilities may have special

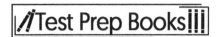

training available to allow exceptions to this list, but it is the responsibility of the nursing assistant to know what is allowed within their scope of practice.

If the nursing assistant is ever in doubt as to whether a task is within their scope of practice, the nursing assistant should contact a supervisor immediately to clarify facility policy. Sometimes due to time constraints or misunderstanding, the nursing assistant may be asked to do things outside of their scope of practice. It may not seem like a big deal at the time, but it could have serious consequences if an error is made. Practicing outside of one's scope of practice may lead to resident harm, liability on the part of the nursing assistant, and disciplinary action up to certification revocation.

Interdisciplinary Team Member Roles

Other members of the health care team include nurses, doctors, respiratory therapists, speech therapists, occupational therapists, physical therapists, nutritionists, and dietitians. Each one of these individual team members has been educated in a certain specialization that serves an aspect of the resident's care.

The **doctor** diagnoses the resident and recommends pharmacological, surgical, and other therapeutic interventions. The **nurse** interprets the doctor's orders, carries them out, performs ongoing resident assessments, makes nursing diagnoses, and carries out nursing interventions. The **respiratory therapist** focuses on the respiratory care of the resident and administers respiratory medications and treatments. **Physical** and **occupational therapists** work with the resident to restore physical ability and the ability to care for themselves. **Speech therapists** are assigned to residents with speech, language, and swallowing difficulties, and work to restore normal function.

There are many other members of the care team that the nursing assistant will encounter and work with. It is important for nursing assistants to be aware of everyone's role in resident care and to collaborate with them to bring about optimal resident outcomes.

Teamwork Principles

Collaboration between interdisciplinary teams is crucial to a holistic resident care approach. The nurse aid must be able to work with all the different teams assigned to the residents in order to deliver effective care. This requires cooperation, mutual respect, and the ability to share the correct information with the right team at the right time. Knowing when to report something to the nurse versus the physical therapist, for example, will help expedite resident care.

Nurse aides play a vital role in healthcare teams. They hold a close relationship with patients due to the amount of time they spend helping them with routine daily care. Therefore, they must collaborate and cooperate with other medical providers, such as nurses and physicians, to understand their patients' diagnoses and needs.

Nurse aides play a critical role in the logistics of patient care, including transporting patients to various areas of a medical facility (e.g., surgery, restrooms). They must ensure that each patient's unique needs are addressed as they are transported safely to the correct location. This requires reliable and accurate communication with the entire healthcare team. In addition, the nurse aide also communicates patient needs to the rest of the healthcare team. Since nurse aides help patients with dressing, grooming, and so on, they may be the first person who notices if a patient needs extra care or is in distress. Therefore, they should be prepared to advocate for the patient, share information that they have noticed, and be

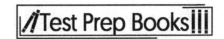

they should be prepared to advocate for the patient, share information that they have noticed, and be prepared to assist other care providers in delivering interventions as needed. Since nurse aides spend so much time with patients, their customer service skills are important. Patients should be served with respect and compassion, as patient satisfaction is highly correlated with both quality of care and overall health outcomes.

Care Planning Process and Implementation

In nursing, the nursing assistant is instrumental in helping to carry out the developed plan of care. The plan of care begins with the nurse's assessment of the resident, followed by recommended nursing interventions. These interventions are then evaluated for their effectiveness and modified based on resident response, starting the whole care planning process over again.

Nurse Aide's Responsibility to Provide Care According to the Care Plan

An example of care performed according to a nursing care plan is when a resident is assessed by the nurse to be at risk for skin breakdown. Recommended interventions would include turning and repositioning the resident every two hours, providing regular perineal care and incontinence care, and ensuring that an adequate amount of the meal tray is consumed by the resident. The nursing assistant assists with all these activities, and they document when the resident is turned, the intake and output record, and when baths and perineal care are performed.

Interpersonal Relations/Communication Skills

The nursing assistant is not only responsible for understanding and mastering the skills of basic physical care of the resident, but they must also be able to communicate with residents and other members of the health care team in an effective and collaborative way.

Communication Principles

There are certain principles nursing assistants need to keep in mind when practicing effective communication. At a basic level, communication consists of a sender, a message, and a receiver. If any of these three components are compromised or a barrier exists, communication is hindered.

The nursing assistant must display respect for the person they are communicating with, such as a nurse or resident. The nursing assistant must be supportive, allowing the resident and family to make their own informed treatment decisions without coercion, unnecessary insertion of the nursing assistant's opinion, or judgment. The nursing assistant should seek to align their own goals for the day with the resident's and health care team's goals, so that cooperation and collaboration are facilitated.

Communication Types

There are several different types of communication, including verbal, written, and nonverbal. **Verbal communication** occurs when two parties are speaking out loud; this can be in person, through video technology, or over the phone. **Written communication** can be through physical or digital writing or printing, such as e-mails, faxes, and instant messages. **Nonverbal communication** is transferred through one party's observations of the other party's body language and facial expressions.

Factors Affecting Communication

Good communication depends on a number of factors. Do the speakers speak the same language? Language can be a barrier to communication and can be overcome with a translator. Sometimes, a family member can help with communication. Cultural barriers exist in communication as some cultures have certain beliefs about how one should talk, who should do the speaking, and how much one should speak.

The nursing assistant should be careful not to create **nonverbal barriers** to communication with residents and coworkers. An example of a nonverbal barrier is the nursing assistant having a personal smartphone in hand and scrolling through social media while a resident or coworker is trying to talk to them. This action suggests the nursing assistant is not paying attention and does not care about what is being said, which inhibits good communication.

Physical barriers to communication may exist, such as a resident having a speech, hearing, visual, or other sensory impairment. The resident may have cognitive difficulties understanding basic communication brought on by illness, change in level of consciousness, or dementia.

Therapeutic Communication Techniques

Overcoming barriers to communication requires practicing therapeutic communication. **Therapeutic communication** is a type of communication that assists the resident in the healing process rather than hindering it. There are a number of useful communication techniques the nursing assistant can employ to aid in therapeutic communication.

Sometimes, silence is the best way to get clarification from a resident, or simply asking them to clarify when one does not understand. The nursing assistant may offer themselves to support the resident without providing personal details, by sympathizing and saying, "Yes, I have been through something similar." The nursing assistant may ask the resident to summarize their thoughts or identify a theme when stories go on at length. This helps redirect communication in a positive direction.

Asking the resident how certain events made them feel is a way to investigate the resident's emotional status. The nursing assistant may give information about their role and make observations, such as "I noticed you seem tense," to open the door to more fluent conversation. Giving the resident praise and recognition without overt flattery is a way to show support, such as complimenting a noticeable effort during a physical therapy session. The nursing assistant may want to determine the chronological order of events, which can be helpful for reporting information.

24

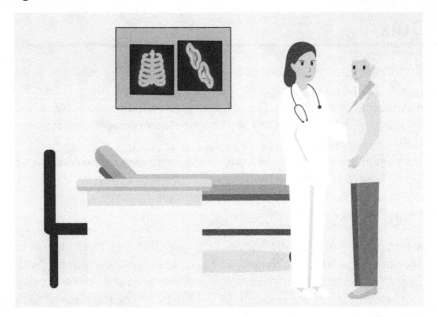

Employing therapeutic communication aids smooth collaboration and cooperation between members of the health care team. Incorporating smart, simple, therapeutic communication techniques and overcoming barriers to communication are important parts of achieving this goal.

Practice Quiz

1. The nursing assistant measures the resident's oxygen saturation to be 89%. The resident is receiving supplemental oxygen at 2 LPM via nasal cannula. The nurse aide checks the position of the probe and re-checks the oxygen saturation; it is still 89%. The resident is calm and comfortable in bed, watching TV. He tells the nursing assistant that he has COPD and that this is a normal finding for him. What should the nursing assistant do?
    a. Take the resident at his word, and then document the finding in the resident's health record.
    b. Call a code and bring the crash cart into the resident's room.
    c. Alert the nurse to the finding to clarify that it is normal.
    d. Notify the nurse manager of the finding.

2. The nursing assistant begins her shift and finds out that a well-known celebrity has been admitted to another unit but does not know why. The nursing assistant wants to know what room the celebrity is in and find out the reason for the admission. According to HIPAA, what should the nursing assistant do?
    a. Nothing. The celebrity is not her resident, so the celebrity's care is none of her business. Looking into the celebrity's chart would be a violation of HIPAA, subjecting her to disciplinary action.
    b. She should look up the celebrity's record in the electronic health record just to see what room the celebrity is in, but no further information beyond that.
    c. She should ask around the unit to see if any other nurses or aides have any details.
    d. She should access his electronic health record and peruse the celebrity's test results to determine the admitting diagnosis.

3. What is one example of nonverbal communication that assists therapeutic communication?
    a. Making good eye contact
    b. Scrolling through one's phone
    c. Giving a look of boredom or disinterest
    d. Looking at the door constantly

4. Which of the following is the proper abbreviation for "weight"?
    a. lb
    b. kg
    c. wa
    d. wt

5. When employing proper lifting technique, which of the following should the nursing assistant do?
    I. Balance on one foot
    II. Avoid twisting and awkward positions
    III. Lift with the legs, not the back
    IV. Try to lift residents alone as much as possible without asking for help, so as not to interrupt other nursing assistant's work

    a. All of the above
    b. Choices II and III
    c. Choices II, III, and IV
    d. Choices I, II, and III

Answer Explanations

1. C: The nursing assistant should clarify with the nurse to be certain that this oxygen saturation is normal for this resident. Calling a code is not necessary as the resident is not in distress. Alerting the nurse manager is an incorrect use of the chain of command. If the finding is new to the nursing assistant, they should clarify with the nurse rather than taking the resident at his word.

2. A: Accessing anyone's health record that the nursing assistant is not caring for and for non-medical reasons is a violation of HIPAA, and the nursing assistant is putting herself at risk for disciplinary action. Trying to access information from other members of the health care team is the same concept and a violation.

3. A: Making good eye contact shows the person that the nursing assistant is interested in the resident's message. The other options are all nonverbal barriers to therapeutic communication.

4. D: The most commonly used abbreviation for weight is "wt", not "wa." Kilograms (kg) and pounds (lb) are both measurements of weight.

5. B: Choices II and III are excellent techniques to employ when lifting residents. Asking for help when one needs it will help the nursing assistant avoid injury. Balancing on one foot is not recommended.

Promotion of Safety

Potential Hazards in the Healthcare Environment

Safety in healthcare is extremely important and should be a top priority, not only for the patients but also for the healthcare workers. Potential hazards for employees include infections, bloodborne pathogen exposure or contact with infected bodily fluids, chemical and drug exposures, respiratory hazards, injury related to poor lifting techniques, and hazards during stay in a facility. Such hazards can cause infections, falls, trauma or injury, burns, drug side effects, chemical exposure, fire, and violence.

The four main types of workplace hazards are physical, ergonomic, chemical, and biological. **Physical hazards** pertain to the environment surrounding the nursing assistant and can include tripping hazards, spills, frayed electrical cords, and exposed equipment parts.

Ergonomics refers to how efficiently people work in their environment. For the nursing assistant, this can include efficient lifting techniques and body positioning when moving patients. The nursing assistant is at risk for injury if poor lifting techniques are used, the facility in which they work does not have ergonomically designed equipment available for use, or if the nursing assistant is fatigued or overworked. Proper body posture is important in preventing injury. Incorrect lifting technique, straining, bending, or twisting into awkward positions all contribute to workplace injuries. This is especially true for caregivers such as nurses and nursing assistants, who perform countless tasks involving lifting and positioning patients throughout the day.

Chemical hazards include an overexposure to toxic cleaning products, toxic vapors, toxic fumes, and carbon monoxide gases.

Biological hazards come from working with animals, plants, or people. An example of a biological hazard of working with sick patients is the increased risk of becoming infected with the same organism that is infecting the patient. The nursing assistant will be exposed to bodily fluids of patients and be in close, intimate contact with the patient in order to take care of them.

Risk factors for healthcare worker injury include:

Repetition: motions done over and over again, frequently

Force: how much physical effort it takes to lift or pull someone or something

Awkward positions: stressful positions, such as twisting, reaching high, kneeling, leaning over, and squatting

Strategies to reduce the chance of injury when moving a patient include:

- Make sure enough staff is available to help with a move or a lift.
- Try to lift from the legs and not from the back, bending at the knees and not the waist.
- Raise or lower the patient's bed height before a transfer or lift.
- Know the weight of equipment, patients, or anything else before attempting the move.
- Use transfer aids and assistive devices such as Hoyer lifts, slings, pads, or chucks.

28

- Don't fight gravity. Lower the head of the bed before boosting a patient up in bed.
- Have the patient help as much as they are able.

To lift objects properly:

- Stand close to the object or load.
- Place feet wide apart with one foot slightly in front of the other.
- With both feet flat on the floor, bend slightly at the knees.
- Maintain a neutral or straight back and bend a little at the hips.
- Keep loads close to the body.
- Avoid twisting the back muscles. Feet and legs should be used for turning.
- Do not lift above shoulder height or below the waist level.
- Keep work surfaces (desk, countertop, or computer) slightly higher than waist level when standing.
- Push objects rather than pull them.
- When pushing or pulling, keep stomach muscles tight and use the arm muscles.
- When standing for long periods, wear comfortable shoes and stand on a mat. Also, frequently change leg positions by putting one foot up on a stool for a while.

Nursing assistants will be educated on the lift and transfer equipment available in their facility, and this equipment will be used every day to ensure the safety of patients and staff. Using **transfer devices** will greatly reduce the risk of lower-back stress and injury. Transfer devices eliminate manual lifting and transfers, as well as manual transfers in confined spaces, and they reduce the number of transfers needed per task. For example, it may normally take three steps to move a patient without a transfer device. With a transfer device, however, the task can be completed in only one step. Types of **protective transfer devices** include hoists, walking belts with handles (called **gait belts**), shower chairs, repositioning devices, and weighing devices that use slings. Examples of **repositioning devices** may be a draw sheet, a roller board, or a sliding sheet. Beds can have scales built in so that a patient can be weighed while staying in their bed. Also, there are scales that are large and wide, which will accommodate a wheelchair-bound or morbidly obese patient.

Another way to maintain a healthy back and to keep muscles strong is to stay physically fit with regular exercise and a nutritious diet. Strong muscles and flexible joints can help prevent back injury. Aerobic exercise three times a week for at least twenty minutes combined with regular weight lifting to maintain muscle strength is ideal. Getting adequate rest, nutrition, and stretching in between workouts will prevent injury, improve energy, and increase flexibility.

Common Injuries of Residents

Skin Tears and Shearing

Skin tears occur when the skin is pulled with such force that the layers separate. **Shearing** has more to do with friction; the common cause in hospitalized patients is the constant friction between the patient's body and their bed, especially if they are immobilized by their illness. Skin tears can occur when a patient is pulled up in bed, during transfers, during a fall, or during normal movement from routine daily tasks, like toileting or dressing. Tape removal from gauze dressings or clear, sticky dressings can also cause skin tears. The majority of skin tears happen on the arms. Elderly patients are especially

at risk for skin tears due to decreased elasticity of the skin; decreased layer of fat padding under the skin; and increased risk of falls related to weakness, gait, and coordination issues.

Preventing skin tears can involve dressing residents in long sleeves, using pillows for padding, keeping their skin clean and moisturized, using gentle adhesives, and using proper lifting and transfer techniques.

Tears and shearing injuries can lead to more serious conditions, such as **pressure ulcers**. Turning and repositioning is vital to maintaining skin integrity. Patients at risk for compromised skin integrity should be turned or repositioned every two hours, and have their elbows, heels, and head raised off the bed with pillows to promote circulation to these at-risk areas. Pressure ulcers can be prevented by being diligent with positioning and padding while in the bed, in a chair, or in a wheelchair. Keeping linens and clothing dry will keep the resident's skin clean and dry. It's important to change soiled sheets and clothes quickly, not only for patient's comfort, but also in order to prevent skin injuries. Urine or bodily fluids can break down the natural oils on the skin fairly quickly, leading to sores or tears. Additionally, if the top layer of skin is broken, maintaining cleanliness will decrease the chance of an infectious organism entering the ulcer.

There are many types of treatment options once a skin tear occurs, depending on where the tear is located and its severity. Care facilities will have different supplies available for the nurses to utilize and these items will become familiar. Topical products, which are put directly on the skin, include certain barrier creams or petroleum-based creams. These will help with the pain and protect the area so that healing can occur. Advanced wound-care dressings, such as hydrogel pads or nonstick pads, can be used to cover the tear. Clear, sticky dressings should be avoided because of the risk of causing additional tears with removal. A skin tear will heal best when it is kept dry, clean, and moisturized.

Falls

Falling is the number one cause of injury for residents and the leading cause of death due to injury in the elderly. Because of the risks associated with falls and the frequency of falls, there is a lot of research and money invested in fall prevention at healthcare facilities. Statistics show that one-third of people over sixty-five years of age fall at least once per year. Eighty-seven percent of all broken bones are due to falls. When a fall happens in the elderly, their quality of life and mobility are never fully restored. Many fall victims are hospitalized, which can lead to other problems such as hospital-acquired infections, pneumonia, or complications from surgery.

Falls can cause broken bones, bruises, tears, internal and external bleeding, and head injuries. Fall prevention includes many factors of the individual's environment and their overall physical health. If the physician is concerned that the patient may be at risk of falling, they will evaluate medications and dosages, order physical therapy, and review the plan of care in order to prevent fall injuries. Physical and occupational therapies are especially helpful if patients are living at home or if they are staying in a rehabilitation facility. Residents who have the greatest risk for falls will usually have assistive devices like canes, walkers, wheelchairs, and reachers/grabbers. Also, these residents will need assistance with all transfers from one place to another, such as from bed to a chair.

Spills

A spill can occur anywhere and at any time in a hospital or facility. Because they make the floor slippery and create a major fall hazard, spills can pose a risk to residents.

Falls in healthcare facilities may result from spills left unattended. This is a hazard to both healthcare workers and patients alike. The results of a fall after slipping on a spill include sprains, strains, dislocations, tears, bruises, contusions, concussions, fractures, cuts, burns, lacerations, punctures, and abrasions. These falls may affect the upper or lower body, head, neck, back or trunk.

For the nursing assistant, this can potentially result in the loss of valuable days at work, medical bills, and long-term injury. For the patient, this may extend their hospital stay, worsen their condition, and increase their medical bill.

The maintenance team of the hospital will primarily be in charge of preventing and notifying facility workers of spills, but the nursing assistant should be able to assist in ensuring the safety of their fellow coworkers and patients. The nursing assistant may do this by ensuring that "Wet Floor" signs are in place when appropriate, warning coworkers and patients if a spill has occurred and where, and ensuring that a plan is in place to clean up a spill. The nursing assistant may even help clean up the spill if appropriate. As soon as a spill is noticed, the nursing assistant should cover, clean, and report the spill to the appropriate person.

Each facility will have a specific dress code in place for employees. Slip-resistant shoes will often be a part of that code for the specific reason of protecting the nursing assistant from injury. Residents also will be issued a pair of socks with rubber treads on the bottom to help them ambulate across slippery floor surfaces.

Burns

Scalding burns are the most common type of burn. They can occur in patients at mealtimes if food or beverages are too hot. Extra precautions should be taken and supervision should be required for residents who need assistance with meal preparation and feeding. Additionally, scalding burns can occur when bathing or washing with scalding water. It is important to check the temperature of the water in the residents' bathrooms. Candles or open flames are not allowed in most facilities. Radiators should be covered. If an elderly resident does sustain a burn, they are more vulnerable to infection and, in severe cases, body-fluid loss and shock. They may need to be hospitalized immediately for fluid replacement or even sent to a facility specializing in burn treatment.

Bruises

Bruises or **ecchymosis** are caused by blunt force or clotting abnormalities that cause capillaries under the skin to leak blood into the tissue, causing a discolored area. Bruises can range in color from blue, brown, or purple to even green and yellow depending on the stage of healing. Bruising can occur in patients as a result of bumping into objects, multiple or failed intravenous-access attempts, medication side effects, or falling. Significant bruising that occurs without a known cause could indicate an underlying medical condition, such as a blood-clotting disorder. Bruising can also be a result of physical abuse from a caregiver, a family member, or another resident. If suspicious bruises are noticed, it is

important to ask the resident questions about the bruising. Family members should also ask staff or caregivers about bruises they notice on their loved one.

Risks Related to Common Injuries

Elderly residents have an increased risk for skin injuries due to the fragility of their skin, decreased circulation, poor nutrition, decreased sensation, mental changes, and altered mobility. As the body ages, the skin becomes thinner due to decreased adipose tissue and has less elasticity. The **epidermis**, which is the outer layer of the skin, is only 0.1 millimeters thick and becomes thinner with time. Loss of collagen as the skin ages decreases the skin's elasticity, making it more vulnerable to friction and force. **Dry skin** is caused by loss of sweat and oil, and also due to a decrease in blood flow to the skin. All of these factors contribute to skin that is fragile and prone to tears. If any skin injuries are observed on a resident, the nursing assistant must notify the nurse taking care of that patient immediately. Injuries will be assessed, documented, treated, and monitored for changes. Residents who require total care have the greatest risk of developing a skin tear or a pressure ulcer.

Risks for developing a skin tear or pressure ulcer include:

- Bedridden patient
- Wheelchair dependent
- Limited mobility
- Spinal-cord injury
- Poor nutrition
- Poor circulation to the skin, commonly due to a heart condition or diabetes
- Dependence on others for care
- Weakened immune system
- Elderly population
- Excessive pressure on the skin or on bony areas

Risk factors for falls include:

- Muscle weakness
- Balance and gait problems
- Dizziness related to low blood pressure, heart conditions, or medication side effects
- Slower reflexes
- Confusion or memory loss
- Foot problems and/or unsafe shoes
- Vision problems
- Safety hazards around the home or room, such as stairs, rugs, corners, poor lighting, clutter, and slippery surfaces
- History of falls (Patients who have fallen before are two to three times more likely to fall again.)

Risks for spills are as follows:

- The nursing assistant may encounter a spill hazard arising from possible sources including outdoor or indoor walking-surface irregularities, poor drainage from facility pipes and drains, or the presence of a slippery substance on the floors of the facility.

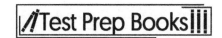

- If at any time the nursing assistant must take a patient outside, the nursing assistant should be especially mindful of outdoor walking-surface irregularities. This can be anywhere the ground is uneven or there are potential areas where the nursing assistant or the patient can slip and fall. The nursing assistant should stay with the patient, be aware of the surroundings, use assistive devices when necessary, and use common sense and good judgment about when and where to walk.

- Flooring inside a facility may vary from carpet to vinyl tiles to concrete. These surfaces all have the potential to become damaged, uneven, and ultimately a slipping hazard. The nursing assistant should be mindful of indoor surfaces that are hazards, report new damage, and ensure proper warning signs are near the hazardous area in order to prevent coworkers and patients from slipping.

- Sometimes, standing water may be noticed near an area where a facility drain or pipe has become improperly aligned, damaged, or disconnected. Outside the facility, sidewalks may gather water where a downspout from a facility gutter ends. In either of these cases, if a spill presents hazardous conditions, the nursing assistant should report it to the appropriate person so it may be cleaned and safe conditions restored to the walking surface.

- Slippery substances that may be accidentally spilled or gather on the floors of the facility include water, grease, oil, food, or other fluids. Areas where food is prepared, places where equipment is stored, bathrooms, drinking fountains, and entrances to a building during times of rain and snow may all contain spill hazards. The floors of patient rooms and hallways must be specially monitored for spills, as these are where patients walk the most. The patient may be disoriented with a decreased level of consciousness as a result of illness and/or medication side effects. Because of these factors, the patient needs the nursing assistant's help to navigate safely about their room and the facility, avoiding hazardous spills.

Risks of a burn injury include:

- Altered mental status such as dementia or Alzheimer's disease
- Elderly person living alone
- Parkinson's disease or tremors in the hands
- Smoking
- Drug or alcohol intoxication (can lead to disorientation, altered judgment, and/or careless, erratic behavior)
- Decreased sense of smell (may not smell smoke and be alerted to a fire)
- Hearing loss (may not hear smoke detectors or warning of a fire)

Risks for bruising include:

- Elderly population
- Frail, thin skin
- Blood-thinner medications that cause slower blood clotting times, resulting in quicker and easier bruising
- Altered mental status or disorientation (may cause a person to be unsteady or to be unaware of their surroundings)

- Environmental hazards in the patient's room, such as corners of tables, throw rugs, furniture, or cords that could cause tripping and bumping
- Visual or other sensory impairment (may cause falling or bumping into objects)

Safety and Comfort

Comfort Needs of the Resident

This section discusses positioning, comfort, and injury prevention for the resident. **Bony areas** of the body should always be padded. These can include the head, elbows, tailbone, and heels. The illustrations below show the pressure points on the body in three positions: sitting, lying on the back, and side lying.

While lying down, the lower back often feels better when the knees are elevated with a pillow. The head of the bed should be raised per the resident's comfort. Remember to offer toileting/bedpan at least every two hours.

When a patient is lying on their back (**supine**), the following actions may be done for their comfort:

- Place pillows under the head, knees, lower arms, and heels.
- Elevate the head of the bed per needs of patient.
- Make sure water, nurse call button, and personal items are within reach.
- Raise all of the side rails on the bed if the resident is unable to get up without assistance.
  -

heels   tailbone   elbows shoulder back of head
blades

Side-lying position:

- Place a pillow under their head.
- Tuck a pillow under the back to keep the resident from rolling onto their back.
- Put pillows between bent legs, knees, and between ankles.
- Place a pillow between arms.
- Elevate the head of the bed, per comfort.

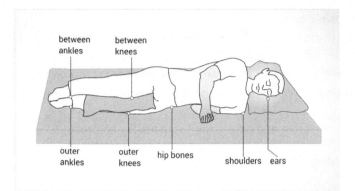

Seated position (in a wheelchair, lounger, or chair):

- Place a cushion or pillow under the patient's bottom if the chair is hard.
- Make sure there is no extra pressure behind the knees. A folded blanket could be used for padding.
- Place folded blankets under the patient's forearms if the arms of the chair are not padded.

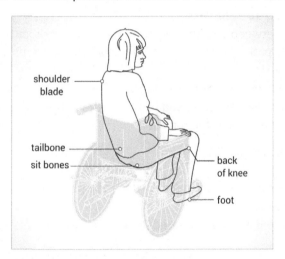

Steps for transferring a patient in bed to a sitting position:

- Explain what is going to happen.
- Bring the side rails down and make sure the bed is locked.
- Place one hand behind the patient's shoulder and the other under their knees.
- Recruit another staff person if the patient is heavy.
- Lift and turn the shoulders and swivel their knees over to the side of the bed.
- Let the patient rest at the side of the bed, keeping a hand on them if needed.

Steps for transferring from bed (sitting) to wheelchair:

- Explain the procedure to the patient.
- Put the wheelchair as close to the bed as possible, with the wheel against the side rail of the bed.
- Make sure the bed and the wheelchair are locked and move the footpads on the chair out of the way (flip them up).

35

- Put nonslip footwear on the patient.
- The aide should stand in front of the patient with a wide leg stance and have the patient put their hands on the aide's shoulders.
- Use a gait belt or grab the patient's waist and help them stand on the count of three.
- Pivot them into the chair and have them back up until they feel the front of the chair behind their legs.
- Lower them into the chair and adjust the footpads for comfort.

Steps for transferring from bed to stretcher:

- Explain the procedure to the patient.
- Recruit at least one other staff member to assist, and more if the patient is heavy.
- Lower the head of the bed and the side rails of the bed and stretcher.
- Make sure both are locked and at the same level.
- Have the patient cross their arms on their chest.
- Have one coworker roll the patient onto their side with the draw sheet while the other aide places a slider board or slider sheet under the patient's back.
- Have the patient roll onto their back.
- Move the stretcher between you and the bed, then pull the slider board or sheet as the second coworker pushes the patient's hip and shoulder from the patient's opposite side. Pull until the patient is fully on the stretcher.
- An additional staff person may be needed to transfer the patient's feet and legs.
- Remove the slider board or sheet if used by rolling the patient onto their side with the draw sheet; then position the patient for comfort.

Steps for moving a patient up in bed:

- At least two aides or caregivers are needed, depending on the patient's size.
- Explain the procedure to the patient.
- Ensure the bed is locked and lower the side rails.

Lower the head of the bed so that the bed is level. Another commonly used technique is to place the head of the bed at a downward angle, called **Trendelenburg position**, to allow gravity to assist if necessary.

- Have the patient cross their arms across their chest.
- Standing on both sides of the bed, each aide grabs the draw sheet with two hands.
- Count to three to ensure a synchronized movement with the assistant and boost the patient up toward the head of the bed.
- If the patient can help, they may bend their knees, lift their head, and push up with their heels while being boosted.
- Position the patient for comfort.

Providing for a resident's comfort level includes their room environment. The temperature of the room should be kept at a comfortable level, plenty of linens should be made available, along with warm blankets if necessary, and even a personal quilt or sweater, if available. Appropriate lighting and a window may help the resident orient to the time of day and enjoy the outdoor view. Residents who have items from home may feel more secure and comfortable. The room can be decorated with family photos or important knick-knacks, as long as there are no candles or items that could cause injury. Keeping the day's schedule in line with the resident's routines and habits as much as possible will help give them a sense of familiarity and independence.

Accident Prevention Including Fall-Prevention Protocols

The majority of accidents that occur in the older population happen in their homes, with falls being the most common accident. Accident prevention involves maintaining a clean home and living area and recognizing potential hazards. In addition, individuals should be knowledgeable and aware of their level of health and their own body's capabilities and weaknesses. Keeping regular appointments at the physician's office and following any medication regime correctly will keep one's health in check. It is important for people to understand and be aware of potential side effects of any medications that they may be taking. Recognizing a side effect could be a way to prevent an accident, especially if it relates to mental status or mobility. For example, blood-pressure medications have the potential to lower blood pressure to the point of the person passing out, ultimately causing a fall. Informal caregivers such as family members should check on elderly family to ensure they are able to continue taking care of themselves and to survey the home for safety hazards.

If an older adult is still living in their home, the following measures should be addressed to avoid accidents related to poisoning, burns, hypothermia, and falls. The main causes of poisoning in adults aged sixty-five and older are medicines and gases. Gases would include carbon monoxide and pipeline gases, such as propane or natural gas for heating the home. Fuel-burning devices should be checked regularly for proper functioning. Chimneys and flues should be cleaned once a year.

Older adults are often on a complicated medication regime involving multiple pills, various dosages, and the different times of the day and week that they should be taken. Medicines should be taken exactly as prescribed, and an organized schedule should be in place to prevent mistakes. One example for organizing medications is a pillbox that has individual compartments for each day of the week.

Burns and scalding in the home can be prevented if water heaters are not set too high, and if the cold water is turned on first. Kettles should be avoided if possible. If necessary, spout-filling kettles, cordless kettles, or wall-mounted heaters can be used instead. Items in the kitchen and the flow of the kitchen should allow for the least amount of distance for carrying hot food or beverages. On the stove, rear burners should be used and handles should be kept away from the edges in order to avoid accidentally knocking a pan off the stove.

An additional accident not often thought of in the older population is **hypothermia**, which means the body's temperature drops below 95 °F. Strategies to prevent hypothermia in the elderly include making sure the home is heated properly in colder weather, providing several layers of clothing, encouraging movement and exercise around the home to increase body heat, and making enough food and drink available.

As previously discussed, falls are the most common accident in the older adult population. Whether the person lives in their home or in a care facility, there are preventative measures that should be put into place.

Fall-prevention interventions include:

- Identification of patients at high risk for falls
- Assessment of the resident's room or environment for hazards that can be removed, such as:
- Rugs
- Slippery floors
- Clutter
- Poor lighting
- Use of assistive devices, such as:
- Canes, used for stability
- Walkers, used for balance because of their wide base
- Reachers or grabbers, used to pick up items off of the floor or reach items on a shelf
- Gait belts, used with an aide or caregiver, placed around the patient's waist to assist in walking or when standing up from a sitting position
- Railings in bathrooms, hallways, and tubs
- Proper footwear is worn, such as rubber-soled shoes
- Staff, family-member, and resident education on fall-prevention strategies
- Assistance for residents with daily activities and routines if necessary
- Stairways that are well lit, have railings, and are lined with nonslip flooring

Fall prevention for bed-ridden patients includes:

- Keep two side rails up at all times when a patient is in bed.
- Keep the call light and personal items on a table within reach of the patient's bed.
- Place bed alarms on the resident's bed to alert the staff of any attempt to get out of bed.
- Offer toileting at least every two hours to prevent patients from getting up without assistance.

Falling with a Patient

Sometimes it becomes necessary to assist a person to the ground safely if it becomes clear that they are about to fall. When standing in front or behind the falling person, spreading one's legs shoulder width apart allows for a wide base of support. Try to keep an arm under their shoulders or under their arms and ease them to the floor. Always attempt to protect their head first and try to direct them away from hard objects, such as furniture.

Healthcare facilities should identify which patients are at a higher risk for falls, as these patients will require special fall precautions. Some facilities have signs on residents' doors that say "Fall Risk," or a resident may wear a certain color bracelet as a reminder to staff and/or family. Keep in mind that all patients or residents are at risk for a fall, especially if they are elderly. Staff will be educated regarding how much assistance is needed for each resident. For example, resident A may be able to walk with assistance or walk with stand-by assistance. Resident B may need assistance x 2, or two staff persons, to help transfer.

Assistance for Ambulation

The types of assistance needed for ambulation are as follows:

Stand by assistance (SBA): This patient does not require any assistance to move and can walk independently, though someone should be standing by to monitor. A gait belt is not required.

38

Contact-guard assistance (CGA): This patient requires an assistant to be within reach in case of a fall. These patients can walk independently but have a high risk for falls.

Minimum assistance (MIN): This patient needs a little support when moving about, and an example would be the use of a gait belt.

Maximum assistance (MAX): This patient is unstable and may not be able to walk or stand without help. At least two staff persons are needed for assistance.

Patients who use assistive devices for ambulation need instruction on how to use them and may need reminders to ensure they are still using the device properly. It is important to stay with a patient who is learning to use an assistive device. A gait belt should be used while the patient is learning to use a walker.

Canes
The purpose of the cane is to help stabilize a leg that is weak. Steps for using a cane are listed below:

- Have the patient place the cane in their strong hand and move the cane out one step while stepping the weak leg out with the cane.
- With their weight on the cane, have them step out with their stronger leg.
- After each step, the patient can rest to ensure they feel balanced.

A Walker Without Wheels
A walker is used to give the patient extra stability when a patient is weak in both legs or has trouble with balance when walking. Steps for use are listed below:

- Instruct the patient to stand inside the walker while holding onto the walker with both hands.

- Have the patient lift and move the walker forward so that the back legs of the walker line up with their toes.

- With their weight on their stronger leg, have the patient take a step with their weaker leg while gripping the handrails of the walker. They should step into the center of the walker.

- Finally, their stronger leg steps up to evenly meet their other leg. They may rest in between steps if necessary.

Care must be taken to ensure that the flooring surface is flat when using a walker or a cane. Trips or falls can occur if rugs or thick carpet get caught in the walker or cane. Some walkers have wheels on the bottoms of the legs so that a patient can push the walker while walking. The wheels may be on all four legs or just the front two legs. The patient's weight is placed on the walker with their hands, and this helps with extra support as they lean forward. These types of walkers are not lifted during walking and allow for a bit faster pace. Make sure while walking that the walker does not move too far ahead of the patient.

Here are steps for moving from a chair to standing with a walker:

- Place the walker in front of the patient and have the patient place their hands on the arms of the chair.
- Assist the patient with standing up.
- Encourage the patient to place one hand at a time onto the handgrips of the walker.
- Ensure the patient feels steady and is not dizzy before walking.

Use of Crutches

Crutches can be used on a short-term basis when a patient has limitations for weight bearing on a leg. An example would be a patient that has a cast or a splint on their ankle, foot, or leg. Putting weight on an injured leg may interfere with healing and may be painful. A physical therapist will be responsible for fitting the crutches. Ensure the crutches are the appropriate length for the patient. The armpit, or **axilla**, rests should fit into the patient's armpit without lifting the shoulders and without causing stooping. The pads should be one to one-and-a-half inches below the axilla. If the crutches are too tall, the patient could trip over the crutches and too much pressure will be placed in their armpits. If the crutches are too short, leaning over will put unnecessary strain on the patient's back. The handgrips should also be adjusted so that the arms are slightly bent at the elbow. The grip should be comfortable.

Crutch Gaits

The **three-point crutch gait** helps with an inability to bear weight on one leg, such as with fractures, pain, or amputation.

- Move both crutches and the weaker leg forward. Then place all weight down on the crutches and move the stronger or unaffected leg forward. Repeat this pattern.
- Good balance is required for this type of gait.

The **two-point crutch gait** is used for weakness in both legs and poor coordination.

- Move the left crutch and right foot together.
- Then move the right crutch and left foot together.
- Repeat the pattern.
- This is a faster gait but difficult to learn.

The **swing-through crutch gait** helps with an inability to bear full weight on both legs.

- Move both crutches forward then swing both legs forward at the same time. The legs must swing past the crutches.
- This is the fastest gait but requires a lot of arm strength and energy.
- It will not be used in the elderly.

The **swing-to crutch gait** is used for patients who have weakness in both legs.

- Move both crutches forward.
- Put weight on both crutches and swing both legs forward together to the crutches. The legs must not swing past the crutches.
- This requires good arm strength, so it most likely will not be used for the elderly.

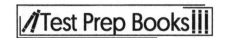

Standing up with crutches:

- Have the patient hold both crutches on their injured side, and then lean forward off of the chair while pushing off with their arm from the chair.
- Once standing, place the crutches under the arms.

Sitting down with crutches:

- Have the patient place both crutches on their injured side.
- Holding the handgrips in one hand, they can use their other hand to brace on the chair as they sit.

Using crutches on stairs should not be attempted until the patient is confident on level ground. Until then, or at any time, the patient can also slide up or down the stairs on their bottom. Also, the railing of the stairs can be used with one hand while holding the crutches in the other arm.

- The crutches should stay on the step the patient is standing on.
- The good leg is brought up to the next step while letting the injured leg lag behind.
- As the patient straightens up to their good leg, they should bring the crutches and their injured leg up onto the step.

Going down steps:

- Have the patient place the crutches on the next step lower and bring their injured foot forward.

- Next, the good foot is moved down to meet the crutches on the lower step. The weight is on the crutches at this time.

Restraint Techniques and Alternatives

Restraints can be defined as anything that is used, done, or said to intentionally limits a person's ability to move freely. Restraints, when applied properly, cannot be easily removed or controlled by the person. In addition to physical form, restraints can also be emotional, chemical, or environmental. Use of restraints is very controversial due to the ethical issue of personal freedom. These are a temporary solution to a problem and must always be used as a last resort. Restraints are used to limit a patient's movement to prevent injury to themselves or others, and they always require a physician's order.

Types of restraints include:

- Physical: vests, wrist restraints, straps, or anything that confines the body
- Emotional: verbal cues or emotions used to coerce the patient to act a certain way
- Environmental: side rails, locked doors, closed windows, locked beds
- Chemical: any medication used to change a patient's behavior

The medical doctor or practitioner is responsible for ordering the use of restraints. Nursing assistants, nurses, and caregivers are responsible for applying restraints safely and for the management of a patient with a restraint. After an order is given, the physician must visit the patient within twenty-four hours of placing the order to assess its further necessity.

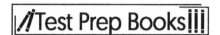

Alternatives to Restraints

Other methods must be tried before restraints. They include:

- Talking with the patient about being cooperative
- Using distractions such as television, music, knitting, and folding towels or cloths
- Placing the patient within view of a caregiver, such as near the main desk
- Having someone sit with the patient
- Moving the patient to a quiet area
- Ensuring that the patient's bathroom needs are being met
- Ensuring personal items are within reach

When to Use Restraints

Each facility will have a specific protocol that must be followed for restraint use. Circumstances under which restraints are used include:

- Signs of patient aggression toward self, staff, or other patients
- Interference with important medical devices, such as an IV or a catheter
- Patient movements that are potentially harmful to their health, or may cause further injury
- Potential for a patient to interfere with a procedure

Applying Restraints

- Always follow the facility's restraint policy.

- Obtain an order from a physician or medical practitioner, unless it is an emergency situation.

- Obtain consent from the patient or from next of kin if the patient is not capable of understanding.

- Explain to the patient what is going to happen, even if the patient is unable to understand due to confusion or dementia.

- Always monitor the patient per facility policy—check the positioning of the restraint every thirty minutes and remove every two hours for range of motion. Remember to reposition the patient and offer toileting every two hours.

- Explain the need for restraints and how long the restraints will be used.

Applying Physical Restraints

Vests have holes for the arms and the opening crosses in the back. The straps will be secured on either side of the bed or chair, depending on the patient's location. Tie it in a quick-release knot to a lower part of the bed that does not move. Make sure that two fingers fit underneath the vest on the patient's chest so that it is not too tight.

Wrist or **ankle restraints** are cloths that wrap around each wrist or ankle. They have a strap that is tied to a lower, immovable part of the bed or chair. Tie it in a quick-release knot. Ensure the restraints aren't too tight and that the patient's arms or legs aren't in an awkward position. Usually a pillow will be placed under the arms and/or the knees and heels.

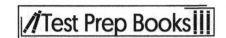

Legal Implications in the Use of Restraints

If restraints aren't used correctly or are used for the wrong reasons, the patient's family can take legal action against the nursing facility. A patient in restraints becomes completely vulnerable and may feel helpless. They are at a greater risk of sexual abuse, elder abuse, psychological abuse, or violence from other residents/patients.

Possible injuries from restraints can include:

- Broken bones
- Bruises
- Falls
- Skin tears or pressure sores
- Depression or fear due to lack of freedom
- Death from strangulation

Risks Factors for Elopement

Elopement is when a nursing home resident wanders away or leaves unsupervised. This is a huge safety issue for the resident. Injury or death could occur from falls or from wandering onto a busy road. Other concerns are exposure to hot or cold weather or lack of food and water. In the United States, statistics say that each year 34,000 people with Alzheimer's disease wander out of their homes or care facilities.

Some causes of elopement include residents with memory problems, such as disorientation, dementia, or Alzheimer's disease. They are prone to wander because they may not be clear on their whereabouts. They may be confused and think that they need to complete routines, such as feeding a pet, going home, or visiting a store. Other causes of elopement include residents who are able to walk independently but have mental impairments. They are more prone to wander than those in wheelchairs, or with limited mobility.

Elopement prevention includes:

- Proper training for staff
- Knowing the residents' habits and tendencies
- Knowing which residents need extra supervision due to mental issues
- Having locked and alarmed doors that are not for resident use
- Quick responses to exit-door alarms

Safety Devices

Safety devices include anything that is used to keep residents safe, or to prevent injury or harm. We discussed several things previously, such as assistive devices, rubber-soled shoes, and bed rails. Below are some other general, facility-wide devices used to prevent falls, wandering, or eloping:

Resident Guard Wander Alert Systems: A radiofrequency bracelet that keeps residents from wandering outside of a certain area. Staff will be alerted when resident reaches a boundary zone.

Bed Alarms: Beds can have alarms attached that alert staff when a resident attempts to get out of bed.

Electronic Tagging: Residents are tracked with a bracelet, or a lightweight device placed on a buckle or watch.

Video Surveillance: Video streaming allows staff to view residents in certain areas.

Infection Prevention and Control

Infections can spread quickly in areas where people are living in close proximity, because germs are easily shared. Individuals who are sick, those recovering from illness, the elderly, and immunocompromised patients are at increased risk for getting an infection. **Immunocompromised** means that an individual has an immune system that is weakened, reducing their ability to fight infection. Patients with acquired immune deficiency syndrome (AIDS), cancer, or immune-system disorders, or those who have undergone a recent tissue transplant, may be at increased risk for getting an infection. Infections continue to be a major cause of death in the elderly population and account for one-third of all deaths in people aged sixty-five and older. In this age group, 90 percent of deaths are from infections from influenza and pneumonia. These two illnesses combined are the sixth leading cause of death in the United States.

Maintaining a Clean Environment

Hospitals and care facilities must be diligent in maintaining cleanliness in order to reduce the chances of spreading infection. Facilities employ staff under the title of environmental services. These employees clean, disinfect, and promote a pleasant environment for residents, staff, and visitors. On a daily basis, environmental service employees may clean and disinfect the main entrance/lobby, visitor/staff restrooms, and offices and therapy rooms. In resident areas, they may clean and disinfect bed rails, bathrooms, call lights, remote controls, phones, cabinets, and door handles. In addition, odors will be controlled.

The definition of **cleaning** is to remove dirt and organic material from surfaces. **Disinfection** involves destroying most of the microbes on surfaces by using chemicals or heat. Disinfecting a surface does not work properly unless the surface is cleaned first. Sterilization removes all microbes from equipment or supplies. Cleaning and disinfecting must be done prior to sterilization.

Levels of risk for certain equipment:

Low-risk items come in contact with a person's intact skin. Examples are stethoscopes, tabletops, and doorknobs. Low-risk items require cleaning with a detergent.

Medium-risk items come in contact with mucous membranes, such as the mouth and nose. These items can include thermometers or respiratory equipment, and they require cleaning with a high-level disinfectant.

High-risk items come in contact with open skin, or broken skin. An example would be surgical instruments. These items have the greatest risk of carrying microbes and must be cleaned and sterilized between uses.

Ways to promote a clean environment:

- Always wear gloves when touching a patient and patient clothing/linens.

- Always wash hands before and after care, even if wearing gloves.
- Change bed linens when soiled, placing them in the proper dirty bin.
- Ensure bed rails, wheelchairs, and shared equipment are disinfected between uses.
- Clean patients' personal areas, such as nightstands or bedside tables.
- Clean up or report bodily-fluid spills right away, per the facility's policy.
- Know the patients' medical history and any infectious diseases they may carry.

Spread of Disease-Causing Organisms

Microorganisms that cause infection can be spread by touching surfaces, equipment, people, and bodily fluids, as well as by breathing in **airborne droplets**, such as those that exit the nostril when a person sneezes. Touching infectious microorganisms followed by contact on the hands, face, mouth, eyes, or with food can spread the germs. A clean environment and good handwashing not only protect healthcare workers from infectious germs but protect the patients as well. Infections can spread from resident to resident, from caregiver to resident and vice versa.

There are three types of infections: viral, bacterial and fungal. **Fungal infections** are caused by spores of fungus that usually affect the skin but also can be inhaled and cause respiratory infections. Examples of fungal skin infections include Athlete's foot, ringworm, and yeast infections. Fungal infections can be spread by touching the lesion or skin area that is infected.

Bacteria and **viruses** are caused by microbes, or microscopic organisms. Both of these types of infection can produce similar symptoms, including:

- Coughing and/or sneezing
- Inflammation (swelling)
- Fever
- Vomiting
- Diarrhea
- Fatigue

Even though bacteria and viruses both must be viewed through a microscope, they differ tremendously in how they infect the body. Bacteria are complex and can reproduce or multiply on their own. They can live in extreme environments, such as heat and cold, and can infect both the bodies of animals and humans. Bacterial infections are usually localized or found in contained areas of the body, such as the sinuses (sinus infection). Most bacteria are harmless and actually necessary to the body. One example is the bacteria in our gut, which is important for digesting food. Bacterial infections are treated with antibiotics, which will either kill the bacteria or stop the growth of the bacteria that has entered the body.

There are many different types of bacterial infections. Some common bacterial skin infections include cellulitis, folliculitis, impetigo, and boils. Foodborne bacterial infections usually cause vomiting, diarrhea, fever, chills, and abdominal pain. Harmful bacteria may be in raw meat, fish, eggs, and poultry, and in unpasteurized dairy products. The bacterial growth can be caused by unsanitary food preparation and handling.

Sexually-transmitted bacterial infections include chlamydia, gonorrhea, syphilis, and bacterial vaginosis. There are many additional types of infections, such as otitis media (ear infection), urinary tract

infections, and respiratory tract infections. Infections in the respiratory tract can be from bacteria or a virus, and they can cause a sore throat, bronchitis, sinus infections, tuberculosis, or pneumonia.

Viruses are different from bacteria in that they need another cell in order to reproduce, or multiply. They attach to a cell in the body and change the cell to make more of the virus. Eventually, the original body cell dies. Viral infections do not respond to antibiotics and are more difficult to treat. Unlike bacteria, most viruses cause infection. The common cold is most often caused by a virus in the rhinovirus family and is an example of a mild virus. An example of life-threatening viruses is the human immunodeficiency virus (HIV). Vaccines do a good job of protecting against viruses such as polio, chicken pox, influenza, and measles. There are antiviral drugs available to treat certain viruses.

Common types of respiratory viruses include influenza-causing viruses, respiratory syncytial virus, and **rhinoviruses**, which is most often the cause of the common cold. Viral skin infections can include **Molluscum contagiosum** (small, harmless bumps on the skin), herpes simplex virus-1 (cold sores), and **varicella zoster virus**, which is similar to the chickenpox. Foodborne viral infections are the most common cause of food poisoning and can include the hepatitis A virus, norovirus, and rotavirus. Viruses that are transmitted sexually include human papilloma virus, hepatitis B, genital herpes (herpes simplex-2), and HIV. Other types of viruses include Epstein-Barr, West Nile, and viral meningitis.

Bacteria and viruses can be spread by:

- Droplet contact from coughing and sneezing
- Contact with infected people
- Contact with infected animals, like livestock, pets, fleas, and ticks
- Contact with infected surfaces, like tabletops or railings
- Contact with contaminated food or water

Microbes can cause acute infections, chronic infections, or latent infections. **Acute infections** last for a short period of time and chronic infections can last for weeks, months, or years. **Latent infections** may not show any symptoms at first and then may reappear or show up after months or years.

Handwashing with soap and water is the number one way to prevent the spread of germs. The soap removes the visible dirt and invisible germs from the hands, and the water rinses them off.

Handwashing steps:

- Remove any jewelry or watches and pull long sleeves up past the wrists.
- Turn on the water and use warm water.
- Place soap in one hand and rub for at least twenty seconds.
- Make sure to rub the top and palms of the hands. Rub between the fingers and around the nails.
- Wash above the wrists.
- If there was contact with bodily fluids, wash for at least one minute.
- Be sure not to touch the sides of the sink during the process (the washing process would then need to be repeated).
- Rinse hands with fingers facing down so that the soap and germs run off rather than back up the arms.
- Dry hands with a paper towel or clean hand towel.
- Use the towel to turn off the faucet.

When to perform handwashing:

- After using the bathroom
- After sneezing or handling tissues
- Before and after eating
- Before entering and after leaving a patient's room
- Before and after feeding a patient
- Before and after performing a procedure on a patient
- Before and after coming in contact with a wound
- After coming in contact with dirty linens or clothes
- After coming in contact with bodily fluids of any kind (blood, urine, vomit, mucus, or stool)
- After leaving a patient's room

Cleansing the hands with an alcohol-based hand sanitizer is also available in healthcare facilities, but it is best to wash with soap and water. Hand sanitizers can get rid of many, but not all, microbes. For example, **clostridium difficile**, commonly referred to as "**c-diff**," is a microbe that is not killed by alcohol-based sanitizers. A c-diff infection causes a patient to have copious amounts of watery diarrhea. In addition to standard infection-prevention precautions, the nursing assistant must wash hands with soap and water before and after caring for a patient with c-diff.

Hand sanitizer should not be used when the hands are visibly soiled, or if bodily fluids have been touched. After several uses of hand sanitizer, oils build up on the hands and should be removed by washing with soap.

Educating patients about cleanliness and proper handwashing will also help prevent the spread of disease. Make sure to assist patients with washing their hands or use a soapy washcloth on their hands throughout the day, especially after toileting and prior to eating. Proper handwashing in the community reduces the number of people who get sick with diarrheic illnesses and respiratory illnesses, such as colds.

Signs and Symptoms of Infections

Infections can be **systemic**, affecting the whole body, or **localized** to just a certain area. If a wound is locally infected, it also can become systemic by spreading into the person's bloodstream. Systemic infections are more serious and more difficult to treat. Therefore, recognizing the early signs of an infection is extremely important. Examples of some systemic infections include influenza, pneumonia, tuberculosis, and hepatitis. Infection symptoms appear because the body is trying to destroy the disease-causing organism. In the older adult population, normal symptoms of infection may not be as visible, which makes diagnosing the infection more difficult. Below are some signs and symptoms of a localized infection, such as a wound infection:

- An area warm to the touch
- Redness and/or swelling of a cut or sore
- Pain
- Pus or drainage from a wound
- Fever (A fever is the only symptom that can be caused by a local infection but affect the whole body.)

Systemic infection symptoms include:

- Fever (does not always occur in elderly population)
- Fatigue
- Nausea, vomiting, or diarrhea
- Chills
- Generalized weakness
- Change in mental status, especially in older adults
- Weight loss
- Decline in patient's ability to function
- Falls
- Increased respiratory rate, faster breathing
- Aches and pains (generally in the head and back)

Pneumonia is one of the leading causes of death in the elderly. Lung illnesses are common in older adults; therefore, detecting pneumonia can be difficult. Common symptoms can include the systemic symptoms listed above and also the following:

- Chest pain, difficulty breathing, or shortness of breath
- Weakness and fatigue
- Productive cough
- Fever, chills, and sweating

Influenza is also a leading cause of death in the elderly population. Signs and symptoms of influenza in adults are similar to systemic infection symptoms but can include stomach symptoms like nausea and vomiting. Cold-like symptoms, such as stuffy nose and cough, may also occur. In older adults, the flu can lead to other health issues and complications, such as dehydration, worsening of existing conditions (e.g., asthma or heart disease), and can even lead to pneumonia. The flu shot can be given to older adults, and it is recommended yearly in the fall season.

Decreasing Risk of Exposure to Disease-Causing Organisms

There are several precautions put into place in healthcare facilities to protect employees, patients, and the community from exposure to infectious organisms. There are different levels of precautions depending on the type of infection or disease that presents itself. Care should be taken with every patient or resident regardless of their health status, always assuming the potential for infection to occur. Protective equipment or supplies, such as exam gloves, are to be used on every patient as a standard precaution. For patients with a known infection, more specific precautions are put in place to prevent the spread of their infection to others.

Standard Precautions
Standard precautions are the basic practices used to prevent the spread of diseases that can be acquired by contact with blood, body fluids, nonintact skin, rashes, and mucous membranes. **Body fluids** include saliva, vomit, stool, secretions, and urine. **Mucous membranes** are moist membranes and include the inside of the nose, the mouth, the anus, and the openings in some of the genitals. Standard precautions are used as a minimum to care for all patients, whether they have a known infection or not. In this way, protection from potential microbes and the prevention of the spread of those potential

microbes are occurring. Examples of simple standard precautions that are used every day would be not sharing a drink with someone or not sharing an eating utensil with another person. In healthcare, handwashing is the first and largest standard precaution. In addition, personal protective equipment should be used. Personal protective equipment will be discussed in the sections below. All individuals, including patients, staff, and visitors, should comply with standard precautions in order to stop the spread of disease. An example of a standard precaution used in the healthcare setting would be wearing exam gloves when changing dirty linens and performing proper handwashing afterwards. Promotion and education regarding a safe healthcare environment is the foundation for preventing the transmission of pathogens.

Below is a list of key components for standard precautions in healthcare facilities:

- Hand hygiene
- Gloves
- Facial protection (eyes, nose, and mouth)
- Gowns
- Prevention of needle stick and injury from sharp instruments
- Respiratory hygiene and cough etiquette (A person with respiratory symptoms should cover their nose and mouth when coughing or sneezing, preferably coughing into an elbow rather than a hand, and they should throw away used tissues and masks, and perform handwashing after contact with any respiratory secretions.)
- Environmental cleaning
- Linens (Linens should be handled and transported in a way that prevents contact with skin and mucous membranes, and doesn't contaminate clothing.)
- Waste disposal (Ensure that waste contaminated with blood or body fluids is disposed of according to regulations.)
- Patient care equipment (Equipment that is contaminated with blood or body fluids should be handled in a way that prevents exposure to clothing, skin and mucous membranes, and transfer to other patients. Clean and disinfect equipment according to policy before use with another patient.)

Transmission-Based Precautions

Transmission-based precautions are used when a known infection is present in a patient. The type of precaution is specific to the way the microbes are spread or transmitted. Types of transmission-based precautions are divided into three categories:

Contact Precaution

Microbes that spread by contact, such as touching contaminated surfaces, require contact barriers. Such barriers include exam gloves and a gown to cover clothing. Before entering the patient's room, care providers put on the equipment, and it must be removed prior to leaving the room. Visitors are also required to wear gloves and a gown when entering the patient's room. Contact precautions should be applied to patients who have the following conditions and/or diseases: draining wounds, pressure ulcers, ostomy tubes or bags, uncontrolled secretions, rashes, or the presence of stool incontinence, which could be caused by norovirus, rotavirus, or clostridium difficile.

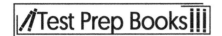

Droplet Precaution

Microbes that spread by droplets from respiratory secretions require droplet precautions. These infections usually affect the respiratory system. Coughing and sputum production will be frequent. Protective equipment used in this type of precaution includes a mask and gloves; however, a gown and eyewear may be used as well. The patient should be instructed to wear a mask if they need to leave their room. Some diseases or conditions that require droplet precautions may include respiratory viruses (e.g., influenza, respiratory syncytial virus) or Bordella pertussis.

Airborne Precaution

Microbes that spread through the air and can be inhaled can last a long time in a room. Some examples of infections in this category are Tuberculosis, measles, chickenpox, and herpes zoster. Both chickenpox and herpes zoster will require airborne precautions until the lesions have crusted over. A fit-tested N-95 or higher-level disposable mask must be worn in this patient's room. Gloves, a gown, and eyewear may also be used. The patient should be instructed to wear a mask if they leave their room. Negative-pressure rooms are usually used for these types of infections. **Negative pressure** means that the air in the room is basically kept from escaping to other rooms when the door opens. This keeps the contaminated air contained in the patient's room.

Patients who are placed in precautions will have a cart outside of their door and a sign to designate the type of precaution needed. Each cart will contain protective supplies for the healthcare worker and single-use items such as stethoscopes. Precaution rooms will be thoroughly disinfected per the facility's protocol between patient uses.

Personal Protective Equipment (PPE)

Personal protective equipment is the technical term for the supplies worn to protect employees from workplace injury or illness. Gloves, gowns, masks, and eye shields are the most common types of PPE in the healthcare environment. Employers are required to provide PPE and to ensure that proper training is available. Training for this equipment should include how to put it on, where equipment is located, when it should be used, how it is removed, and proper disposal. PPE should be put on in the following order, depending on how much protection in needed:

- Gown
- Mask
- Eye wear
- Gloves

When wearing a gown, the opening is in the back and it will secure at the back of the neck and around the person's waist. The gown should be worn on top of the uniform or clothes and must cover all clothing from the neck down to the knees. A new gown should be worn every time the patient's room is entered and must be thrown away when leaving the room. This prevents contamination from spreading into hallways or other patients' rooms.

Masks are placed over the nose, mouth, and chin. First, pull apart the mask from top to bottom so that it will fit the face, and then place the top ridge on the bridge of the nose. This ridge is meant to conform over the nose, and it must be bent and squeezed to ensure a tight fit. Next, pull the lower edge of the mask under the chin. Tie the top ties on top of the head so that the ties go above the ears. Tie the lower ties behind the neck. As with any PPE, use a new mask when entering a room, and remove it when

exiting. Fit-tested respirators, or N-95 masks, are placed in a similar way to regular masks, but the seal must be tighter. Education on the N-95 mask will occur during the fit-testing process.

Eye shields or goggles should cover the eyes, and they should not slip off when bending down. Some eyewear, such as glasses or goggles, is attached to a mask like a shield. When putting on gloves, make sure to pull them above the wrists and above the cuffs of the gown if one is worn.

Removing PPE occurs in this order:

- Gloves
- Goggles
- Gown
- Mask or respirator

Peel off one glove by pulling on the outside of the glove and folding it down. Hold the removed glove in the hand that is still gloved and use the exposed hand to slide the fingers under the cuff, peeling it off. Throw the gloves away in the proper trash. To remove eye protection, grab the sides of the eyewear and throw them away. Avoid touching the front of the eyewear, which is considered contaminated. When removing a gown, reach back and untie the ties. Pull the gown off inside out from behind the neck or back so that exposed hands are kept off of the outside and front of the gown. Once the gown is off, keep the clean, inside part of the gown on the outside and roll it up. Then dispose of the gown in the proper bin. Remove the mask last by untying the ties and not touching the front of the mask. When removing a respirator, or exiting a room in airborne precaution, it is important to close the door before taking the mask off. Handwashing must always be performed after disposing of PPE.

While caring for patients, clean and dirty tasks will be performed. Always work from clean to dirty and change personal protective equipment if needed between tasks. Below are some examples of clean and dirty tasks.

Clean tasks:

- Taking vital signs
- Assessing the patient
- Feeding a patient
- Making a clean bed

Checking urine output in a patient who is **continent** (able to control their bladder)

- Transferring a patient from bed to chair
- Boosting a patient up in bed

Dirty tasks:

- Changing dirty linens
- Bathing a patient
- Changing a diaper or emptying a bedpan
- Providing oral care
- Caring for a wound

Emergencies

Emergencies include numerous physical, environmental, technological, and disaster-related crises. Generally speaking, emergencies in the hospital or medical facility are medical in nature, affecting a person's health or physical body. Disaster-related emergencies are also very important to consider because they can lead to physical and medical emergencies. Environmental emergencies can include tornadoes, hurricanes, flooding, severe storms, and earthquakes. Technological hazards, such as electrical failure or heating/cooling failure of a facility, can also affect a person's physical health. Other forms of disaster could be bomb threats, fire, an active shooter, or terrorism in the area, as well as severe outbreaks of illnesses such as the flu.

Medical emergencies can include choking, cardiac arrest, falls, an unresponsive person, burns, or any life-threatening injury. These emergencies can happen to patients, visitors, and employees.

Emergency and Disaster Response Protocols

Healthcare facilities are required to have disaster preparedness manuals and protocols that specify the steps to follow in any environmental disasters. Good record keeping of patient information, including contact persons during emergencies, is very important. Evacuation routes and exits should be clearly marked and practiced in case of an emergency. For example, during a severe storm, it may be necessary to move patients to interior rooms away from windows or to move patients from upper floors to a lower level for their safety. Patients in long-term care or assisted living who are independent should be educated on the different routes and plans should an emergency occur. All and any staff available will immediately follow protocol and assist with the plan or evacuation as indicated. Patient and employee count, or roll call, will be performed to ensure that no person is left behind or unaccounted for. The Centers for Medicare & Medicaid Services (CMS) developed an emergency preparedness checklist for healthcare facilities. This checklist includes seventy tasks and gives guidance for developing emergency plans. In addition, the checklist provides guidelines for adequate food and water supply, identifies evacuation routes, provides for patient transport, and outlines critical supplies and equipment.

Thunderstorms

It is important to go indoors if a storm is coming, especially when thunder is heard. Lightning can strike up to ten miles away from a storm. Be prepared to bring residents indoors if there is a storm approaching. Once inside, ensure that residents, staff, and visitors stay away from windows and avoid electrical equipment such as computers or landline phones with a cord. Staying away from electrical equipment will reduce the chance of coming in contact with electric shock during a storm. Also, bathtubs, showers, and pools should be avoided to reduce the risk of getting shocked from a potential lightning strike.

Tornadoes

If there is a tornado in the area, it is best to seek shelter immediately. Follow the acronym **DUCK**. Go **d**own to the lowest level, get **u**nder something, **c**over heads, and **k**eep in the shelter or safe place until the storm has passed. It is advised to be in a basement or the lowest level and stay in the center of the building, away from windows. In healthcare facilities, there will be designated rooms or hallways for shelter during a tornado. Education on these safe areas will be taught during training drills.

Power-Outage Emergencies

The power may go out at any time and for any length of time. Power may be out due to a storm, earthquake, fire, tornado, or simply because of electrical failure. If the power goes out in a patient's home or in a healthcare facility, the following areas of concern need to be addressed:

- *Safe and adequate supplies of drinking water.* When power goes out, water filter systems may not work properly. Make sure there is a backup supply of clean water, preferably in bottles or jugs.

- *Food.* Food will be safe in the refrigerator if the power is out for less than four hours. The freezer can stay cold for twenty-four to forty-eight hours, depending on how full it is. During the outage, avoid opening the doors to the freezer and refrigerator so that the cold air does not escape. Perishable items such as milk, eggs, meat, and dairy should be packed and isolated with ice. Any perishable food item that is over 40 °F should be thrown away.

- *Cold.* During the cooler months, make sure that residents wear extra layers and blankets when the heat supply is off during an outage.

- *Heat.* To prevent overheating in a power outage during the summer, residents should drink plenty of fluids, wear loose-fitting clothes, and remove layers if necessary. Open windows if it is safe, so that there is some airflow through the home or building. Also, cool cloths can be placed on the forehead and armpits.

Disaster supplies should be available in facilities and in homes. These supplies can include bottled water, canned or dried food, flashlights, extra batteries, a first-aid kit, and extra blankets. In hospitals, there are emergency outlets that work on back-up generators if the main power goes out for any reason. All essential equipment must be plugged into emergency outlets at all times in case of a power failure. Such equipment might include IV pumps, ventilator machines, cardiac monitors, bed cords, surgical equipment, and computers. There are certain lights that remain lit for safety during a power outage. In patient homes or other healthcare facilities, these back-up systems may not be available. Family members may be asked to take their loved one home during an extended power outage. Sometimes evacuation to a safer facility or shelter may be necessary.

Earthquakes

Earthquakes can occur in any geographic region, but most commonly they occur in areas near fault lines, such as the San Andreas Fault line in California. They can happen without warning anytime during the night or day. Injuries can occur from heavy objects falling, ceiling collapse, debris from buildings, or from falling furniture such as bookcases and cabinets.

The three steps a person should take when an earthquake is happening are:

- Drop down to the ground level (this prevents a fall when the quaking occurs).
- Cover the head and neck using the hands and arms.
- Get under a table or sturdy desk.

If there is no furniture to shelter under, getting next to a sturdy wall or shorter furniture is a good substitute. Glass doorways and windows should be avoided so that injury from broken glass can be minimized. Lastly, the sheltering item, whether it is a table or a couch, should be grasped.

Until the shaking stops, the person should stay with the sheltering item. After an earthquake, the home or facility may need to be evacuated.

Hurricanes

Hurricanes can cause heavy winds, rain, and flooding. Generally, knowledge of pending hurricanes via meteorological reports gives adequate warning and preparation time. Evacuation to a shelter or another healthcare facility may be necessary if a certain facility is near the coast or near the impact of the storm. If evacuation is not required, taking shelter in interior rooms away from windows is advised. As with all natural disasters, emergency kits and survival supplies should be available during and after the storm.

Disease Outbreak

Another type of emergency that can occur in a community or in a geographic region would be infectious in nature. Examples include outbreaks of Ebola or the Zika virus. Influenza can even fit into this category if it is a strain of flu that is not affected by the seasonal flu shot. The World Health Organization tracks infectious diseases worldwide and responds to try and control the outbreak, prevent spread, and treat victims. An epidemic is a widespread occurrence of an infectious disease in a region or community at a certain time. Generally speaking, any advice given by the public health workers should be followed, and vaccines should be administered if available. In the healthcare environment, patients who develop symptoms similar to the disease of focus will be isolated away from others and monitored closely depending on the type of disease. Healthcare providers will be educated on the **level of precaution** (standard, contact, droplet, or airborne) that is required to care for patients affected by the particular disease.

Additional Emergency/Disaster Situations

The response to bomb threats, an active shooter in the workplace, or bioterrorism will be dictated by facility protocol, outlined during an employee's orientation, and practiced during training drills.

Immediate Life-Safety Techniques

In the event of a medical emergency, there are specific steps to take depending on the situation. There will be written policies for these types of emergencies in the workplace that are used for patients, staff, and/or visitors.

Below are some examples of medical emergencies:

- Choking
- Unresponsive or unconscious person or patient
- Excessive bleeding
- Head injury
- Broken bones
- Severe burns
- Seizures
- Chest pain
- Difficulty breathing
- Allergic reactions that cause swelling and/or breathing difficulties
- Inhalation or swallowing of a toxic substance
- Accidental poisoning

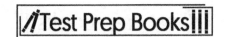

Choking

If someone is choking, the victim will most likely grab at their throat, or they may have a cough that eventually stops, indicating blockage of the airway. If the airway is blocked, they will need the Heimlich maneuver to be performed immediately. Oftentimes people cough and may leave a room to get a drink or to avoid disrupting others. It is best to follow that person to ensure they are not choking.

When someone is choking and conscious, the **responder**, or person at the scene who witnesses and intervenes, should:

- Ask the victim if they are choking and tell them help is here.
- Assist the victim to a standing position.
- Stand behind the victim and wrap the arms around the victim's waist.
- Make a fist with one hand and place the thumb against the victim's stomach just above their belly button.
- Place the other hand on top of the fisted hand.
- Thrust quick, hard, and upward on the victim's stomach.
- Continue this until the food or object comes out of the victim's mouth.
- Do *not* swipe the victim's mouth with one finger, as this could push the blockage further down the airway.

If the victim is still choking and goes unconscious:

- Lower the victim to the floor, shout for help, and have someone call 911.

Begin cardiopulmonary resuscitation (CPR) by following the basic life support steps until **emergency medical services (EMS)** arrives.

Unconsciousness or Unresponsiveness

First, try to arouse the person by shaking or tapping them. If they are indeed unresponsive, call for help, have someone call 911, and proceed to:

- Make sure the patient is lying flat and place a backboard under them for CPR.
- Follow basic life support (BLS) protocol.
- Look and listen for breathing (chest rise).
- Check for a pulse in radial artery (wrist).
- If patient is breathing, stay with them until EMS arrives. If there is a pulse but no breathing, begin rescue breaths. Give one breath every five or six seconds. Check pulse every two minutes.
- If no pulse, begin CPR and continue until EMS arrives.

Direct someone else to get the **automated external defibrillator (AED)** as CPR is continued.

- CPR: Thirty chest compressions then two breaths, repeat for two-minute cycles.
- Chest compressions should be firm and deep, to the rhythm of the disco song "Stayin' Alive," about one hundred beats per minute. This ensures adequate perfusion of organs with blood since the heart is not pumping on its own.
- When the AED arrives, turn it on and follow the prompts for use.

If the patient recovers, turn them onto their left side and continue to monitor them until EMS arrive. Healthcare workers will be trained and certified on BLS, CPR, and AED use.

Excessive Bleeding

Call for help and call 911. Then:

- Have the patient sit down or lie down.
- Use a towel or shirt to hold continuous pressure on the bleeding area.
- Elevate the area above their heart. For example, if the leg is bleeding, have the patient lie down and put their leg on a chair.
- Talk to the patient and monitor their responsiveness. Stay with them until EMS arrives.

Head Injury

Concussions, contusions, and skull fractures are all common types of traumatic brain injuries. Concussions occur when the brain is jarred against the skull, usually during sports, hard contact with another person, or hitting the head on the ground. **Concussions** can cause mental confusion and lead to disruptions in normal brain functioning. The effects of a concussion can show up immediately, or they may not show up for hours or days. Normally, concussions do not cause a loss of consciousness, so it is important to pay attention to other possible symptoms. Another type of traumatic brain injury is a **contusion**, which is a bruise on the brain. This bruise can swell in the brain and cause a **hematoma**, or bleeding in the brain. A skull fracture is a break in the skull bone and can occur with or without brain damage. The following list includes symptoms of traumatic brain injuries:

- Confusion
- Depression
- Dizziness or balance problems
- Foggy feeling
- Double vision or changes in vision
- Tiredness
- Headache
- Memory loss
- Nausea
- Sensitivity to light
- Trouble remembering and concentrating

If a patient has a known head injury, or they stated that they hit their head, stay with the patient and call for a supervisor. Monitor the patient for mild symptoms from the list above. If the symptoms are not serious, the patient may require a visit from the physician. If the patient is elderly or has other serious health issues, hospitalization may be required to rule out more serious consequences from the head

injury. The pie chart below depicts the leading causes of traumatic brain injury, with falls being the largest percentage.

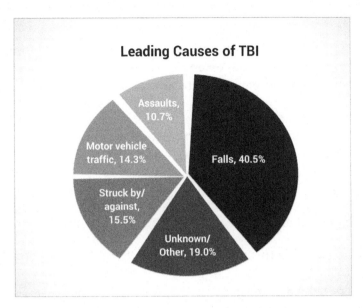

Symptoms of a head injury that are more serious and require immediate emergency treatment include:

- Unequal pupils
- Convulsions
- Fracture of the skull or face
- Inability to move legs or arms
- Clear or bloody fluid coming from the ears, nose, or mouth
- Loss of consciousness
- Persistent vomiting
- Severe headache
- Slurred speech and distorted vision
- Restlessness and irritability

If any of the above symptoms appear after a head injury, call for help and call 911.

Broken Bones (Compound Fractures)

A **compound fracture** is a fracture in which the bone is protruding through the skin. Other symptoms include pain, swelling, deformity in the fractured area, and bruising. This is the most serious type of fracture and requires immediate attention. The following comprises first aid for fractures:

- Call for help and call 911, especially if a fracture in the head, back or neck is suspected.
- Don't move the patient unless they are in danger of further injury.
- Keep the injured area still and stay with the patient.
- Treat any bleeding by holding pressure with a towel or gauze.
- Look for signs of shock in the patient (shallow, fast breathing, or feeling faint) and lay them down with their feet elevated.

- Wrap ice packs in a towel and ice the injured area.
- Wait for EMS to arrive.

Burns

Burn injuries can range from mild to severe, but the initial treatment for all burns is the same. **First-degree burns** affect the top layer of the skin, **second-degree burns** affect two layers, and **third-degree burns** affect all three layers. Call for an emergency response if:

- The burn is through all the skin layers.
- The person is a baby or elderly and the burn is severe.
- The hands, feet, face, or genitals are burned.
- The burn is larger than two inches or is oozing.
- The burn is charred and leathery, or has white, brown, or black patches.

Initial treatment for all burns includes:

- Remove the source of the burn, put out the fire, smother the burning area, or have the person stop, drop, and roll.
- Remove any hot or burned clothing.
- Remove clothing that is tight and remove jewelry (burns can swell very quickly).
- Hold the burned area under cool, running water for twenty minutes.
- Use two cold cloths if running water is not available. Alternate holding them on the area every two minutes.
- Do not put ice on the burn.
- Keep the patient warm by covering the rest of the body.
- Wrap or cover the burn loosely with gauze, or a use a sheet for large areas.
- If EMS has been called, stay with the patient and keep them warm until help arrives.

Seizures

Seizures have many symptoms depending on the type of seizure. Some symptoms include jerking motions, shaking, unconsciousness, stiffness, and blank staring. If someone is having a violent seizure, the steps to follow include:

- Protect the victim's head by moving hard objects out of the way and placing a blanket under their head.
- Loosen clothing around their neck.
- Do not try to hold them down and do not try to put something in their mouth.
- Get help to control bystanders so that the victim has some space.
- When the seizure is over, have the victim lie on their side and make sure their airway is open.
- Call 911 if the seizure lasts more than five minutes, if the victim has other medical conditions, or if the person has never had a seizure before.
- People with known epilepsy may have seizures that are short and frequent, so calling 911 may not be necessary.

Chest Pain

Chest pain can be a symptom of a heart attack or other serious heart or lung condition. Prompt attention is necessary so that the person can be treated before serious heart damage or death occurs.

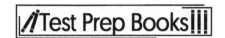

Chest Pain

Chest pain can be a symptom of a heart attack or other serious heart or lung condition. Prompt attention is necessary so that the person can be treated before serious heart damage or death occurs. Chest pain can also be a result of a lung infection, excessive coughing, broken ribs from an injury, anxiety, indigestion, or muscular injury. If the patient has not fallen or does not have any outward physical signs of injury to the chest area, assume that the chest pain is cardiac related. When someone complains of chest pain, do the following:

- Have the person sit down and ask where the pain is located.
- Call for the supervisor immediately.
- Assess if they have any injuries on or near their chest.
- Call 911 (if not in a medical facility) if the pain lasts more than a few minutes, or they have the following symptoms:
- Pain in the arms, shoulders, back and chest
- Difficulty breathing
- Fatigue
- Nausea
- Sweating
- Dizziness

If there is oxygen available, a respiratory therapist or nurse will place a **nasal cannula** in their nose and give between two and four liters of oxygen.

- If available and the person is not allergic or taking any blood-thinner medication, the nurse will have the person chew a regular-strength aspirin. Aspirin helps the blood flow to the heart.
- Stay with the person until EMS arrives.
- If the person becomes unconscious, follow BLS guidelines and initiate CPR.

Difficulty Breathing

Breathing difficulties or shortness of breath can be caused by many factors, such as asthma, bronchitis, pneumonia, heart conditions, pulmonary embolism, anxiety, or exercise. People may occasionally have shortness of breath because of an underlying condition that is being monitored by a physician. They may take medication for this symptom and be able to continue to live relatively normal lives. However, if a person has sudden difficulty catching their breath, and it is not relieved with rest, change of position, or their inhaler medication, immediate attention is required. Do the following if a person begins to struggle with breathing:

- Call for help and have the person sit up in their chair or in their bed.

- Instruct the person to try to take slow breaths, inhaling though their nose and exhaling out of their mouth.

- Continue to talk to them reassuringly and soothingly. Anxiety can actually make breathing even more difficult.

- If their breathing becomes easier and they seem to calm down, have a physician see them as soon as possible, especially if this is something new for this person.

- If breathing continues to be difficult, call 911 (if not in medical facility).

- A nurse or respiratory therapist will place oxygen on the patient with a mask or nasal cannula, if available.

- Stay with the patient until help arrives and monitor their level of consciousness and breathing rate.

Allergic Reactions

Allergies can cause many symptoms from mild to severe. Some examples of mild symptoms might include itching, redness on the skin, hives, sneezing, runny nose, and itchy eyes. Wheezing may occur and may be treated with a prescribed inhaler. Life-threatening allergic reactions include swelling of the tongue or throat, difficulty breathing, and anaphylaxis, which is a systemic reaction. **Anaphylaxis** is rare but can lead to death if it is not recognized and treated quickly. Allergies to foods, medications, latex, and insect bites can cause anaphylaxis. Normally a person who has serious allergic reactions will have an epinephrine pen, or "epi-pen," with them at all times, to be administered in case of a reaction. If the following symptoms associated with anaphylaxis are observed outside of a medical facility, call 911. Otherwise, report any of the following symptoms to the nurse:

- Difficulty breathing
- Swollen tongue or throat tightness
- Wheezing
- Nausea and vomiting
- Fainting or dizziness
- Low blood pressure
- Rapid heart beat
- Feeling strange or sense of impending doom
- Chest pain

Call 911 even if an epi-pen has been administered for the allergic reaction. Reaction symptoms can continue to occur or can reoccur later.

Poisoning

Poison can be something eaten, inhaled, or absorbed in excess, or exposure to toxic substances. This type of emergency can happen to patients and employees. If there is an accidental poisoning and the person is awake and alert, call the poison-control hotline at 1-800-222-1222. Stay on the phone with poison control and stay with the victim. Try to have the following information available for the responders:

- Weight and age of the victim
- The label or bottle of the substance taken
- The time of exposure to the substance (how long it has been)
- The address of where the victim is located

If the person goes unconscious or is not breathing, call 911.

Many chemical labels, such as cleaning supplies, have warning labels and instructions for dealing with toxic exposure. The eyes may need to be flushed with water, for example. Read labels but also call for

60

Many chemical labels, such as cleaning supplies, have warning labels and instructions for dealing with toxic exposure. The eyes may need to be flushed with water, for example. Read labels but also call for help. In healthcare facilities, protocols for chemical spills or exposure exist so that clean up and injury can be dealt with quickly. Always follow the policy provided by the facility or workplace.

Evacuation Procedures

During or after a disaster situation, evacuation of patients may be necessary. Designated shelters or facilities should be predetermined and written in disaster/emergency protocols. Additionally, an outside meeting place should be determined in case of a low-scale evacuation, such as during a fire. Staff and assisted-living residents (independent) should know the evacuation route and meeting place, and these should be practiced with drills. Nonambulatory residents need to be evacuated by staff in an organized manner so that each staff member has a role in the evacuation. Large-scale evacuations include transferring to another facility or shelter.

Evacuation from a Fire

In assisted-living facilities, once the evacuation from a fire has begun and the fire department arrives, give them a list of people that are missing. Also, give them a list of who is nonambulatory and their locations inside the building.

In nursing-home facilities, a staged evacuation is needed so that all residents are accounted for and assisted out of harm's way. Residents in rooms adjacent to the fire should be evacuated first and moved to the other side of fire doors. Fire doors or safe zones should be predetermined by the facility. Evacuate any additional residents' rooms as needed.

It is important to know and account for the residents and essential items. The following is necessary during any disaster and evacuation:

- Copies of medical records, phone numbers, and medication binders
- Critical supplies, such as prescriptions and medical supplies
- Binders for each resident that include personal information
- Any medications it is possible to take along
- Oxygen tanks (twice the number normally used if relocating to another facility)
- Food (enough for three meals a day for three days)
- Water (one gallon per person per day, for three days)

Staff should be familiar with the following:

- The building's evacuation and emergency plan
- Recognized fire hazards
- Two routes out of their work area
- The building's safety systems and equipment

Evacuation Drills

For large-scale evacuations, the areas of immediate risk should be evacuated first, followed by a systematic approach for the rest. All doors should be closed when leaving. Drills should be conducted once a quarter. There should be a logbook that contains the dates, times, and sections in the building where the drills took place. The logbook will be reviewed yearly as required by the Fire Department.

Drills should be treated as real evacuations and should take place on every shift so that all staff members have a chance to participate. A drill should be announced ahead of time to alert staff and residents. Drills should involve potential fires in varying sections of the building so that different exit routes can be tried. Elevators should not be used during an evacuation unless the fire department says to do so. Following the drill, discuss and critique how it went so that changes can be made. Drills should also involve evacuation for all types of disasters, including weather emergencies.

Relocation Sites

For relocation sites for evacuations, there should be two potential sites. One close in distance and one out of the area. These sites can be set up as reciprocal sites, meaning that the other sites may use the facility if they need to relocate. The sites should be suitable for all weather conditions. Bedding/beds may need to be supplied.

Facilities that may require evacuation and transport include hospitals, nursing homes, dialysis centers, assisted-living facilities, and psychiatric treatment facilities. In an emergency disaster situation, it must be assumed that ambulances may not be available for transportation due to the number available and their use for other emergencies during the crisis. Also, it must be assumed that some disasters will happen without pre-warning, and quick decisions will need to be made. In general, EMS agencies will manage the medical transportation in a region. In addition to potential ambulances, buses (school, commercial, etc.) may be considered for large-scale patient evacuation and transportation. Buses should be equipped with appropriate equipment and supplies for safe patient transfer. Each facility is responsible for tracking the movement and relocation of their patients. Contacting extra available medical personnel is as important as transport. All staff should be contacted and recruited for assistance during a crisis, if they are able to do so. Additional nonemployee lists of personnel such as registered nurses (RNs), certified nursing assistants (CNAs), or licensed practical nurses (LPNs) may volunteer to assist and care for patients during the evacuation and transport process.

Fire Prevention and Safety

Recognizing fire hazards in the workplace is important in the prevention of fires and the promotion of safety for residents and employees. Staff will be trained on the fire policy and regular drills should be performed so that each staff person's role is known and practiced. Below are some potential workplace fire hazards:

Candles may not be allowed in certain facilities. If they are allowed, make sure they are never left unattended, are not within reach of children or pets, and are not placed near windows or material that could burn.

- To mitigate electrical hazards, unplug appliances when not in use and keep them clean and in good working order. If there is concern that a piece of electrical equipment is not working properly, report it and stop using it. Keep three feet of space around heaters. Do not overload outlets with too many cords, and do not pinch cords behind devices or furniture. Do not use cords that are cracked or broken.

- Use of a stove and cooking appliances may not be allowed in certain facilities, but these guidelines are useful for anyone that may be cooking:

- Never leave cooking unattended.

- Never leave cooking unattended.

- Don't cook if too sleepy or if taking medication that causes drowsiness.

- Use back burners on the stove to prevent spills and burns.

- Turn handles away from the front of the stove.

- Don't leave towels or potholders laying on the stovetop.

- Keep the oven and stove clean and wipe up spills.

- In case of a grease fire, do not use a fire extinguisher. Smother the fire in the pot or pan with a lid and turn off the burner.

- For an oven fire, turn off the oven and leave the door closed.

- For a microwave fire, leave the door closed, turn off the microwave, and unplug it.

- Healthcare facilities are smoke-free, but there may be designated smoking areas outside. Ensure that guests or employees use the appropriate area and extinguish the cigarette completely.

- Do not allow smoking near someone who is using oxygen, because oxygen can increase the strength of a fire

Each year, there are many structure fires in health care facilities. These fires happen in nursing homes, hospitals or hospice houses, mental health facilities, and doctors' offices or clinics. Cooking equipment is the primary cause of fires. Other causes of fires include clothes dryers or washers, intentional fires, smoking materials, heating equipment, electrical distribution or lighting equipment, and playing with a heat source.

Employees will be educated on the location of fire alarms, any alarm systems that are in place, sprinklers, and fire extinguishers. The danger of a fire is mainly from the smoke it creates. Smoke can travel quickly in a fire and can affect areas in a building that are not close to the fire itself. With elderly and sick residents, lack of mobility inhibits a quick escape; therefore, proper evacuation and rescue planning is essential. When responding to a fire or an alarm, always treat it as a true emergency. Call 911 even if an alarm system is monitored and activated, to ensure that help is on the way. If it is a false alarm, the fire department may still search to make sure everything is safe.

In case of a fire, follow the acronym **RACE:**

R - Rescue yourself and others away from the fire.

A - Activate the fire alarm or call 911 if it has not already been done.

C - Contain the fire (close doors or windows).

E - Extinguish the fire (with fire extinguisher or smothering with a blanket).

Do not attempt to use a fire extinguisher if the fire is too large or if the area around the fire is unsafe. Extinguishers have about ten seconds of power in them. To use a fire extinguisher, use the acronym **PASS**:

> P - Pull the pin.

> A - Aim at the base of the fire.

> S - Squeeze the handle.

> S - Sweep from side to side.

There are several classes of fire extinguishers, depending on the type of fire that is burning.

Class A is for regular combustible materials, such as wood, paper, plastics, and cardboard. The geometric symbol on this type of extinguisher is a green triangle.

Class B is for liquid combustibles, such as gasoline, kerosene, grease, and oil. The geometric symbol is a red square.

Class C is for electrical fires that involve appliances, outlets, circuit breakers, and wiring. Never use water because of the risk of shock. The geometric symbol is a blue circle.

Class D extinguishers are for chemicals and are usually found in chemical laboratories. Such chemical fires may involve magnesium, titanium, potassium, and sodium. The geometric symbol for this extinguisher is a yellow decagon.

Class K is for fires involved with cooking oils. These extinguishers should be found in kitchens and restaurants. The geometric symbol is a black hexagon.

Most common types of fire extinguishers:

- Water extinguishers, or air-pressurized water (APW), are for Class A fires only and can cause damage if used on the wrong type of fire. Do not use on grease, electrical, or Class D (chemical) fires.

- Dry chemical extinguishers can be used for combination fires of Class A, B, and C.

BC is the regular type of dry chemical extinguisher. It is filled with foam made of sodium bicarbonate or potassium.

ABC is the multipurpose extinguisher and the one found in most facilities.

- Carbon dioxide (CO_2) extinguishers are used on Class B and C fires.

Practice Quiz

1. Which of the following is the best way to prevent the spread of infection?
   a. Keeping the mouth covered when coughing or sneezing
   b. Disinfecting shared patient equipment
   c. Practicing proper hand hygiene
   d. Avoiding contact with infectious patients

2. What are the correct steps to follow when using a fire extinguisher?
   a. Pull the pin, Squeeze the handle, Aim the nozzle, Swirl around the fire
   b. Pull the pin, Aim at the base of the fire, Squeeze the handle, Sweep from side to side
   c. Squeeze the handle, Aim at the base of the fire, Pull the pin, Sweep from side to side
   d. Stand back, Pull the pin, Squeeze the handle, Sweep from side to side

3. When preparing to transfer a patient from their bed to a wheelchair, what is the first step to take?
   a. Ensure that the bed is locked.
   b. Inform the patient about what is going to happen.
   c. Get another staff member to help.
   d. Have the patient sit up in bed.

4. When attempting to lift something heavy, which of the following should not be done?
   a. Keep the legs straight and bend over to use back muscles.
   b. Spread legs apart and bend at the knees.
   c. Stand close to the object.
   d. Use only feet and legs to turn.

5. An aide is caring for a patient in their home. Which of the following items should the aide recognize as a fire hazard?
   a. Multiple electrical cords plugged into a power strip
   b. A pack of matches on a coffee table
   c. A potholder lying on the stove
   d. A toaster left out on the counter

See answers on next page

Answer Explanations

1. C: All of the answer choices are types of standard precautions, but research has shown that proper hand hygiene using soap and water or alcohol-based hand rub (if appropriate) is the best way to prevent the spread of germs.

2. B: Use the acronym PASS to answer this question. The pin should always be pulled first. Choices *A*, *C*, and *D* are not listed in the correct order or with the correct wording. The correct directions and order are: Pull the pin, Aim at the base of the fire, Squeeze the handle, and Sweep from side to side.

3. B: Anytime a task or procedure is about to occur, the patient should be informed first. All of the other options are part of the procedure, but the first step is to explain the task to the patient. Another staff person may not be needed, the patient may not be able to sit up in bed on their own, or they may wonder why they are being asked to sit up.

4. A: When lifting a heavy object, the lower back should not be strained; therefore, bending over and using the back muscles should be avoided. Choices *B*, *C*, and *D* should be done when lifting. Stand close to the object, bend at the knees with legs apart, and use feet and legs to turn if needed.

5. C: Anything flammable that is on top of a stove should be moved off of the stove surface to avoid a fire if the burners are turned on. Keep in mind that this patient is in their own home. All of the other choices are acceptable and pose no immediate fire hazard. Multiple cords should be plugged into a power strip, and a toaster left on the counter is not a hazard. The pack of matches on the table could be a hazard, but the patient is still living independently and may still be capable of using matches correctly. If there are no children in the home, the matches are not of immediate concern.

Promotion of Function and Health of Residents

Personal Care Skills

Feeding

A nursing assistant may have to feed a resident who is unable to eat independently. Before assisting a resident with their meal, make sure they have received the correct meal based on their dietary orders. If the resident's meal does not correspond to their prescribed diet, remove their tray and notify the licensed nurse immediately so the meal won't be delayed for too long.

It's essential for a nursing assistant to know a resident's dietary status and to carefully adhere to any restrictions. For example, if a resident is ordered to have nothing by mouth (**NPO**) prior to surgery, and they consume something (including liquids), the surgery might have to be postponed or canceled. Allowing a resident to consume food outside their prescribed diet is detrimental to their nutritional status, overall health, and well-being.

Residents with **dysphagia** (trouble swallowing) are at a high risk for aspiration. When feeding a resident with dysphagia, make sure that all liquids are adequately thickened according to their dietary orders before feeding. The resident should be seated upright, fed slowly, and checked for complete swallowing with each bite. Residents at risk for aspiration should remain in an upright position for at least thirty minutes after eating.

Residents who are visually impaired may also need assistance with meals. The **clock method** helps them become more independent at mealtime. This method involves describing each food's position on the plate as corresponding to a number on the face of a clock, which helps residents understand where a particular food is located. For example, by placing the meat at the twelve o'clock position, the vegetable at four o'clock, and the starch at eight o'clock, residents can then feed themselves and get more enjoyment from their meal.

It's important that mealtime be a pleasant experience for all residents, regardless of their abilities. A nursing assistant is responsible for ensuring that foods are both visually appealing and at the proper temperature, as well as for promoting independence whenever possible.

Bathing

Bath care is provided to residents for hygienic purposes and to promote circulation and relaxation. A resident's mobility status determines the level of assistance they need with their bath. Residents who are fully mobile and not at risk for falls can shower or take tub baths with little or no assistance. A **partial bath** is when only some areas of the body are cleansed. For residents needing assistance, baths can be given in a shower (using a shower chair) or in a tub, depending on availability, ability, and preference.

Residents who are unable to leave their bed require a **bed bath**. Not all residents require a full bath every day; however, frequent perineal care (at least twice daily) is always necessary for adequate hygiene. A resident's skin should be inspected during bathing, and any signs of redness, bruising, or irritation should be reported to the nurse. When assisting a resident with bathing, always start with the

67

cleanest areas of the body and progress to the most soiled. For example, start with the face and end with the perineal area. When giving a bed bath, the bath basin water and washcloths can be changed during the bath, if necessary. If for any reason the bath is interrupted, dry off the resident and cover them to avoid overexposure and/or discomfort.

After bathing, it's important that the resident's skin be dried thoroughly, taking special care to dry areas that tend to remain damp. Under the arms, under the breasts, between fingers and toes, and in skin folds are all areas prone to remaining damp and at risk for skin breakdown if not dried properly. Powders and excessive lotions are generally unnecessary to maintain healthy skin.

Perineal Care, Including Catheter

Perineal care should be provided for residents during routine AM (morning) and HS (hour of sleep/bedtime) care, and throughout the day as needed. Residents who have bladder and/or bowel incontinence, are experiencing diarrhea, and have mobility limitations need frequent perineal care to promote adequate hygiene and to prevent skin breakdown and infection.

When performing perineal care on a female resident, always wash the genitals from front to back to avoid introducing an infection into the urinary tract. When performing perineal care on an uncircumcised male resident, gently pull back the penis' foreskin to allow for thorough cleaning of the tip. To lessen a resident's discomfort, always provide them with as much privacy and coverage as possible when providing perineal care.

For residents with indwelling catheters, perineal care is like that of any other resident except that care must be taken _not_ to pull on the catheter and cause them any discomfort or harm. When cleaning the resident, the exposed portion of the catheter can be wiped down with a damp washcloth. When cleaning the catheter, begin wiping at the end closest to the resident and progress down the tubing, away from the resident. Always make sure that the tubing is free of kinks and secured to the resident's leg to prevent accidental dislodging. The catheter bag must also remain below the level of the resident's bladder to prevent urine from running back up into them. The perineal area of residents with indwelling catheters should be cleansed regularly to prevent a urinary tract infection.

Foot/Nail Care

A resident's nails should be kept neat and clean. Inspect fingernails and toenails daily and report any signs of fungus or infection immediately. Nails should be trimmed; however, some facilities have policies that don't allow nursing assistants to clip a resident's nails. If the policy does allow it, take extra care when trimming the toenails of a diabetic resident to avoid causing irritation to the nails or surrounding skin. Diabetic residents are at high risk for infection due to poor wound healing, so small cuts or abrasions to the feet can put them at risk. Patients with diabetes can also suffer from **peripheral neuropathy** (loss of feeling in the extremities), so even if nail trimming isn't permitted by the facility, the feet of diabetic residents should still be inspected daily for signs of infection.

Mouth Care

Mouth care should be performed on residents who are unable to adequately perform mouth care independently. While providing mouth care, inspect the mouth and report any of the following: discoloration, redness, swelling, bleeding, cracking, sores, cracked or broken teeth, and odor. Mouth care should be provided during AM and HS care, as well as after meals. Intubated residents may need oral care more frequently due to the drying of their oral mucosa. Facility policy and/or the intubated resident's condition will dictate how often they need care.

If a resident has dentures, carefully remove them from the resident's mouth and immediately place them in a denture cup to prevent damage.

When performing mouth care on an unconscious resident, position the resident upright (if possible) with their head turned to the side to prevent aspiration. The resident's mouth can be opened by applying gentle downward pressure to the chin. A nursing assistant should never place any part of their hand in a resident's mouth. Next, use oral swabs to swab all areas of the mouth, including the teeth, gums, tongue, and cheeks. Finally, dry the outside of the resident's mouth and apply lip moisturizer if necessary and available.

Dentures should be transported and stored in a denture cup at all times. To clean the dentures, place a washcloth or paper towels in the sink basin to prevent damaging the dentures if they should drop accidentally. Brush and rinse the dentures under cool or tepid water. After providing oral care, place the dentures back in the resident's mouth or store them in a denture cup containing cool or tepid water or denture cleaning solution. Never clean or store dentures in hot water as this can damage them.

Skin Care

A resident's skin should be washed frequently and always dried thoroughly. Lotions can be applied sparingly if permitted by the facility's policy. Some powders can cake in the folds of the skin and promote breakdown, so they are not routinely recommended. During baths and dressing, examine a resident's skin for signs of redness, irritation, bruising, and/or abrasions. Any new or worsening findings should be reported to the nurse immediately.

Toileting

A nursing assistant assists residents with toileting needs during AM and HS care, as well as throughout the day. For residents on a bowel and bladder program, initiate and strictly adhere to this program. If residents need frequent perineal care with toileting, provide this if they are unable to do so for themselves.

Grooming

Daily grooming (including hair care and shaving) is part of the personal care for which a nursing assistant is responsible.

Hair care includes brushing and styling the resident's hair daily and shampooing their hair periodically. When providing hair care, inspect the scalp for any signs of excessive dryness, redness, and/or lesions and report them promptly.

Shaving a resident's face, legs, and/or underarms can be part of a nursing assistant's daily duties, depending on the facility's policy and the resident's needs. Some residents are at high risk for bleeding due to physical conditions or anticoagulation medication. If a resident is at risk for this, take special care to prevent any cuts or abrasions. If available, use an electric razor to avoid causing the resident any harm.

Dressing/Undressing

Some residents need assistance with dressing and undressing. When assisting a resident with this, promote their autonomy by allowing the resident to participate as much as possible. For example, encourage the resident to choose an outfit *they* want to wear.

When assisting a resident with dressing, note any deficiencies and provide support accordingly. Gather the resident's change of clothes before undressing them to avoid overexposure. If the resident has weakness or paralysis on one side, undress that side last and redress it first. For example, if changing the shirt of a resident with right-sided weakness, remove the sleeve from the left arm (the strong side) first, and then remove the sleeve from the right arm (the weak side). When putting on the resident's new shirt, do the opposite: place the right arm in the sleeve first, then the left arm. When dressing a dependent resident, be especially careful not to force the limbs into positions that could cause discomfort or injury. This is because the resident may not be able to feel or express when an injury is occurring.

Residents who need assistance with activities of daily living (such as dressing) typically work with a physical and/or occupational therapist to learn techniques for self-care. When assisting this resident, reinforce therapy techniques and encourage them to participate in their self-care routine to promote as much independence as is appropriate.

Health Maintenance/Restoration

Promoting Circulation and Skin Integrity (e.g., Specialized Mattresses, Chair Cushions, Positioning)

Residents who have had or are at risk for developing pressure sores can use an air mattress or egg crate mattress on top of (or in place of) their traditional mattress to relieve pressure on areas of bony prominence. Special props, cushions, and wedges are used to assist with proper positioning to promote circulation and skin integrity and to ensure the resident's comfort.

Edema is the buildup of fluid in the body tissue, usually resulting from immobility or a medical condition that causes the body to retain excess fluid. Generally, edema is first seen in the extremities. Regularly assess residents for edema during AM and HS care since new onset or worsening edema can indicate a serious underlying condition. Residents who are able to ambulate should be encouraged to do so to prevent or lessen edema. Residents who are unable to ambulate should be assisted with range of motion exercises. Elevation of edematous extremities (if not contraindicated) can help relieve edema and provide comfort to the resident.

Nutrition and Hydration

Basic Nutritional and Hydration Needs

Well-balanced nutrition and proper hydration are essential for regaining and/or maintaining good health. If not nourished and hydrated adequately, a resident won't heal properly from disease, accident, or surgery, while an older resident's health will deteriorate rapidly. A balanced diet of whole grains, proteins, vegetables, fruits, and healthy fats should be made available to residents. Assist the residents with meals as needed and report any changes in their eating habits. For example, if a resident is unwilling or unable to eat a meal, report this information to the nurse.

It's also essential to monitor a resident's hydration status for signs of dehydration. Residents can become dehydrated if they lose fluids more quickly than they replace them. Dehydration can occur quickly and, if untreated, is common in residents with diarrhea, vomiting, and/or fever since these conditions result in rapid fluid loss.

Signs and symptoms of dehydration include:

- Thirst
- Headache
- Dry mouth
- Lightheadedness or dizziness
- Low blood pressure
- Accelerated heart rate
- Dry skin
- Decreased and/or concentrated urinary output
- Constipation

Any signs or symptoms of dehydration should be reported immediately. However, sometimes a resident can experience dehydration without showing or reporting any signs or symptoms. Therefore, it's essential to accurately record a resident's fluid intake and output. If the output is significantly greater than the intake, it can signify that the resident is (or is in danger of becoming) dehydrated.

Significant changes in a resident's weight (i.e., the gain or loss of two or more pounds) from one day to the next can be a sign of a nutritional and/or hydration imbalance. For instance, a resident with congestive heart failure who gains more than two pounds overnight might be experiencing fluid overload. This has serious adverse effects on the body and can quickly lead to death if untreated. Report weight fluctuations like these to the nurse immediately.

Factors Affecting Dietary Preferences

Residents can have particular dietary preferences based on culture, religion, or general values. For example, some religions require that foods be prepared and/or served in a particular way. Some religions also restrict the consumption of pork or beef, while some individuals simply don't eat meat at all. Whenever possible, a resident's dietary preferences should be acknowledged and respected.

Factors Affecting Dietary Intake

Many factors can affect a resident's dietary intake. Aging, injury, and health conditions can all impact a resident's ability to consume certain kinds or consistencies of food. For example, a resident who's suffered a stroke can have **dysphagia** (trouble swallowing) and be at risk for aspiration. Because of this, they might need a diet consisting of thickened liquids to prevent aspiration. Another example is an older resident with missing teeth who has a limited ability to chew and, therefore, requires a softened diet. There might also be residents who are unable to consume any food by mouth and require tube feedings.

When residents have conditions that affect their intake, they can easily lose their desire to eat. To promote adequate nutrition, always make the presentation of meals and the atmosphere surrounding them as pleasant as possible. Monitor the resident's dietary intake and report any significant findings to the nurse.

Specialized Nutrition and Hydration Care

Therapeutic diets are prescribed for residents based on their physical condition, nutritional status, and possible upcoming procedures. Following are commonly ordered therapeutic diets:

Regular Diet: No dietary restrictions

Nothing by Mouth (NPO): Resident is not to have any food or drink when this diet is ordered.

Clear Liquid Diet: Resident can consume clear liquids such as water, coffee, and tea (without milk or cream), as well as clear fruit juice, popsicles, gelatin, and clear broth.

Full Liquid Diet: In addition to clear liquids, the resident can have any liquid that can be consumed through a straw. This includes pureed soups, ice cream, and meal replacement shakes.

Mechanical Soft Diet: Resident is only given pureed foods.

Other commonly ordered diets are based specifically on a resident's individual nutritional needs as determined by a physician or dietitian. These include: diabetic, low sodium, low residue, high residue, heart healthy, low cholesterol, gluten free, and lactose free.

Monitoring residents' nutrition and hydration, based on their physician's recommendations as well as the patient's response to the therapy, is a critical part of patient care. Residents should have a variety of foods that can meet their specific dietary goals, as interesting and balanced meals increase the likelihood that residents will adhere to their prescribed nutrition therapy. Residents should also be monitored during their mealtimes to see if they need additional assistance with holding utensils and feeding themselves, or if they appear to not be eating or drinking well. Many health conditions increase the risk of patients not being able to accurately assess their hunger and thirst levels, leading to an increased risk of malnourishment and dehydration. Residents should regularly be monitored for signs of these issues, including sudden weight loss or weight gain, dry skin, dry mouth, a sunken appearance, and fatigue. Some residents may benefit from intravenous hydration support or nutrition supplementation through vitamins or liquid meals.

Sleep and Rest Needs

Sleep and rest are essential to optimal health and healing. Residents can have difficulty sleeping. Whenever possible, plan the resident's care routine to correspond with periods when the resident is awake. Care activities should be grouped together when appropriate to avoid disturbing the resident more than necessary. Although residents need adequate rest periods, they should be encouraged to get out of bed and participate in activities when they're able, which aids in better rest. For a resident who's unable to leave their bed, encourage them to perform active range of motion exercises.

Residents in unfamiliar surroundings, or in facilities with constant lighting and noise, can become disoriented to day and night. Provide these residents with as many environmental cues as possible, such as dimming the lights and keeping the noise level low at night, turning the lights on and opening curtains and blinds in the morning, etc. Performing activities of daily living on a set schedule can also help the resident to stay oriented.

Elimination (Bowel and Bladder)

Normal Elimination Patterns

Elimination patterns can vary from resident to resident, and each resident usually has their own pattern. When providing care, it's important to be aware of a resident's toileting needs and be available to assist them.

If a resident is taking in fluids and nutrients, they should be producing output. When assisting with toileting, always document the resident's output. Any elimination of bodily fluids by the resident (including urine, stool, and emesis) is counted towards their output. Stools are counted and recorded in the daily stool count, and any remarkable characteristics (e.g., excessive wateriness or dryness, unusual color, unusual odor) should be reported to the nurse.

When measuring urinary output, note and report any unusual color, consistency, or odor of the resident's elimination, as this can indicate an underlying condition. For example: cloudy urine can be a sign of infection; pink or red urine can be a sign of bleeding; and urine with a fruity odor can be a sign of high blood sugar. Normal urine output should be clear and yellow in color.

Promoting Elimination

If assistance with toileting is delayed or a routine is changed, incontinence can occur. Try to be available for the resident at regular intervals for routine elimination. When assisting a resident with toileting, always allow adequate time and privacy.

Bowel and Bladder Training

A bowel and bladder program is a routine that's established with a resident to prevent incontinence. This is accomplished by anticipating the resident's toileting needs and providing toileting assistance at regular intervals. The resident's meal schedule, fluid intake, and activity level must be observed and taken into consideration when planning this program. To help establish a routine and promote bowel and bladder training/retraining, be proactive and anticipate the resident's toileting needs.

Aides can anticipate needs by monitoring the resident's bowel and bladder habits, such as through a data log. These logs help to highlight triggers that result in incontinence and to quickly spot any changes in the resident's normal habits that could also require changes to their toileting routine. Finally, aides should have a plan for accidents, including how to manage the issue with the resident in a compassionate and dignified manner, a process for timely and adequate clean up, and preventing health issues that could result from incontinence (e.g., infection).

Mobility, Including Bed Mobility

Promoting Mobility and Proper Positioning

Assisting a resident with mobility and positioning are frequent duties of a nursing assistant.

Proper positioning is important for a resident's comfort and safety. Some of the common resident positions are:

High Fowler's Position: The head of the resident's bed is raised sixty to ninety degrees and the knees are either flexed or extended out straight.

Fowler's Position: The head of the resident's bed is raised forty-five to sixty degrees.

Semi-Fowler's Position: The head of the resident's bed is raised thirty to forty-five degrees.

Supine: The resident is lying on their back.

Lateral: The resident is lying on their side.

Prone: The resident is lying on their stomach, with their head turned to the side.

When positioning a resident in bed, always raise the entire bed high enough to avoid bending over while assisting the resident. Be sure to lower the head of the bed to its lowest position before leaving the resident.

Promoting Function, Including Prosthetic and Orthotic Devices

A nursing assistant should encourage residents to be as mobile as possible and help them correctly use assistive devices such as canes and walkers. Residents with prosthetic limbs should be given assistance with, and access to, these devices. When assisting a resident with a prosthetic limb, always note any redness or irritation that occurs where the prosthetic limb contacts the skin.

Safe Transfer Techniques

When transferring a resident, the safety of the resident and the nursing assistant are of the greatest importance. Incorrectly performed transfers can cause injury to both. Be mindful of proper transfer techniques and body mechanics, such as keeping a straight back, bending at the knees, avoiding twisting at the waist, and, most importantly, asking for additional help if needed.

When assisting a resident out of bed, always make sure that the bed is in the lowest position. Then, assist the resident to sit upright on the side of the bed with both feet on the floor. While the resident remains in this seated position, make sure they aren't lightheaded or dizzy from the position change. If the resident needs significant physical assistance other than stabilization, an assistive device should be considered. To assist the resident in standing, the nursing assistant should stand in front of the resident, place their knees in front of the resident's knees, and hug the resident under the arms for lifting. Then instruct the resident to help as much as possible. If transferring the resident to a chair after assisting them to stand, both the nursing assistant and the resident should take small steps, pivoting around to the chair. Make sure the backs of the resident's knees are touching the front of the seat before lowering them into the chair.

When transferring a resident, make sure that all wheels are locked on the bed and/or chair before moving the resident.

Devices that Promote Mobility (e.g., Braces, Walkers, Wheelchairs, Gait Belt, Trapeze)

A nursing assistant should encourage residents to use available assistive devices, such as canes, walkers, and wheelchairs. Before leaving a resident's room, make sure any assistive device that the resident uses independently is within their reach. Residents with lower-body immobility who still have upper-body strength might have a bed equipped with a trapeze. A **trapeze** is an assistive bar that hangs above the resident's bed and enables self-repositioning. Residents who are able should be encouraged to use the trapeze.

The use of assistive devices such as **gait belts** (also known as **transfer belts**) benefits both the nursing assistant and the resident. When transferring or walking with a resident who needs assistance, it's advised to use a gait belt to prevent falls. When using a gait belt to assist a resident to walk, fasten the belt around their waist and hold it with both hands while standing to the side and slightly behind the resident. If the resident loses their balance and begins to fall, never attempt to catch them. Instead, continue holding the gait belt, bend at the knees, and slowly lower the resident to the floor.

Range of Motion Techniques

Range of motion exercises involve moving the body's limbs in particular ways to keep the joints healthy and flexible. **Active** range of motion exercises are performed by the resident independently. **Passive** range of motion exercises are done for residents who are unable to perform active ones. When performing passive range of motion exercises, gently guide the resident's limbs through their range of motion. Never force the limbs, as this can harm the resident.

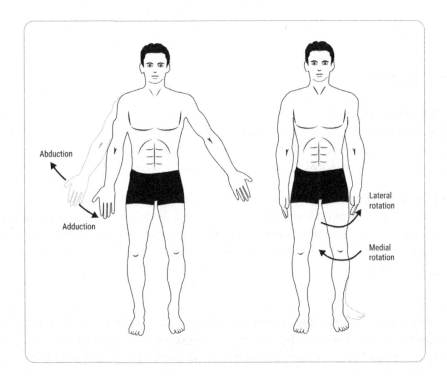

With the resident resting in the supine position, take each joint through its range of motion. **Adduction** is the movement of a limb toward the midline of the body. **Abduction**, the opposite of adduction, is the movement of a limb away from the midline of the body. **Lateral rotation** is the rotation of a limb along the long axis of the joint away from the midline of the body. **Medial rotation** is the rotation of a limb along the long axis of the joint toward the midline of the body.

Flexion is the bending of a limb at the joint, while **extension** is the straightening of a limb at the joint.

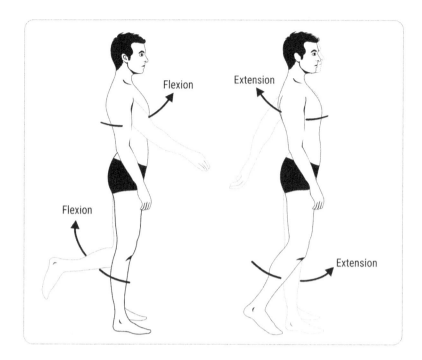

Effects of Immobility

Circulation and Skin Integrity

Residents with limited mobility are at risk for compromised circulation and/or skin breakdown. A nursing assistant helps residents reposition themselves frequently (at least once every two hours), which prevents pressure sores and promotes adequate circulation.

Pressure sores (also called **bedsores** or **pressure ulcers**) are areas of skin breakdown that manifest when pressure on the skin minimizes circulation in that area. These usually occur over bony prominences such as the heel, ankle, coccyx, elbow, knee, or hip. Residents with pressure sores generally have some degree of immobility and are unable to reposition themselves frequently. Pressure sores are categorized by the following four stages:

Stage I

The skin of the affected area is unbroken, generally red, and warm to the touch. Skin discoloration remains even after the resident is repositioned and the pressure is relieved from the site. Residents may have associated pain. Stage I pressure sores can be difficult to recognize in residents with dark skin.

Stage II

Damage or loss of skin through several layers (partial thickness) with shallow ulceration of the skin, abrasion, or blistering.

Stage III

Full thickness skin loss (epidermal and dermal layers) with ulceration that can be deep enough to expose fatty tissue; however, muscle, bone, and tendon are NOT visible. Tunneling might also be seen in residents with Stage III pressure sores.

Stage IV

Full thickness tissue loss (epidermis, dermis, and underlying tissue damage) with deep ulceration and possible tunneling. Muscle, bone, and/or tendon are visible and palpable with Stage IV pressure sores.

To help prevent pressure sores, keep the resident's skin clean and dry, and reposition the resident at least every two hours. Whenever available, use assistive positioning devices such as pillows and wedges to help relieve pressure on bony prominences. These bony areas should not be massaged in residents who have, or are at risk of having, pressure sores. Clothing and bed linens should be straightened often to avoid wrinkles that can quickly lead to pressure sores in at-risk residents. Report any indication of skin breakdown to the nurse.

Deep vein thrombosis (DVT) refers to a blood clot in the body's deep veins, most commonly in the legs. Redness, swelling, and sometimes pain in an extremity can be signs of DVT. Residents with DVT are at risk for a **pulmonary embolism (PE)**, which occurs when a blood clot in the deep vein breaks off, travels to the lungs, and cuts off blood flow. Do not massage red or swollen areas in the extremities, as this can result in a clot breaking off and causing a pulmonary embolism.

Residents who are immobile are at an increased risk for developing DVT. If possible, residents should be encouraged to ambulate to avoid DVT. If a resident is unable to ambulate, assistance with range of motion exercises should be provided. **Anti-embolism stockings** (also called **thrombo-embolus deterrent hose** or **TED hose**) and **sequential compression devices (SCDs)** are commonly used for residents who are confined to their beds. Both of these help to promote circulation in the lower legs and prevent blood pooling.

Elimination (Bowel and Bladder)

Immobility can lead to problems with elimination. Residents who are unable to care for their own toileting needs are at risk for incontinence. Be attentive to a resident's toileting needs and attempt to establish a routine with the resident. Immobility can also lead to constipation. If not contraindicated, a resident who is at risk for constipation should be encouraged to increase fluid intake. Residents can be reluctant to increase fluid intake because of their inability to self-toilet, so encourage the resident to increase their intake and be available for their toileting needs.

Sleep and Rest Patterns/Needs

Residents with immobility can have altered sleep patterns because of their limited ability to be physically active. Pain, discomfort, anxiety, stress, and certain medications are also common issues that can disrupt sleep. Older residents, as well as residents who are healing from illness or injury, require frequent rest and sleep periods. However, they should be encouraged to be active when they're able. Assist residents in establishing daily routines and encourage them to participate in daily living activities as much as possible. For instance, if a resident can sit in a chair for a meal rather than remaining in bed, encourage and assist them to do so. As another example, if a resident is able (with assistance) to transfer from using a bedpan to using a bedside toilet, encourage and assist them to do so. Any activities a resident can participate in will benefit their sleep, rest, and overall well-being. However, be attentive and careful not to overtire the resident. Any resident complaints of sleeplessness should be reported to the nurse.

Self-Image

When residents lose mobility, they can experience a sense of loss of independence. They can become isolated, depressed, and/or withdrawn and might begin to develop a negative self-image. Encourage these residents to participate in activities of daily living and give them as many opportunities as possible for autonomy.

Strength and Endurance

Residents who experience immobility can begin to lose muscle strength and endurance. If the immobile resident isn't cared for properly and their muscles aren't used, the muscles can begin to **atrophy** (weaken), the joints can begin to stiffen, and **contractures** (muscle shortenings) can develop. To prevent this from occurring, a nursing assistant performs passive range of motion exercises with immobile residents during times of care, such as bathing and/or dressing. Residents who are able to perform active range of motion exercises are encouraged to do so.

Activity Tolerance

While residents should be encouraged to participate in activities of daily living as much as possible, be careful not to overtire them. A resident's daily routine should be planned carefully. Activities should be spaced so that there's ample opportunity to participate as well as adequate rest periods in between.

Comfort

A nursing assistant should provide immobile residents with as much comfort as possible. Reposition residents no less than every two hours and use positioning devices such as pillows and wedges to promote proper body alignment and circulation and to reduce issues of skin breakdown.

Use of Assistive Devices

Residents are provided with assistive devices such as walkers, canes, and crutches that enable them to participate in activities of daily living. Encourage residents to use these assistive devices and leave the devices within reach of the resident if they're able to use them independently.

The primary benefit of assistive devices is to promote autonomy and independence in residents, which is correlated with a higher sense of well-being. They can prevent higher-risk activities, such as falls, from occurring. These devices can also enhance basic activities, such as magnifying reading material so that the resident is better able to enjoy a familiar activity.

Age-Related Changes

Cognitive Changes

As people age, their cognitive abilities can change. Memory, attention, decision-making, speech, and language can all be affected. Older residents may experience changes in their ability to make timely and/or sound decisions. They might lose their ability to perform common everyday tasks because of memory and/or attention decline, and their speech can become unclear. Awareness of these deficits doesn't always accompany changes in cognition. If a resident is aware of their cognitive decline, it can cause frustration and/or a feeling of loss. Be aware of a resident's cognitive functioning and work to accommodate their needs. When assisting a resident who is struggling with decision-making, give them ample time to perform tasks. Don't rush them into making decisions. Speak slowly and clearly to a resident who is experiencing a decline in their speech and language cognition. Changes in cognition are generally gradual, so any sudden significant changes could be related to something other than normal aging and should be reported to the nurse immediately.

Psychosocial Changes

As a person ages, changes in social structure and relationships occur. The elderly experience loss of peers and the inability to continue familiar hobbies or work. They are often forced to move out of their homes and into care facilities due to financial issues or physical changes. They also experience a decrease in their mental and physical capacities. Residents in long-term care facilities (especially older residents) frequently experience the loss of autonomy and the loss of and/or changes in relationships. This puts them at risk for isolation, loneliness, and depression.

The nursing assistant should be present with an empathetic understanding of the resident and their emotional needs. It's important to allow the resident as much independence as possible. Familiar belongings such as family pictures and sentimental objects should be allowed in the resident's room and may provide comfort to the resident.

Physical Changes

As people age, they also experience physical declines. Common physical changes include the following:

- Decreased circulation
- Decreased lung elasticity
- Decreased skin elasticity and moisture
- Reduced healing capacity
- Slower digestion
- Constipation
- Urinary retention and/or incontinence
- Decrease and/or loss of senses

Psychosocial Needs of Residents

Fundamental Human Needs

All humans have similar fundamental needs. **Maslow's Hierarchy of Needs** describes a person's needs in levels, starting with the most basic and important ones. Maslow stated that all humans progress in a similar pattern through these levels of need. The first, most basic level of need must be met before a person can progress to the second level and, until the second level of need is met, a person cannot progress to the third level, and so on.

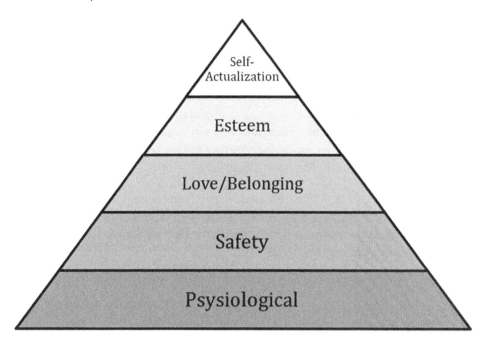

Physiological Needs are the most basic ones. They include water, food, air, clothing, shelter, sex, and sleep. Until these basic needs are met, an individual cannot progress to the next levels, which are:

Safety Needs: Physical safety, job security, and stability

Social Needs: Family and relationships

Esteem Needs: Achievements, reputation, and responsibility

Self-Actualization: Reaching one's full potential, creativity, and authenticity

Emotional Support Strategies

As a nursing assistant, it's important to recognize when a resident is experiencing changes in their social structure and/or relationships, and to provide the resident with opportunities for new social interactions, developing new relationships, personal growth, and achievement. While assisting the resident with daily care routines, offer emotional support by taking the time to talk with and listen to the resident.

Intervention Strategies

When people are placed in long-term care facilities, they face many changes. They can experience the loss of autonomy, privacy, and control, as well as the loss of relationships and social roles. Whenever possible, give residents the opportunity to participate in the planning of their daily routines to give them a sense of control. Also, encourage them to interact with their environment and with other residents to foster new social roles and relationships. If appropriate, give the resident privacy and opportunities for time alone.

Moving into a nursing home is a major adjustment. It is often accompanied by a sense of grief for the resident and guilt for family members. Almost all residents go through an adjustment phase that can be marked by depression and struggle as residents contend with living in a new environment that they may not have chosen, the idea that they cannot live autonomously, and losing many familiar comforts and routines. Some residents may take six months or longer to adjust. Effective intervention strategies can include incorporating familiar items (e.g., photos, furniture, favorite books) and routines into the resident's new living quarters, promoting social events, fostering a community atmosphere among residents, and offering psychosocial therapies, such as counseling, art therapy, and other active endeavors (with modifications for those who need it). Residents are typically in nursing home facilities because they need support with routine activities, but nurse aides who allow the opportunity for independence and privacy wherever it is safely possible can help the resident's outlook. Encouraging regular visits from friends and family members can also support the resident's adjustment. Providing education regarding the resident's adjustment to family members can also help, as family members can serve as a support system for the resident. Family members may also need support with feelings of guilt or resentment. Providing an outlet to address these concerns can indirectly benefit the resident as well.

Practice Quiz

1. A nursing assistant is providing care for a resident. Which of the following should be reported to the nurse immediately?
   a. While giving the resident a bed bath, the nursing assistant notices that the resident's bed linens are soiled and need to be changed.
   b. While dressing the resident, the nursing assistant notices that the diabetic resident has a small abrasion on the bottom of their foot.
   c. While being given a partial bath, the resident requests that their hair be washed.
   d. An ambulatory resident who's been experiencing diarrhea for several days requests additional perineal care supplies.

2. While performing a bed bath, a nursing assistant notices that the resident has a new area on their left heel that's red and warm. Which action should the nursing assistant take?
   a. Immediately stop the bed bath, cover the resident with a blanket, and report the findings to the nurse.
   b. Dry the area thoroughly, apply a thin coat of lotion, massage the heel for at least ten minutes, and report the findings to the nurse.
   c. Complete the bed bath (make sure to dry the resident thoroughly), position the resident so there's no pressure on the left heel, and report the findings to the nurse.
   d. Complete the bed bath, apply a thin coat of lotion to the resident's feet, put socks on them, and report the findings to the nurse.

3. When performing HS oral care for a resident with dentures, which action should the nursing assistant take?
   a. Remove the resident's dentures, clean them with cool or tepid water, place them in a denture cup with cool or tepid water or denture cleaning solution, and leave the cup on the bedside table within the resident's reach.
   b. Remove the resident's dentures, clean them with hot water, place them in an empty denture cup, and leave the cup on the bedside table within the resident's reach.
   c. Remove the resident's dentures, wrap them in a paper towel, and place them on the bedside table within the resident's reach.
   d. Remove the resident's dentures, clean them with cool or tepid water, wrap them in a washcloth, and leave them by the sink until the resident is ready for AM care.

4. A nursing assistant is providing AM care to a resident who has suffered a stroke and has right-sided weakness. When dressing the resident, which action should the nursing assistant take?
   a. Before dressing the resident in the new clothing, the nursing assistant should remove all of the resident's old clothing to prevent cross contamination.
   b. The nursing assistant should first undress and redress the resident's upper body, then undress and redress the resident's lower body.
   c. When removing the resident's pants, the nursing assistant should remove the pants from the left leg first and then the right leg.
   d. When redressing the resident in clean pants, the nursing assistant should place the left leg in the pants first and then the right leg.

5. Which of the following findings should the nursing assistant report to the nurse?
   a. During afternoon rounds, the nursing assistant empties 400 cc of clear yellow urine from the resident's urine catheter bag.
   b. During AM rounds, a resident requests that the nursing assistant helps them ambulate to the toilet.
   c. During AM rounds, the nursing assistant measures and disposes of 200 cc of clear yellow urine from a resident's bedside toilet.
   d. During HS care, the nursing assistant empties 100 cc of cloudy yellow urine from a resident's bedside urinal.

See answers on next page

Answer Explanations

1. B: Diabetic residents are at risk for infection due to poor wound healing. Any cuts, abrasions, or irritations to the skin should be reported to the nurse. In Choice *A*, the resident's bed linens are soiled, so it's the nursing assistant's responsibility to change the linens. While the nursing assistant can report this to the nurse, it doesn't need to be reported immediately. For Choice *C*, unless contraindicated, the nursing assistant can wash the resident's hair during their bath if the resident has requested it. Again, the nursing assistant can choose to report to the nurse that the hair has been washed, but it's unnecessary to report the event immediately. For Choice *D*, if the resident is experiencing diarrhea, the nursing assistant can expect that the resident might need additional towels, washcloths, and soap for frequent perineal care.

2. C: The area that's red and warm on the resident's left heel might be a developing pressure sore. The nursing assistant should finish the resident's care and then report the finding to the nurse. In Choice *A*, while the findings should be reported to the nurse as soon as possible, it's not necessary to stop the bed bath. In Choice *B*, the area should be dried thoroughly, but a developing pressure sore should never be massaged. Finally, in Choice *D*, the bed bath can be completed prior to the findings being reported to the nurse, but lotion should not be applied to areas of developing pressure sores.

3. A: The resident's dentures should be removed, cleaned with cool or tepid water, and then stored in a denture cup with cool or tepid water (or denture cleaning solution) within the resident's reach. For Choice *B*, dentures should never be cleaned with or stored in hot water since hot water can damage them. In Choice *C*, a resident's dentures should never be stored in a paper towel because they could accidentally be thrown away. Dentures should always be stored in a denture cup. In Choice *D*, if a resident is unable to put their own dentures in their mouth, or the resident doesn't wish to keep them within reach, storing them by the sink is acceptable. However, they should never be stored in a washcloth. A washcloth can be used to handle dentures while cleaning them to prevent accidental damage, but dentures should always be stored in a denture cup.

4. C: When dressing a resident with a weakness or paralysis on one side, the weak side should always be undressed last and redressed first. In Choice *A*, unless the resident has soiled his clothes, it's unnecessary to remove all of their clothes prior to redressing them. The resident should be covered up as much as possible to avoid discomfort and/or overexposure. For Choice *B*, the order of the upper- and lower-body dressing is unimportant as it relates to the resident's right-sided weakness. There might be a valid reason to start with the upper body, but it isn't related to the right-sided weakness. In Choice *D*, this is the opposite order. The nursing assistant should place the right leg (the weak side) into the pants first.

5. D: This finding should be reported to the nurse because the urine is cloudy. Urine should be clear and yellow in color. Choice *A* is a normal finding. If the resident's output is being measured, the amount of urine emptied should be recorded in the intake and output record, but it doesn't need to be reported to the nurse. Choice *B* (assisting a resident to the toilet) is a regular responsibility for a nursing assistant and doesn't need to be reported to the nurse. Choice *C* is also a normal finding that doesn't need to be reported.

Basic Nursing Care Provided by the Nursing Assistant

The nursing assistant is an important member of the health care team who provides basic nursing care to patients at the facility in which he or she works. The following will be a discussion of the basic care provided by the nursing assistant, including recognizing normal and abnormal situations, an overview of the human body and its functions, and what to do when a patient's condition worsens.

Routine, Chronic, Non-Life Threatening Situations

Observation and Reporting of Physical Changes

One of the most important roles of the nursing assistant is to be an additional set of eyes and ears for the health care team. This entails monitoring the patient, recording observations, and reporting to the nurse when abnormal signs and symptoms appear. A knowledge of basic human anatomy and how the body functions is necessary to know what is normal and abnormal in a patient. The nursing assistant can collect this information while performing routine vital signs and other tasks involving the patient.

Basic Anatomy and Functions of Body Systems

The human body is made up of systems of cells, tissues, and organs that work together to perform all the various functions necessary to sustain life.

The **cardiovascular system** (sometimes known as the **circulatory system**) is one of the most important systems of the body. This system is made up of the heart and the vessels carrying blood to and from the heart. The **heart** pumps blood through blood vessels called **arteries** to the lungs to pick up oxygen, and then out to the rest of the body to distribute it. **Veins** carry blood back to the heart. The **capillary beds** in the tissues are where the arteries and veins meet and where oxygen exchange occurs. Blood carries oxygen in the red blood cells. Oxygen is necessary for the cells of the body to perform their functions, without which they would cease to function and die.

The **pulmonary** or **respiratory system** is how the body obtains oxygen from the outside environment. It consists of the lungs and the respiratory passageways that travel from the mouth and nose to the lungs, including the trachea and bronchial tree. The **diaphragm** is a muscle necessary for breathing, located beneath the lungs and above the organs of the abdomen. By contracting and relaxing, the diaphragm changes the pressure in the lungs in order to pull air in and push air out. Oxygen exchange occurs when air reaches the **alveoli**, which are tiny sac-like structures at the ends of the airways. Oxygen is exchanged for the waste product carbon dioxide and then travels through the pulmonary blood vessels back to the heart to be pumped out to the rest of the body.

The **neurological system** consists of the brain, spinal cord, and peripheral nerves. The neurological system interprets sensory input from the external environment, such as taste, smell, sight, hearing, and touch. It also regulates and adjusts the internal environment of the body, such as maintaining temperature and increasing or decreasing heart rate. The neurological system controls motor function as well, directing body movement, maintaining balance, and performing reflexes.

The **endocrine system** is comprised of glands that secrete chemicals called **hormones.** Hormones travel through the bloodstream and directly influence the function of almost all the different tissues and organs of the body in response to environmental and metabolic changes. The glands of the endocrine

85

system include the hypothalamus, pineal gland, pituitary gland, thyroid, parathyroid, adrenal glands, testes in males, and ovaries in females. The **pituitary gland** secretes growth hormone that influences growth and development, such as height and weight. The pituitary gland also influences other glands of the endocrine system to secrete their hormones. The **reproductive glands**, the testes and the ovaries, secrete hormones that regulate semen production, ovum production, and many other human sexual and reproductive functions.

The **integumentary system** consists of the body's largest organ, the skin, and the hair, nails, and exocrine glands that exist within it. The integumentary system serves as a protection for the internal environment of the body from the external environment. The integumentary system insulates the body from temperature changes in the external environment, protects from trauma and infectious agents, and sends sensory input to the neurological system for interpretation. The nails protect the ends of the digits and are useful for gripping and scraping. Hair also helps insulate the body and prevent ultraviolet radiation from hitting the skin. The exocrine glands secrete substances such as sweat and oil to regulate temperature and eliminate waste products.

The **musculoskeletal system** includes the bones and the muscles of the body. This system, supplied by the neurological system, is responsible for the movements and structure of the body, allowing the body to perform many different actions such as sitting, standing, running, and jumping.

There are three different types of muscle tissue: smooth, cardiac, and skeletal. **Smooth muscle** is under involuntary control, meaning one cannot consciously control its contraction. Smooth muscle is located in various parts of the body, including the intestines. The intestines make a movement called **peristalsis**, a contraction that moves food along the gastrointestinal tract. This movement allows for absorption of nutrients and fluid, and ultimately elimination of waste products from the body.

Cardiac muscle makes up the heart, an organ that is almost entirely muscle. Cardiac muscle is also involuntary, beating from a few days after conception until the day of death. When cardiac muscle contracts as an organ, it creates the pumping action that pushes blood from the heart to the tissues and organs of the body for oxygen perfusion.

Skeletal muscle is responsible for voluntary movement. This type of muscle is under voluntary control, meaning one consciously controls the contraction and relaxation. Skeletal muscle is located all along the skeleton, on the arms, legs, skull, chest, and abdomen.

The **reproductive system** is a series of glands, organs, and structures in the human body that controls sexual function and the ability to reproduce. In males, this consists of the testes, prostate, and penis. In females, this includes the ovaries, uterus, and vagina. Both male and female reproductive systems are largely under hormonal control, the major hormones being estrogen and progesterone in females and testosterone in males.

The **renal system** includes the kidneys, ureters, urinary bladder, and urethra. The kidneys regulate fluid and electrolyte balance in the body and produce urine as a waste product that is collected in the bladder and eliminated through urination.

The **digestive system** starts at the mouth, where food enters the body. After chewing, food travels down the esophagus and into the stomach, followed by the small intestine and the large intestine. After nutrients and fluids are absorbed, fecal matter is eliminated as a waste product.

The **lymphatic system**, comprised of lymph nodes and lymphatic circulation, works with the circulatory system as a major part of the immune system to fight infections. Lymph nodes are located throughout the body; prominent locations include the neck, armpits, and groin.

Observable Body Functions

Now that the nursing assistant is familiar with the basic structures and functions of the body, this knowledge can be applied in the context of the collection of vital signs and other tasks performed while caring for patients.

The **vital signs** that will be routinely obtained from the patient include heart rate, blood pressure, pulse oxygenation, rate of respirations, and temperature. Heart rate is a reflection of the speed at which the heart is beating. A normal heart rate for an adult is between sixty and one hundred beats per minute. A heart rate higher than one hundred is called **tachycardia**, while a heart rate less than sixty is called **bradycardia**. Athletes may have a lower resting heart rate as a result of conditioning with exercise. Tachycardia occurs normally during exercise, so the patient should be at rest to get an accurate measurement of resting heart rate.

Heart rate can be collected manually by **palpating**, or feeling, the pulse with the index and middle fingers. The most common site of pulse palpation is at the radial artery, located below the thumb on the inside of the wrist. Heart rate can also be determined via auscultation, which means to listen through a stethoscope placed over the heart.

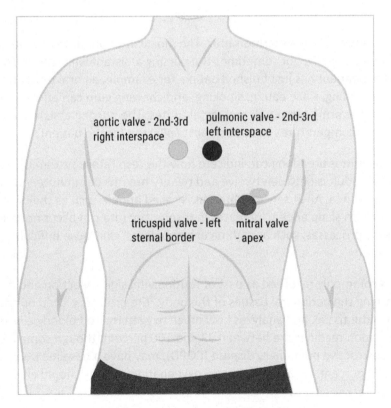

Auscultation sites for a patient's heart rate

Measuring the patient's blood pressure is another method of assessing the patient's cardiovascular system for normal function. Blood pressure is measured in millimeters of mercury (mmHg) and reflects the force that blood has on the blood vessels. Blood pressure readings will consist of two numbers, called systolic blood pressure and diastolic blood pressure. The **systolic blood pressure** is the top number and represents the highest point of pressure on the vessel walls. The **diastolic blood pressure** is the bottom number and represents the pressure while the heart is at rest, which is the lowest point of pressure on the blood vessel walls. In an adult, normal systolic blood pressure is greater than 90 and below 120, and normal diastolic blood pressure is greater than 60 and less than 90. **Hypertension** is described as higher than normal blood pressure, and **hypotension** is lower than normal.

Most facilities will have automatic blood pressure collection machines, in which a cuff is placed around the patient's arm, an arrow is aligned with the patient's brachial artery (located on the inner aspect of the patient's elbows), and the machine inflates and deflates, measuring pressure internally and giving a reading on a screen. The nursing assistant should know how to collect a manual blood pressure, as machines are not always accurate. This involves placing the same cuff over the patient's brachial artery; inflating the cuff to 200 mmHg; listening for the absence, return, and diminishing sounds of the brachial artery as the cuff is slowly deflated; and recording the pressure readings on the **sphygmomanometer** (technical name for a manual blood pressure collection device). Patients should relax their arms, and their legs should not be crossed, since this can compress blood vessels and affect the reading.

A normal temperature in a healthy adult is around 98.6 degrees Fahrenheit. An elevated body temperature is called a **fever** and often indicates that the body is fighting an infection. A temperature below a patient's normal temperature is called **hypothermia**, and usually occurs as a result of a cold environment.

Temperature may be collected via a **thermometer**. The most common route of obtaining a body temperature in a patient is orally, but sometimes the nursing assistant will need to consider an alternative route. If the patient has just finished eating, for example, an oral temperature is not best for obtaining an accurate reading, since eating, smoking, and chewing gum can affect accuracy. Alternatives include **axillary** (under the arm), temporal, and rectal routes. The nursing assistant may check with the nurse to determine how temperatures have been best collected for the patient.

The rate at which a patient is breathing can indicate how the respiratory system is functioning. A normal rate of breathing for an adult is between twelve and twenty breaths per minute. An increased rate of breathing is called tachypnea. An absence of breaths is called **apnea**, such as the brief pauses in breathing in a patient with sleep apnea. Increases in respiratory rate can occur normally, as during exercise. Some disease processes, such as asthma exacerbations, can cause difficulty breathing, which is called **dyspnea**.

Pulse oxygenation is commonly recorded as part of routine vital sign collection and is a reflection of how much oxygen is reaching the peripheral tissues of the body. The probe is placed on the patient's finger, shines a light through the tissue, and analyzes how much oxygen the red blood cells are carrying. Normal pulse oxygenation readings are between 93 and 100 percent, though some patients, such as those with chronic obstructive pulmonary disease (COPD), may have a baseline pulse oxygenation reading of less than 90 percent. An abnormal pulse oxygenation reading should always be reported to the nurse.

The nursing assistant will observe the function of both the digestive and urinary systems through observation of intake and output. Intake is the amount of food and drink consumed by a patient, and output is the amount of waste, such as urine and stool, produced by a patient. The nursing assistant will record the amount the patient ate, the amount of fluid ingested by the patient in milliliters, the amount and characteristics of bowel movements, and the amount of urinary output. Intake and output records help the health care team assess the patient's overall health and nutrition. Variations in intake and output give clues to possible bodily dysfunctions.

The nursing assistant may be required to obtain a patient's height and weight. This data reflects the patient's nutrition and hydration status, and potentially the patient's growth and development. Height and weight information is used to calculate body mass index and helps members of the health care team determine appropriate interventions, such as nutritional needs and the correct doses of medications.

Height and weight can be obtained using a scale and wall height indicator. If the patient is unable to get out of bed, there are assistive devices available in some facilities that may be able to measure the patient's weight in a sling, while only slightly lifting them out of bed. Otherwise, the nursing assistant will assist the patient to stand on the scale and record the reading. Any extra equipment, such as a heart monitor, should be removed before weighing to get the most accurate weight. For height, have the patient stand against the wall with the height scale with their heels touching the wall. Place the measuring device on top of the patient's head and record the measurement. For a patient who is bedfast, a measuring tape may be an appropriate way of collecting height information.

While assisting the patient with the activities of daily living (ADLs), such as eating, getting dressed, and bathing, the nursing assistant will be able to observe the integumentary system. The patient's skin integrity consists of information about the skin that the nursing assistant can see, smell, and feel. The nursing assistant will observe the skin of the client and note if it is intact, dry, moist, and/or clean. Patients who are immobile are at risk for compromised skin integrity, which includes pressure ulcers. Pressure ulcers commonly occur on the **bony prominences** of the body, where the weight of the patient's body exerts pressure, such as the lower back, elbows, and heels.

The musculoskeletal system controls how well the body coordinates movement and is able to maintain an erect posture. The nursing assistant can make observations about the patient's movement and mobility as they assist the patient in activities of daily living. The nursing assistant will assist with moving the patient in the bed, transferring the patient to a chair or wheelchair, and walking, depending on the patient's abilities and diagnosis. The nursing assistant should observe how the patient moves and how much assistance is needed, making special note of changes, such as increased weakness.

Nurse aides monitor various behavior changes relating to a resident's dietary intake. First, they should monitor if a resident is experiencing any issues with the physical intake of food, such as the ability to adequately coordinate utensils from plate to mouth, chewing and swallowing (especially if dentures or other oral devices are involved), and gastrointestinal distress that occurs after eating. Additionally, aides can note if a patient appears to be eating more or less than normal, as this can indicate mood disorders, stress, cognitive loss, or hormonal changes. Some residents may also have allergies or personal preferences regarding foods, and aides can note any concerns.

Noting the patient's vital signs, normal physical abilities, intake and output, and skin integrity, as well as changes that occur in any of these categories, is a valuable contribution to the health care team's ability to care for the patient and detect problems early.

 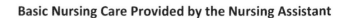
Observation and Reporting Behavioral Changes

The nursing assistant not only collects vital signs and observes any changes in the patient's physical state, but must also monitor the patient's psychological state as well. This includes behavioral changes such as confusion, disorientation, emotional fluctuations, changes in mood, and common defense mechanisms during periods of stress.

Mental Status Changes

In an unfamiliar environment, a patient may experience mental status changes such as confusion. A patient may be uncertain of certain facts about him or herself and the environment that would otherwise be apparent under normal circumstances. The patient may seem bewildered, unclear, or disoriented. If the nursing assistant observes a new onset of confusion in the patient, it must be reported to the nurse immediately.

Potential causes of sudden confusion include low blood sugar, stroke, psychosis, seizure, head injury, fatigue, and electrolyte imbalances. If there is any change in the status of a patient, the nursing assistant can request an additional set of vital signs be obtained to further investigate the issue.

Some patients may be confused at their baselines, meaning they are consistently at roughly the same level of confusion. As with other baselines, confusion should not be assumed as a normal finding in a patient. When the patient's normal mental status has changed, or the nursing assistant is unsure if confusion is typical in a particular patient, immediate reporting of the change is necessary.

There are certain interventions that the nursing assistant can employ to help prevent or alleviate confusion. The nursing assistant can help ensure the patient gets adequate rest by planning tasks around the patient's resting schedule. For example, if the patient is normally accustomed to taking a nap at a certain time and the nursing assistant keeps the patient awake to give a bath, it may lead to agitation and confusion. Keeping the lights and television on at night may lead to disturbed sleep and overstimulation, causing confusion. Maintaining a peaceful environment for the patient will help decrease episodes of altered mental status.

Residents may have myriad health issues that could contribute to mental status changes, either directly from the health issue itself or from medication used to treat the issue. Additionally, residents are vulnerable to age-related mental status changes; unfortunately, they are also vulnerable to potential abuse and neglect that can cause mental distress. Finally, residents are likely to experience anxiety, fear, and sadness due to the adjustment that comes with changing living environments. If an aide notices symptoms of mental status change, such as panicky or frenetic behavior, depressed mood, rumination, clamminess, or becoming easily startled, the aide can help in several ways. First, they can involve clinical care providers to determine if the changes are due to an underlying medical or pharmaceutical issue. Second, the aide can provide a supportive ear and safe space for residents to voice any concerns. Finally, aides can benefit tremendously by learning and employing simple techniques that have been proven to help acute mental status changes, such as breathing exercises, incorporating specific activities that the resident enjoys into care, and encouraging favorite friends and family members to visit.

Reality Orientation/Validation Techniques

Part of confusion in a patient is **reality disorientation**, in which a person becomes confused about identity, location, time and date, and/or the circumstances leading to the present situation. A person may be confused about one or all of these points. Through questioning, the nursing assistant can determine exactly about which points a person is disoriented about.

A simple way to rate a patient's orientation is on a scale of one to four, based on the **four points of orientation** (person, place, time, and situation). For example, if a patient knows who he is, but does not know where he is, what time it is, and why he is there, the nursing assistant would report that the patient is "alert and oriented times one." If the patient knows who he is and where, but is confused about the date and time and the circumstances that brought him to his situation, his orientation would be rated as "alert and oriented times two" or abbreviated as "A&O X2." The nursing assistant can assist the patient who is confused and disoriented by validating and clarifying points of confusion. The nursing assistant can gently remind the patient of their name, the time of day and date, the location, and the reason for being there. If reorientation is done in a kind and respectful manner, it has the potential to calm and reassure the patient. It is important to keep in mind that confusion is unintentional, and that a confused patient may be especially vulnerable and even frightened. The nursing assistant has the opportunity to show compassion to such patients.

Emotional Stress

Illness and unfamiliar surroundings are stressors. A person fighting an illness in a hospital or facility is often under an unusual amount of emotional stress. Some will cope with a change in circumstances differently than others. Factors affecting patients' levels of emotional stress include how long it has been since a condition was diagnosed, how well they have adapted to the change in their routine, and how well they have been able to maintain personal relationships and to care for themselves. The sense of a loss of independence can be a factor in emotional stress.

When one is experiencing emotional stress, the manifestations may be subtle and gradual, or immediate and dramatic. Patients experiencing emotional stress may be overcome by intense feelings of sadness or despair, leading to crying. They may become easily agitated if the nursing assistant attempts to start an activity with them, such as getting dressed or eating a meal. Patients may try to exert control over a situation through aggressive communication, such as making demands or shouting. Patients may not realize their actions are being driven by emotional stress and may initially appear unreasonable.

Patients experiencing emotional stress may also exhibit physical symptoms. Physical and emotional health often affect each other. Emotional stress can have bodily manifestations and may lead to sleep disturbances; gastrointestinal symptoms such as nausea, loss of appetite, vomiting, diarrhea, and constipation; or musculoskeletal symptoms such as headaches and body aches. Similar to behavioral signs of emotional stress, patients may not realize their physical symptoms might be linked to emotional stress.

Patients experiencing emotional stress need empathy from the nursing assistant and health care team. This can entail taking the time to inquire about feelings and offering a listening ear. Talking about, recognizing, and being aware of emotional stress can be therapeutic for patients. Patients may find comfort in simply verbalizing their feelings, or they may come to a realization or conclusion by speaking out loud.

Increased emotional stress may be manifested as aggressive communication. If a patient believes that their needs are not being met, or their concerns are not being acknowledged, it can lead to feelings of frustration and anger. Attempts should be made to establish healthy communication and interactions with the patient. The nursing assistant should not reciprocate aggressive behavior when exhibited by a patient. If the nursing assistant is having difficulty interacting with a patient who is emotionally stressed and is unable to determine a solution, he or she should consult the nurse and/or nurse manager, according to the appropriate chain of command. Sometimes involving a third person to mediate a conflict is enough to come to a resolution. The nurse or nurse manager may also come to an alternative solution, such as reassigning a patient to a different nursing assistant.

Any sudden change in emotions should be reported to the nurse. Emotional stress can have a negative impact on healing and wellness and should be managed to minimize detrimental effects.

Mood Status Changes

Along with experiencing emotional stress, a patient is also susceptible to experiencing mood status changes. The same factors that cause emotional stress, such as change of location, new illness, or change in routine, may affect the mood of the patient as well. The patient may experience anxiety about a new situation involving a major lifestyle change. A patient may be afraid that life will not be the same after a chronic illness diagnosis, and that he or she may not be able to adapt to changes. A period of adjustment to a life change may also be a period of sadness for a patient.

Psychiatric diagnoses are not uncommon accompaniments of physical diagnoses. For example, a patient who suffered a stroke several months ago may still be learning to cope with decreased mobility. Because she is physically unable to go out and visit her friends like she used to, her social interactions have been limited as well. What starts as feelings of sadness may progress over time to depression in some patients. A loss of independence or change in situation may eventually result in a patient developing symptoms of psychiatric disorders such as depression or generalized anxiety disorder.

Patients experiencing depression may have feelings of sadness, lack of energy, fatigue, and loss of interest in normal activities. Patients with depression may withdraw socially from others. They may be resistant to participate in group activities or physical or occupational therapy. They may also be resistant to visitors or prefer to remain in bed instead of interacting with others. If the nursing assistant notices these symptoms and they are a change in the patient's previous status, this should be reported to the nurse. Undiagnosed depression can negatively affect the patient's ability to heal from physical ailments.

Patients experiencing anxiety disorders may exhibit both physical and mental symptoms. Physical manifestations of anxiety can include increased heart rate, elevated blood pressure, or gastrointestinal upset, including loss of appetite, nausea, vomiting, constipation, diarrhea, and/or indigestion. Patients may pace around their rooms or the halls of the facility. They may speak quickly and almost uncontrollably at times. A panic attack may cause the patient to sweat, feel hot, and experience shortness of breath. During a panic attack, a few or several of these symptoms may worsen to the point that the patient is overwhelmed with anxiety.

The nursing assistant should be aware of these symptoms and their possible indications and report them to the nurse for further assessment and diagnosis. While calming and reassuring the patient during an intense episode of mood change, it is important for the nursing assistant to provide a relaxing and peaceful environment. This can be achieved by speaking in a comforting tone of voice, decreasing stressful stimulation, and genuinely listening to the patient's concerns.

Defense Mechanisms

Patients experiencing confusion, disorientation, emotional stress, and/or mood changes may display some sort of defense mechanism. In psychology, a **defense mechanism** is a way that humans protect themselves from perceived emotional pain. A patient, for example, may feel threatened or pained by a current situation in a hospital or facility after a new illness has been diagnosed. She may attempt to protect herself from the disturbances that these changes will cause in her life. There are several different defense mechanisms, some more effective than others. More primitive defense mechanisms, such as denial, are generally less effective than more developed ones. Defense mechanisms are learned from early childhood to adulthood and are often employed without conscious choice. However, more productive ways of coping with potential emotional stress can be learned and used deliberately.

Denial is one of the most common defense mechanisms. Denial occurs when a person refuses to acknowledge that anything is wrong or causing stress, and instead attempts to proceed as if nothing has happened. In a patient with a new diagnosis of illness, this may manifest as a disregard of illness, refusal to follow a health care provider's advice, and noncompliance with a treatment plan, such as not taking medications prescribed for the condition. Some patients employ this defense mechanism for a long time, to the detriment of their health and wellness.

Regression is a defense mechanism in which, faced with new and daunting circumstances, the person reverts back to a previous stage of development in an attempt to avoid confronting a situation. In children, a behavior such as **nocturnal enuresis**, also known as wetting the bed at night, may return during a stressful period of life, despite the child having previously stopped this behavior. In adults, attempting to revert to immature behavior may be a manifestation of regression, such as a financially responsible adult gambling large amounts of money at a casino shortly after the death of a parent.

Along with regression, **acting out** is another primitive defense mechanism in which a person performs a radical act or behavior in response to a stressful life situation. This would be an activity that is unusual for the individual, such as getting a tattoo—even though the individual had never expressed a desire for a tattoo before—and regretting it immediately after. Another example of acting out is an individual who binge drinks one night after a stressful life event, though she does not normally drink alcohol.

When a person uses the defense mechanism of **dissociation**, he or she disconnects from the present reality and loses him or herself in another activity. In an attempt to avoid the stresses of real life, a person may become so absorbed in another representation of him or herself that he or she loses track of time or self. This may go on for a period of time, and it may be difficult to break the person's habit of dissociation.

Compartmentalization occurs when a person behaves in a way that is contrary to their normal set of values. Compartmentalization is a form of dissociation, though to a lesser degree. People may perform an activity they normally would not condone, such as shoplifting, and later fail to acknowledge that this behavior is contrary to their normal values.

A particularly detrimental defense mechanism for relationships is **projection**. When a person is projecting, he or she misattributes negative feelings to another person. People may lack insight into their own situation and find it difficult to acknowledge a challenging new reality, causing them to project feelings onto other people.

An interesting defense mechanism that a patient experiencing emotional stress may display is **reaction formation**. In this case, the patient may experience negative feelings about a situation, but instead of talking about it or thinking through it, he or she reverses the emotions and acts as if the feelings about a situation are positive. While this mechanism might appear harmless, it demonstrates a lack of emotional insight. Reaction formation does not acknowledge feelings or the reason behind them and, as a result, does not attempt to rectify a situation.

When a person uses the more developed defense mechanism of **repression**, he or she unconsciously ignores the negative emotions and feelings until they are forgotten. The patient may completely forget about a negative event that occurred, such as a heart attack, and the events that led up to and followed it. This can be detrimental to emotional health, since it does not allow the individual to develop a more appropriate response to a similar situation in the future.

Similar to projection, **displacement** is a defense mechanism in which negative emotions are expressed at the wrong object or person. For example, a patient may have strong negative feelings toward a specific doctor or nurse, yet feel powerless in expressing them for whatever reason. Instead of dealing with the frustrations with the specific doctor or nurse, he or she unjustly directs anger at the nursing assistant or another health care staff member.

Intellectualization is a defense mechanism in which the patient focuses on thinking about the situation, rather than acknowledging the associated emotions. For example, a patient may feel grief at the loss of a loved one, but instead chooses to focus on the details of the funeral and estate arrangements. The patient ignores the feelings of sadness and loss, and instead busies the mind with details and planning. A productive emotional response is one in which feelings are acknowledged and recognized.

Rationalization is a defense mechanism in which a person previously felt one way, was faced with a change in situation, and instead of expressing disappointment and pain, finds a reason for the situation to have changed in order to move on. This is a more developed response than many other mechanisms of defense. For example, a patient may have liked her diabetes management routine that she was on at home because she was still able to eat certain foods that weren't good for her blood sugar. After an episode of hyperglycemia and a hospitalization, she has to change her routine at home. Instead of feeling sadness that she will no longer be able to eat certain foods as often as she would like, she declares that she never liked those foods anyway and that it will be easy to give them up.

Undoing is a defense mechanism in which a person does something that he or she regrets, and then tries to reverse the action with the opposite action. For example, a patient who was mean to a nursing assistant yesterday and told him that he was a terrible nursing assistant may feel badly about saying such a thing. To undo the action, she spends the entire next shift being excessively friendly toward the nursing assistant to make up for her hurtful behavior.

Sublimation is a mature defense mechanism in which untowardly actions, impulses, and desires are channeled into a positive activity. A patient who has been diagnosed as an alcoholic, for example, may still feel a strong desire to drink despite consciously having decided that it is not good for him. Instead of succumbing to the impulse to drink, he has a planned activity to divert himself, such as jogging or calling a friend. People who use sublimation may use any number of different productive activities to divert themselves from acting on a negative impulse or when put in a stressful situation. They may use humor, fantasy, physical activity, or social support to get them through the difficult periods of temptation.

Compensation is a way of focusing on one's strengths when faced with a weakness. A patient who has trouble managing her high blood pressure may have a weakness for salty, high-fat foods, which she needs to eat less of in order to maintain a healthy blood pressure. Instead of feeling sad and helpless about her weakness, she instead focuses on how well she is able to resist sugary foods. While she still needs to work on her weakness, she is not wallowing in it. She is reinforcing a positive self-image, which will strengthen her will and discipline overall. There is such a thing as over-compensation, in which too much emphasis is placed on one's strengths without being realistic and acknowledging one's weaknesses. This can lead to reality distortion and an inaccurate perception of oneself.

Assertiveness is one of the most developed forms of defense mechanisms, in which a person strikes a healthy balance between passiveness and aggression. When one is passive, one does not speak up for or defend oneself when one has an emotional need. Aggressive communicators do not think of the needs of others but are solely focused on their own needs. An assertive person has the ability to respect the needs of others while still being able to communicate their own needs, emotions, and struggles in order to find healthy solutions. This is a valuable skill developed over time. Both the nursing assistant and the patient should practice assertive communication as part of a mutually respectful relationship.

Acute Emergency Situations

There will be times when a patient's condition will decline rapidly and emergency intervention will be required from the health care team. The nursing assistant needs to be familiar with these crisis situations and what their role is during these times to best serve the patient.

Chest Pain

When a patient complains of chest pain, it is not necessarily an emergency situation, but it must be immediately reported to the nurse in order for timely intervention to occur.

Chest pain can be an indicator of many different problems, potentially involving the cardiovascular system, respiratory system, gastrointestinal system, or even the musculoskeletal system.

Descriptions of a patient's chest pain may vary, indicating different causative factors. The patient may describe the chest pain as sharp, burning, dull, achy, tight, stabbing, squeezing, or crushing.

If the chest pain arises from an issue in the cardiovascular system, the cause could be **coronary artery disease (CAD)**, in which the vessels in the heart become obstructed with plaques, and oxygen supply to the heart muscle is decreased or blocked completely. When chest pain occurs in this situation, it is called **angina**. Patients may have chronic stable angina, in which they are known to have CAD. This is a medically stable condition. In these cases, chest pain is usually expected and manageable with medications and rest.

Another cardiovascular cause of acute chest pain is **myocardial infarction (MI),** or more commonly known as a heart attack. In this case, the chest pain is a medical emergency. Patients experiencing a myocardial infarction may describe their chest pain as crushing and severe, with possible radiation of pain to the left arm. Their chest pain may be accompanied by sweating, nausea, shortness of breath, or sudden weakness.

Also, a patient with chest pain may be suffering from **myocarditis**, in which the muscle of the heart becomes infected and inflamed. This condition can mimic the symptoms of a heart attack, though the oxygen supply to the heart muscle is never actually compromised. A patient in this situation may have other signs of infection such as fever, tachycardia, and dyspnea.

Other cardiovascular causes of chest pain may include **pericarditis** (inflammation of the pericardium), **hypertrophic cardiomyopathy** (cardiac muscle disease), mitral valve prolapse (the flaps of the mitral valve do not close properly as the heart contracts), and **coronary artery dissection** (a serious medical emergency in which a coronary artery has separated, causing severe internal bleeding).

Sometimes chest pain can occur as a result of a problem with the respiratory system, since the lungs are located on either side of the heart in the thorax. Causes of chest pain arising from the respiratory system include **pleuritis**, in which the **pleura**, or lining of the lungs and chest, become inflamed. Pleuritis may cause a sharp sensation upon breathing, coughing, or sneezing.

Pneumonia, another infection of the respiratory system that affects the lungs, may also cause the same type of sharp chest pain as pleuritis. However, it may sometimes be a deeper ache in the chest. Pneumonia is typically accompanied by other signs of infection, such as fever, chills, and cough.

Acid reflux, or **gastroesophageal reflux disease (GERD),** is a common cause of chest pain that can be mistaken for a heart attack. In this condition, acid from the stomach is not properly contained by the upper sphincters of the stomach, causing a burning sensation and potential damage to the esophagus. This symptom is called **heartburn**, but can be mistaken for the chest pain of a heart attack. Remember that the heart and esophagus are anatomically next to each other.

If the nursing assistant encounters a patient reporting chest pain at any time, this symptom needs to be reported to the nurse immediately. The nursing assistant may prepare to collect a set of vital signs and potentially assist if the situation progresses to a cardiac and/or respiratory arrest situation. The patient may need to be transferred to a unit with closer monitoring, such as a telemetry or intensive care unit (ICU). If a patient transfer is needed, the nursing assistant will collect the patient's belongings and prepare him or her for transport.

Cardiac Arrest

The term **cardiac arrest** refers to a situation in which a person's heart stops pumping blood effectively. It is important to note that this differs from the term "heart attack," in which the heart may still be functioning to some extent, but oxygen supply has been significantly decreased or cut off completely. Cardiac arrest is a medical emergency, and immediate intervention is necessary to restore the heart to its function and revive the patient.

Cardiac arrest may be caused by a number of different conditions affecting the heart, though other systems may be causative factors as well. One of the most common causes of cardiac arrest is the interruption of normal electrical rhythm of the heart, which then interferes with the heart's ability to pump blood. Some common **arrhythmias** involved in cardiac arrest include **ventricular tachycardia**, in which the ventricles of the heart are contracting too quickly and not pumping effectively, or **ventricular fibrillation**, in which the ventricles are quivering and not pumping any blood at all.

Potential precursors to arrhythmias and/or cardiac arrest include scarring of the heart muscle, heart disease, cardiomyopathy (thickening of heart muscle), medications regulating heart rhythm, increased blood pressure, heart failure, electrical abnormalities (e.g., Wolff-Parkinson-White, long QT syndrome), substance abuse, respiratory failure, and shock.

Decreased blood flow to the brain results in decreased oxygenation of brain tissue, which causes the patient to lose consciousness and become unresponsive immediately. A nursing assistant is required to have cardiopulmonary resuscitation (CPR) certification as part of training, so the signs of cardiac arrest and what to do if the situation arises should be familiar. When a patient becomes unresponsive (does not respond to tapping, shaking, or verbal cues) and there are no signs of breathing, the first thing the nursing assistant should do is call for help. This can be done by shouting "help," activating the patient's call light if the nursing assistant is in the room, or activating a code blue or equivalent. Many facilities have specially trained teams who respond to such emergencies. Timely intervention makes an impact on patient outcomes.

After activating the emergency response system, the nursing assistant should start performing CPR. Note: If in a hospital, the standard procedure for cardiac arrest will be different, since greater resources (such as crash cart, code team, and a team of specialized doctors and nurses trained for code situations) are available. The nursing assistant should know the facility's protocol for medical emergencies, such as cardiac arrest, and be aware of the appropriate course of action.

If CPR is required, the nursing assistant will start performing chest compressions. These chest compressions should be delivered to the center of the chest, with appropriate depth so as to achieve adequate pumping action and appropriate rate. Chest compressions should be performed at a rate of about 100 compressions per minute, and at a depth of about two inches. It can be helpful to count compressions out loud as they are being performed.

Chest compressions should be performed until an **automatic external defibrillator (AED)** arrives and indicates that compressions should be stopped. The AED should be switched on immediately upon arrival and will provide visual and voice prompts. An AED uses electricity to activate the heart's natural electrical system. The nursing assistant should be familiar with an AED and how to operate it correctly. Most systems use two pads that can be attached to the patient's chest to analyze the heart rhythm and deliver an electrical shock if necessary. Once the pads are attached, the AED will assess heart rhythm and, if necessary, an automated voice will tell the health care team to deliver a shock (which can be done by pushing a button on the box).

The nursing assistant and all other health care workers should stand away from the patient and not make contact with the patient or the bed while the shock is being delivered to avoid accidental electrocution.

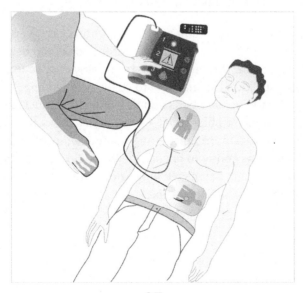

Respiratory Distress

The nursing assistant may encounter a situation in which a patient is suddenly unable to breathe or is doing so with great difficulty. This is called **respiratory distress**. **Acute respiratory distress syndrome (ARDS)** is a specific kind of respiratory distress. With the proper medical intervention, this emergency situation can potentially be resolved within days to weeks.

Causes of ARDS are various and can include aspiration, where a patient breathes vomitus or food into the lungs. Patients with a decreased level of consciousness or decreased ability to chew and swallow should be especially monitored for aspiration.

A patient with pneumonia has a fluid collection in the lungs that can potentially worsen into ARDS. Also, ARDS can be in patients who have recently had a lung transplant and are having issues accepting the new lung tissue. This can lead to respiratory distress, septic shock, or a disseminated infection that has reached the bloodstream and caused a widespread immune response.

The basic physiology of ARDS is as follows: fluid in the air sacs of the lungs (**alveoli**) builds up to the point that oxygen exchange is severely inhibited or is not occurring at all. The blood then becomes **hypoxemic** (not containing enough oxygen), and the tissues and organs of the body do not receive enough oxygen and cannot carry out their basic metabolic functions.

A patient who is going into respiratory distress will complain of shortness of breath. They will appear to be struggling to "catch a breath," their blood pressure may drop, and they will be attempting to take breaths at a rapid rate. Difficulty breathing is sometimes called **dyspnea**, and increased rate of breathing is called **tachypnea**. Feelings of anxiety may accompany difficulty breathing.

When a nursing assistant witnesses a patient with worsening breathing, this should be reported to the nurse immediately. An emergency response team may be activated, and if the patient's oxygenation cannot be restored via nasal cannula or oxygen mask, the patient may need to be intubated and placed on a ventilator until proper oxygenation and breathing are restored. This will likely require that the patient be transported to the ICU or other unit that cares for patients on ventilators. The nursing assistant should prepare transport materials, be on hand to take vitals if necessary, and make him or herself available for any other assistance needed to stabilize the patient.

An important vital sign to monitor during an emergency respiratory distress situation is **pulse oxygenation**. This vital sign is acquired using a pulse oximeter and should be part of the nursing assistant's routine vital sign collection. The **pulse oximeter** is fairly easy to use; one simply places the probe on the patient's finger and allows the machine to collect the reading. The reading is collected by shining a light through the patient's capillary beds and detecting how much oxygen is being carried by the hemoglobin molecule, part of the red blood cell. If the nursing assistant encounters an unexpected reading, always try at least one or two more times using the following interventions: squeezing and rubbing the patient's hands and arms gently to encourage blood flow to the fingers (cold hands may indicate decreased blood flow, meaning decreased hemoglobin for the monitor to detect), trying a different finger, and checking to make sure the probe is placed correctly and in the optimal position.

Difficulty Swallowing

A nursing assistant may encounter patients who have difficulty swallowing. A patient who has difficulty swallowing has **dysphagia**. Dysphagia can arise from a number of different causes and puts the patient at risk for aspiration, which will be discussed in the following section. Nursing assistants should be aware of the signs of dysphagia and know how to prevent complications.

When a person swallows, this process involves chewing food adequately and moving it from the mouth to the esophagus, a tube leading to the stomach where the food may then begin to be digested. The elderly, infants and toddlers, and people with neurological deficits may have trouble with swallowing, although it can affect any person.

Dysphagia usually arises from either the nervous or muscular components of the swallowing process. Sometimes there is a physical block between the mouth, throat, or esophagus through which food and fluids cannot pass.

Causes of muscular and neurological problems with swallowing include patients who have had a cerebrovascular accident, or stroke, an injury to the brain or spinal cord, which coordinate the swallowing process, or other neurological system diseases, including polio, multiple sclerosis (MS), muscular dystrophy, or Parkinson's disease. At times, the esophagus of the patient may spasm uncontrollably, meaning the muscle is contracted without relaxing. Swallowing is a muscular activity, and any condition negatively affecting muscle control can cause dysphagia.

Physical blockades to swallowing include scarring on the esophagus caused by gastroesophageal reflux disease (GERD). The scarring narrows the esophagus, making swallowing difficult. An inflammation of the esophagus that can cause dysphagia is called **esophagitis**. Gastroesophageal reflux can also cause nausea and sometimes vomiting in place of or in addition to dysphagia.

The nursing assistant will recognize a patient has trouble swallowing when the patient reports he or she cannot get food down on the first try, feels like food or pills are stuck in the throat, or starts gagging, coughing, or choking when trying to swallow. There are varying degrees of dysphagia, and some older adults especially may have trouble swallowing as a chronic problem.

It's important for a nursing assistant to report any suspicion of dysphagia to the nurse so the team taking care of the patient can be made aware of the situation. Certain interventions, such as a swallow evaluation done by speech therapy, may be ordered. The patient may be placed on a special diet such as a **mechanical soft diet**, in which foods are ground, blended, pureed, or otherwise mechanically broken down to ease passage from the mouth to the stomach. Patients who have difficulty swallowing should have the heads of their beds elevated when eating. Liquids may be thickened before drinking to aid in swallowing.

Choking/Aspirations

Aspiration is when foreign materials such as food or fluids enter the lungs accidentally while a patient is eating or drinking. Aspiration is sometimes a life-threatening condition, since the lungs cannot perform adequate oxygen exchange when they are impeded with foreign substances. The nursing assistant should know the signs and symptoms of aspiration and what to do during such an emergency.

When a patient aspirates, fluid travels down the trachea and into the lungs, rather than down the esophagus and into the stomach. In normal swallowing, the epiglottis is the protective tissue that blocks food and fluids from entering the airway. When a person has a lower level of consciousness or has a weakened swallowing or gag reflex, the epiglottis does not function properly to protect the airway from foreign substances.

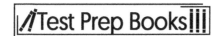

A patient who has aspirated will likely do so while eating or drinking, so mealtime is a time to be cautious and vigilant toward patients who are at risk. Risk factors for aspirating include a lowered level of consciousness, in which the patient is not fully awake and/or oriented. Patients who have experienced a stroke in the past may have developed dysphagia because of a loss of motor function, which puts them at risk for aspirating.

If a patient is intubated with an **endotracheal tube**, this added device could increase the risk for aspirating because it holds the airway open. Intubated patients should receive nutrition through means other than oral feeding. Other risk factors for aspiration include a decreased gag reflex, decreased tone in the esophageal sphincters, alcoholic or drug intoxication, and side effects of medication that affect the level of consciousness.

Patients who are at risk for aspiration should have the head of the bed elevated to at least forty-five degrees, sometimes ninety degrees, so that they are sitting upright both during and after eating. This angle promotes effective swallowing, in which food and fluids travel to the stomach instead of the lungs. A patient who lays flat on their back, or completely supine, is at greater risk of aspirating.

It is important that those who are at risk for aspiration are identified early in their admission or hospitalization to prevent an emergency situation and worsening of their overall condition. If the nursing assistant suspects that the patient has difficulty with swallowing, this should be reported to the nurse immediately.

Signs of potential aspiration include choking or gagging while eating or drinking; continued coughing for a long time after meals; fever after an episode of gagging, choking, or vomiting; wheezing; and/or rapid breathing. The nursing assistant should stop food and fluids immediately after seeing these signs or suspecting aspiration may have occurred. A collection of vital signs may be necessary, particularly respiratory rate and pulse oximetry to see if there is a compromise in oxygenation.

Precautions that may be taken for a patient who is at risk for aspiration may include signage in the room and on the patient's chart indicating the risk, an altered diet with softened foods, supervision during meals, and thickening liquids. Sometimes taking in fluids through drinking straws is restricted, depending on the amount of fluid a patient can safely consume at one time without aspirating. These restrictions to reduce risk of aspiration are usually determined with the help of a nutritionist, speech pathologist, nurse, and/or physician.

When a patient is suspected to be at risk for aspiration, a speech therapist will likely be consulted to do a swallowing evaluation. This may include a radiographic study called a **barium swallow evaluation**, in which the patient is observed swallowing sips of barium, and the pathway the barium takes is observed via X-ray. Some patients have what is called **silent aspiration**, in which they moderately aspirate all the time without any signs or symptoms. These patients will still need interventions to prevent a progression to **aspiration pneumonia**, in which aspirated particles accumulate in the lungs.

Vomiting

When the contents of the stomach are forcefully ejected outside of the body through the mouth, it is called **vomiting**. Vomiting can occur during a patient's hospitalization or admission to a facility and may even be the cause of admission. Vomiting is usually a symptom of an underlying condition. The nursing assistant needs to be aware of what to do when a patient is vomiting and the signs to watch for that indicate whether the patient's condition is worsening.

Vomiting can be caused by a number of different underlying conditions. **Gastritis** is a condition in which the lining of the stomach becomes inflamed due to an infection or irritation. **Gastroenteritis** is often vomiting caused by a virus. Bacteria may cause vomiting in the case of food poisoning. A person can ingest an inflammatory bacterium, which irritates the lining of the stomach and causes vomiting. Common bacteria associated with gastrointestinal upset leading to vomiting include Staphylococcus aureus, Salmonella, Campylobacter, Escherichia coli, and Clostridium botulinum.

Patients who suffer from **peptic ulcer disease (PUD)** may experience vomiting as a result of irritation of the ulcerations in their stomach. Patients with gastroesophageal reflux disease (GERD or acid reflux) can experience nausea and vomiting as a result of the presence of acid in the esophagus and general irritation in the gastric tissues.

Vomiting is not always caused by a problem in the gastrointestinal tract, however. Sometimes the cause may be neurological, stemming from a problem in the nervous system. People who suffer from migraines may experience nausea and vomiting as a side effect of their intense headache. Inner ear problems such as vertigo, labyrinthitis, Meniere's disease, and motion sickness may trigger a vomiting response. Vomiting may occur in patients who have had a concussion or other blunt trauma, electrolyte imbalances, and heat stroke.

Some vomiting may be brought on by other stimuli. Certain sights, sounds, or other sensations may stimulate the central nervous system, causing nausea and vomiting response. For example, the sight of a gruesome wound or a strongly unpleasant smell may stimulate a person to vomit.

Patients admitted to a hospital or facility with organ failure or other disease may experience vomiting as a part of their illness. Hepatitis, gallbladder disease, pancreatitis, Crohn's disease, and renal failure can all cause vomiting as a result of pain, gastrointestinal upset, electrolyte imbalances, or other causes.

Patients who have cancer and are undergoing chemotherapy will commonly experience nausea and vomiting as a side effect. **Chemotherapy** attacks healthy tissue in the body as well as the cancerous tissue, which creates a noxious environment in the body, potentially causing vomiting. Patients receiving chemotherapy may also develop nausea and vomiting as conditioned behaviors even after treatment has stopped.

A **bowel obstruction** can cause vomiting. The blockage of the bowel prevents undigested food and fluids from moving forward along the gastrointestinal tract. This causes nausea and vomiting.

Hormonal fluctuations and imbalances can also cause nausea and vomiting, as evidenced by the experiences of some pregnant women.

Vomiting can be dangerous if it is prolonged, since it can cause dehydration and malnutrition. Vomiting should be monitored by the nursing assistant, recorded in the patient's chart, and reported to the nurse. The characteristics of the vomitus should be especially noted, since these can be a clue to help determine the cause.

Vomitus containing blood could indicate internal bleeding. The nursing assistant should note the blood's color and appearance in the vomitus, whether it is bright red, dark red, liquid, or has the appearance of coffee grounds. All of this can help determine the source of the bleeding and how long the blood has been in the stomach.

When appropriate, patients should be encouraged to take in fluids whenever they can tolerate them to restore hydration. The patient may be placed on intravenous fluid therapy in the meantime to prevent dehydration.

Seizures

Abnormal discharges of electrical signals in the brain may cause a patient to have a seizure. A **seizure** is characterized in a few different ways, including convulsions, disturbances in the sensory system, and potential loss of consciousness. There are a number of different causes of seizures. The nursing assistant needs to be able to recognize when a patient is having a seizure and know what to do next.

The brain is a complex organ of the body that controls many different bodily functions. Because of its complexity, electrical abnormalities may have different manifestations depending on the part of the brain in which they occur. Thus, seizures, a result of disrupted electrical activity, can occur in a number of different ways.

There are several different types of seizures: grand mal or generalized tonic-clonic, absence, myoclonic, clonic, tonic, and atonic. A **grand mal seizure** causes the patient to go into a state of muscle rigidity, convulsions, and unconsciousness. An **absence seizure**, which typically occurs in children unnoticed, is where the patient loses consciousness for a short period of time, sometimes staring into space, and is verbally unresponsive. A **myoclonic seizure** causes part of the body to make sporadic jerking movements. A **clonic seizure** involves rhythmic and repetitive jerking movements throughout the body. **Tonic seizures** are characterized by a rigidity and overall stiffness of the muscles throughout the body. The final type of seizure, **atonic**, is where the patient loses muscle tone completely throughout the body.

Other symptoms of a seizure include twitching motions, falling down, biting of the tongue, loss of bladder and possibly bowel control, stiffness, repetitive motions, staring, tingling, dizziness, and mood changes.

Patients may be diagnosed with **epilepsy**, in which they have a nervous system disturbance making them prone to frequent seizures. Epilepsy can be managed and seizures decreased in frequency or avoided altogether through lifestyle and pharmacological management, such as avoiding known seizure triggers and adhering to a medication regimen. Epilepsy may be preceded by a stroke, brain trauma, or a brain tumor as well.

Epilepsy is not the only cause of seizures. In fact, seizures are associated with numerous different conditions, including the following situations:

- People withdrawing from alcohol or drugs
- Abnormal levels of sodium or glucose in the blood circulation
- Fever (especially in children)
- Blood pressure that is dangerously high
- Abuse of street drugs, side effect of medication, heart disease, electric shock, and brain infection

There is sometimes no known cause of a seizure, in which case it is called **idiopathic,** or of unknown origin.

There are a number of different things that the nursing assistant should do when a patient is having a seizure. The first is to alert the nurse and the health care team immediately in order to get their assistance in stabilizing the patient and activating the emergency response system if necessary.

The nursing assistant should try to prevent any injury in the patient. If possible, the nursing assistant should try and lay down the person to prevent falling. The person's head should have a pillow or some other form of cushioning around it. Tight clothing should be loosened. The patient should be turned to one side to prevent aspiration should vomiting occur. It is not helpful to try and restrain the person, since this is mostly ineffective and could cause further injury. The biting of the tongue may be upsetting, but do not attempt to place anything in the person's mouth, since this could pose a choking or biting risk. Any hazardous objects should be removed from the immediate vicinity if possible.

Changes in Mobility, Speech, and Signs of Stroke

The nursing assistant will potentially encounter a patient experiencing a stroke. A stroke is a medical emergency involving damage to the patient's brain tissue that requires immediate intervention. Knowing the signs and symptoms of a stroke and what causes one, as well as what to do in the case of a stroke, will help the nurse aid better assist the patient and the health care team.

A stroke is medically termed a **cerebrovascular accident**, in which blood flow is restricted to a part of the brain resulting in serious, potentially long-term, or even life-threatening symptoms. A stroke can be **ischemic**, in which blood flow is blocked by a clot, or **hemorrhagic**, in which a blood vessel has broken. There are also **transient ischemic strokes (TIAs)**, in which blood flow is only temporarily blocked to an area of the brain, causing short-term symptoms that may completely disappear.

A person who has been diagnosed with high blood pressure, smokes cigarettes, has problems controlling their cholesterol, has abdominal obesity, is an alcoholic, is under a lot of stress, and/or leads a sedentary lifestyle may be at risk for a stroke. Other risk factors include diabetes, blood disorders, especially those involving clotting, cocaine or other street drug use, and intracranial aneurysms.

Symptoms of stroke include difficulty speaking or understanding what is being spoken; difficulty swallowing; numbness, tingling, and/or loss of function in an extremity; facial numbness, tingling, or twitching; drooping of one side of the face; and other sensory and motor deficits.

It is important for the nursing assistant to note the time when symptoms began. This time of system onset will be important for determination of treatment type. Some anti-clot medications can only be administered within a certain time frame to achieve maximum effectiveness.

An easy, commonly used system of evaluating for stroke in a patient is the "**Act FAST**" system. This system uses the acronym "FAST" to describe four key things to look for to determine if a patient has experienced a stroke. "F" is for face; when the person is asked to smile, does one side of the mouth or face droop? "A" is for arms; when asked to raise the arms, does one arm drift noticeably downward? "S" is for speech; when the patient is asked to repeat a simple phrase, is the speech of the reply slurred, or is he or she unable to perform the task? "T" is for time; if any of the previous three answers were yes, emergency intervention is immediately necessary.

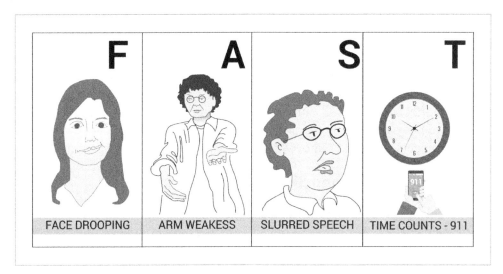

Note: Some facilities may not want the nursing assistant to do a full stroke assessment and may reserve this for the nurse. In either case, the nursing assistant should alert the nurse at the first sign or suspicion of a stroke.

A patient who has had or is having a stroke will need to be taken for diagnostic imaging of the brain using computer tomography or CT scanning. After a stroke has been determined, the decision of whether to give the patient an anti-clot medication will be made. Again, this depends on onset and type of symptoms, as well as what type of stroke is being experienced.

Depending on the severity of the symptoms, after a patient has recovered from the initial stroke, he or she will most likely need rehabilitation to regain lost function from the brain tissue damage that has occurred. The patient will also need an evaluation concerning their medication and lifestyle to help prevent a future stroke.

After reporting the stroke symptom(s) to the nurse, the nursing assistant should be prepared to take a set of vital signs and potentially prepare the patient for transport to a higher level of care.

Diabetic Situations

Diabetes is a common diagnosis among patients in the United States. It is a disease in which the body's natural insulin response to blood glucose is compromised, causing hyperglycemia. **Hyperglycemia** is a dangerously high blood sugar that can damage the organs and tissues of the body.

The nursing assistant will become accustomed to taking care of patients with diabetes. These patients may have a special diabetic diet that restricts or counts carbohydrates; may need blood sugar levels taken before meals, upon rising, and before going to bed, depending on their specific orders; and will need special care in case their blood sugar becomes dangerously low or high.

Insulin is a hormone secreted by the pancreas in the body. No other organ secretes insulin. The **pancreas** is positioned behind the stomach in the body, making it conveniently situated to assist with the absorption and distribution of glucose that enters the body. Glucose enters the body through the food that one eats, is a type of sugar, and is necessary for metabolic functioning in the body. Insulin works in the blood stream to allow glucose to be absorbed into the cells of the body.

When the insulin response is compromised, as is the case in diabetes, it is no longer effective in moving glucose from the bloodstream into the cells of the body. The glucose then accumulates in the blood stream with nowhere to go, and the resulting state is called **hyperglycemia.** The cells of the body need glucose to survive and are unable to function if they are unable to obtain glucose from the bloodstream.

There are two main types of diabetic emergencies: **hypoglycemia**, in which the blood sugar is too low; and **hyperglycemia**, in which the blood sugar is too high.

Hypoglycemia is when the blood sugar of a patient drops below 70 milligrams per deciliter (mg/dL). Patients may develop this if they have had too much insulin or have not ingested enough dietary glucose. This can sometimes occur in a hospital or facility if a patient misses meals due to scheduled tests or procedures. The nursing assistant should be vigilant about the patient getting regular meals and if not, work with the nurse to keep him or her aware of the situation so that insulin dosages can be adjusted or meals can be obtained.

Symptoms of hypoglycemia include decreased level of consciousness, tremors, fatigue, excessive sweating, dizziness, and syncope (fainting). The patient may also become anxious, report blurred vision, headache, or have slurred speech.

If the nursing assistant sees signs of hypoglycemia, this should be reported immediately to the nurse. The nursing assistant should expect to collect a blood glucose reading and a set of vital signs. The nurse will likely administer prescribed oral glucose, IV dextrose, or perhaps parenteral glucagon to correct the blood sugar.

Hyperglycemia is a blood sugar level greater than 200 milligrams per deciliter. Normal blood sugar recommendations are usually between 70 and 130 milligrams per deciliter, but symptoms of hyperglycemia may not manifest until the blood sugar level is greater than 200 milligrams per deciliter. Hyperglycemia may go unnoticed since the patient may not have symptoms of high blood sugar. It is therefore important to obtain blood sugar levels as necessary, even if the patient is not showing symptoms.

Hyperglycemia can be caused by the patient not having adequate insulin and/or anti-diabetic medication management, ingesting more glucose than normal, illness that changes normal routine, or a personal crisis that has occurred causing emotional stress in the body.

The nursing assistant should recognize the most common symptoms of hyperglycemia: an increased need to urinate, called **polyuria**, and excessive thirst, called **polydipsia.** If hyperglycemia has caused complications such as **diabetic ketoacidosis** (an acidotic metabolic state in the body), a patient may display these two symptoms, as well as nausea, abdominal pain, fruity-scented breath, and/or confusion.

Diabetic ketoacidosis is a metabolic imbalance that can cause a condition called **diabetic coma**, when the blood sugar becomes so high that the patient loses consciousness. If diabetic coma is not treated, the patient may not survive.

If signs and symptoms of either hypoglycemia or hyperglycemia are present in the patient, the nursing assistant must report this immediately to the nurse in order to stabilize the patient's blood glucose.

Sudden Onset of Confusion or Agitation

Patients who have entered a facility or hospital may experience periods of confusion or agitation. This may be an acute situation for the individual or part of an ongoing diagnosis of dementia or Alzheimer's disease. A severe and acute situation that involves confusion and agitation is called **delirium**. The nursing assistant should be aware of these different situations, their causes, and what can be done to assist the patient back to normal functioning.

Confusion and agitation are symptoms of an underlying condition or disease. Patients who once were oriented to whom they were, where they were, what circumstances brought them to the facility, and the time may become confused on one or all of these points. They will suddenly not understand and become uncertain about the facts of their situation.

A patient who is agitated may display an acute anxiety about seemingly small details of their stay at the hospital or facility, perhaps even becoming verbally or physically abusive toward staff. In either of these situations, if the confusion and agitation are new, they should be reported to the nurse immediately for further investigation. Usually if the cause can be found, the situation can be corrected.

Delirium is a mental disturbance involving confusion, decreased awareness of surroundings, and sometimes agitation that causes a patient to lose focus and attention. This condition is usually transient in nature, not lasting for long if appropriate interventions are applied. Delirium usually occurs in the presence of an illness, as a sign of drug toxicity, and in situations of dehydration, where the body's fluids and electrolytes are out of balance. A patient who is older, has Parkinson's disease, dementia, or a history of stroke may be at a greater risk to develop delirium.

Patients with dementia or Alzheimer's disease may be prone to periods of heightened agitation or confusion. A person with these conditions is also more prone to acute periods of delirium. **Dementia** is a chronic, long-term condition that involves decreased cognitive ability over time, while delirium happens quickly and usually does not last long.

The nursing assistant should work with the rest of the health care team to create an environment around the confused patient that is conducive to calm, collected behavior. This includes making the environment around the patient as stable as possible, without bright lights, loud and/or sudden noises, and unexpected interruptions to the patient's expected routine.

Including items in a patient's room such as family photographs and other familiar objects can be visual reminders to the patient about their circumstances.

If the patient has sensory deficits such as visual or hearing loss, the nursing assistant should ensure that these are addressed. The patient's hearing aid batteries should be kept refreshed, glasses and dentures in a place where they can be easily accessed, and assistive walking devices such as canes or walkers at hand if appropriate. Granting the patient as much freedom and familiarity as possible will assist the patient in functioning while in the facility.

The nursing assistant can help patients with confusion and agitation by listening to their needs, maintaining a calm, collected, and professional attitude, talking about what the daily tasks and expectations are, and reorienting the patient whenever necessary. The nursing assistant must work with patients based on their cognitive abilities to assure that they can work with the health care team effectively without becoming overwhelmed and confused.

Family members and/or friends of the patient are valuable resources when dealing with confusion, especially if it is a long-standing issue. The patient's loved ones may have developed some tips and tricks for helping the patient regain orientation that can be used by the health care team.

Changes in Levels of Consciousness

A patient in a hospital or facility may experience varying levels of consciousness based on their condition. A person's **level of consciousness** refers to their ability to be aroused, awake, and responsive to the surrounding environment. Procedural sedation also affects the level of consciousness.

The nursing assistant should be aware of the different levels of consciousness, what is normal, and when to alert the nurse of a change.

LEVELS OF CONSCIOUSNESS

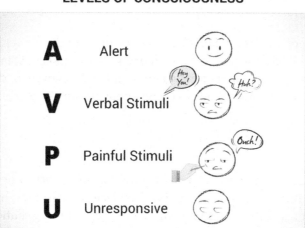

As the illustration shows, there are four basic levels of consciousness. The first is **alert**, in which the patient is awake, responsive to verbal stimuli, and is a normal finding. The next level down would be a patient who is only responsive to **verbal stimuli**, followed by a patient who is only responsive to **painful stimuli.** Painful stimuli include shoulder shaking, a mild pinch, or a sternal rub. The final stage is **unresponsiveness**, in which neither verbal nor painful stimuli arouse the patient.

In addition to the four main levels of consciousness, there are terms to describe specific states of **altered levels of consciousness (ALOC). Lethargy** is when a patient is drowsy and not as aware of surroundings as they normally would be. A **somnolent** patient is very sleepy, can be awakened, but will return to sleep if left alone. A patient in a **stupor** will awaken from sleep only upon painful stimuli, but then return to sleep after the stimulus has discontinued. A coma is a state of sleep in which the patient cannot be awakened either by verbal or painful stimuli. **Delirium**, as was discussed in the section on confusion, has to do with an acute onset of severe confusion and disorientation.

A **coma** is an altered level of consciousness in which the patient is completely unarousable. There are a number of different reasons a patient may be in a coma, including structural disorders of the brain such as abscesses or tumors, seizures that disrupt the brain's electrical activity to an extent that consciousness is lost, and metabolic disorders such as diabetic ketoacidosis or hepatic encephalopathy. Disturbances in a patient's fluid and electrolyte balances, as is the case in hypercalcemia, hyperglycemia, and hyponatremia, among others, may cause a coma. Infections such as meningitis, encephalitis, and sepsis can put a patient into a coma.

There are a number of different causes for a decreased level of consciousness. Drugs, whether medications or street drugs, can cause a decreased level of consciousness. Patients experiencing blood sugar fluctuations, both high blood sugar and low blood sugar, may have their level of consciousness affected. When the brain does not get enough oxygen for various reasons, the level of consciousness is decreased. Other potential causes of a decreased level of consciousness include dementia, brain injury, heat stroke, kidney failure, liver disease, and shock.

The nursing assistant should determine from the patient's reports and medical records what their normal level of consciousness is. Due to underlying conditions, the patient may always maintain an altered level of consciousness. When the level of consciousness changes unexpectedly, this finding should be reported to the nurse immediately.

After reporting the finding of a decreased level of consciousness to the nurse, the nursing assistant should expect to take a set of vital signs, perhaps a blood glucose, and assist in any way to correct the underlying cause of the change. The patient may need supplemental oxygen, correction of electrolytes such as glucose or sodium, intravenous fluids to correct dehydration, or medications to correct other causative factors.

Falls

Risk for falls is a serious consideration for all patients entering into a facility or hospital. A fall can cause injuries that worsen the patient's condition and may even lead to death. The nursing assistant should be able to identify patients at risk for falls and implement the proper fall precautions to ensure the patient's safety.

A fall may occur for a number of reasons. Older adults are at risk for falls more so than younger people due to weakening muscles and bones. This weakness in the musculoskeletal system leads to an unsteady gait and poor balance. People with a weak musculoskeletal system may not be able to correct themselves as quickly or with as much agility when they lose their balance, nor can they catch themselves as well when they fall, leading to greater injury.

Fluctuations in blood pressure may cause a person to fall, especially if the blood pressure becomes too low. Blood pressure is a reflection of how well the heart is pumping oxygen-rich blood to the tissues of the body, especially the brain. If the brain is not getting enough oxygen from the blood as a result of low blood pressure, among other causes, the person may fall as a result of dizziness and/or fainting. **Orthostatic hypotension** occurs when blood pressure drops suddenly as a result of a change in position, such as from sitting to standing, and does not immediately compensate.

Low blood sugar may cause a decreased level of consciousness in an individual. The brain not only needs oxygen, but it also needs an adequate supply of blood glucose to maintain consciousness and regulate movement and coordination. When blood sugar becomes too low, the resulting altered level of consciousness may cause a person to lose balance and fall to the ground.

Patients in an unfamiliar environment may become confused when in bed or navigating themselves around their room. Confusion is common among hospitalized individuals, resulting from medication side effects and the effects of illness. A patient may suddenly attempt to get out of bed or try and walk to the bathroom, not remembering that they are attached to an intravenous pole, urinary catheter, and/or many other types of equipment, depending on their condition. This brief moment of confusion and unexpected obstacles can lead to a fall and injury.

Patients with sensory deficits may be at risk for a fall, such as those with visual and hearing impairments. Visual impairments may prevent a patient from seeing obstacles in their path. Hearing impairments may prevent a patient from hearing warning sounds or words.

There are certain measures, called **fall precautions**, which can be put in place for a patient who is at risk for a fall. The nursing assistant can create an uncluttered, well-lit environment for the patient. Rooms that are full of clutter, equipment, and obstacles put the patient at risk for a fall. In the same way, if the lighting is not adequate for the patient, they may trip on an unseen object and fall.

Placing the call light in the patient's reach and talking to the patient about using it when needing any sort of assistance can prevent a fall. Some hospitals have a "Call Don't Fall" sign in the patient's room, indicating the patient and family should ask for help using the call light when necessary.

Patients who have displayed confusion and impulsive behavior that may put them at risk for a fall, such as suddenly attempting to get out of bed when they are not physically able or need assistance with equipment, should have special precautions put in place. A **bed alarm** is a device that sets off an alarm when the patient tries to get out of bed unassisted. It is a pad with a sensor that is placed under the patient's buttocks or under the fitted sheet of the bed; the bed itself may be equipped with an alarm device.

Some patients will be put on what is called a **low bed**, a bed that can be lowered close to the floor. This ensures that the patient will not accidentally slide or roll out of bed if they try to get out of bed before the health care staff can assist.

Bleeding

Blood is a common sight in hospitals and medical facilities. There are a number of different ways a patient can bleed with varying degrees of severity. Depending on the amount of blood and the severity, bleeding can quickly become an emergency situation. The nursing assistant needs to be aware of the different types of bleeding, what to report to the nurse, and ways to assist to control the bleeding.

Blood is a type of connective tissue that is circulated throughout the body to transport oxygen and other nutrients. Blood is vital to maintaining life and metabolic activities. When blood circulation is compromised, the whole body suffers. In the case of bleeding, blood is lost from the body and replenishment is necessary to restore bodily functions. Blood runs to almost all parts of the body, meaning essentially all parts of the body can bleed, and the vessels of blood that supply them can rupture and leak.

Hemorrhage is a term used to describe a large amount of bleeding and blood loss. This can be internal or external, depending on the cause. For example, a **postpartum hemorrhage** is a life-threatening condition in which a woman who has just given birth continues to bleed uncontrollably.

A **post-operative hemorrhage** is when a person has had a surgery performed and the incision site or internal organs are not surgically closed or connected properly, and this leads to blood loss.

A **hemorrhagic stroke** is a stroke caused by excessive bleeding in the brain, possibly caused by blunt force trauma or excessive anti-coagulant medications.

Gastrointestinal (GI) bleeding is a type of bleeding in which a part of the GI tract begins to bleed and possibly hemorrhage. The manifestations of a GI bleed vary depending on the source of the bleed and its location on the GI tract. If the bleeding is coming from the lower GI tract, such as the colon, the patient may have blood in the stool. If the bleeding is coming from the upper GI tract, such as the stomach, the patient may throw up blood, called **hematemesis**. Upper GI bleeds may be caused by ulcerations and esophageal varices, while lower GI bleeds may be a result of colitis, hemorrhoids, or diverticular diseases.

A patient may also experience bleeding from the respiratory tract, in which blood is coughed up. Coughing up blood is called **hemoptysis**. Causes of hemoptysis include bronchitis, tuberculosis, and necrotizing pneumonia, among others.

Some patients may have a coagulation disorder in which they bleed excessively as a result of their blood not clotting appropriately. These patients may have unexplained nose bleeds, excessive bruising, and bleed more than normal from very small skin wounds such as finger sticks for blood glucose measurement.

Whatever the cause of the bleeding, the nursing assistant should report it to the nurse. It is important to note the site of bleeding; the amount of blood; if the blood is in sputum, vomitus, or stool; and the characteristics of the blood. Bleeding should be charted in the patient's medical record. Depending on the facility policy, the nursing assistant may be able to assist in first aid for excessive bleeding. This involves applying firm pressure to the site of the bleed and holding pressure until the bleeding ceases. Pressure assists in blood coagulation and provides a physical barrier to further blood loss. Depending on how much blood was lost, the patient may need a transfusion of blood, platelets, and other intravenous fluids to replenish blood volume.

Burns

A **burn** is an injury to the skin that has varying degrees of severity. The nursing assistant should be familiar with the different types, severities, and treatments for burn victims.

Burns occur when the skin comes in contact with a thermal, radiation, chemical, or electrical source. Essentially, too much heat causes a burn. Burns can be placed into four different categories, depending on their depth. The first category is first degree, then second degree, or superficial, followed by deep partial-thickness, and finally third degree or full-thickness.

Another way to classify a burn's severity is by percentage of the body affected by the burn. This is easier to estimate when one knows how much skin each body part has as a percentage of total skin. For

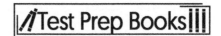
example, it's helpful to know that each arm has about 9% of the skin on the body. The **Rule of Nines** Chart is used for this and is pictured below:

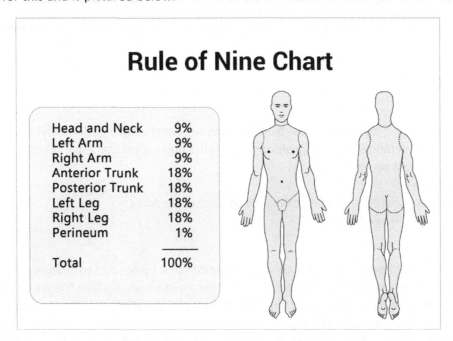

Rule of Nine Chart

Head and Neck	9%
Left Arm	9%
Right Arm	9%
Anterior Trunk	18%
Posterior Trunk	18%
Left Leg	18%
Right Leg	18%
Perineum	1%
Total	100%

A **first-degree** burn only affects the epidermal layer of the skin. A **second-degree** burn, which is sometimes called a **partial-thickness** burn, goes deeper into the dermal layer of the skin. **Deep partial-thickness** burns are a subcategory of second-degree burns, involving deeper layers of the dermis, more scarring, and longer healing time. A **third-degree** burn, also called a **full-thickness** burn, reaches all the way through the layers of the skin into the underlying fat layers. These burns may require skin grafting.

A first-degree burn will appear red and still has the ability to **blanch,** or turn white when pressed. Since nerve endings have not been completely damaged, the patient will still be able to feel pain and tenderness in this area. A second-degree burn also blanches and has pain and tenderness if superficial but may not if the burn is of deep partial-thickness. Depending on the thickness, second-degree burns may or may not have blistering in the area. A full-thickness burn has varying appearances, from white to black to brown and leathery.

Because the protective barrier of the skin has been compromised by a burn, the patient's internal environment is then at further health risks. Infection is a major risk after a burn, as infectious agents can easily invade the deep tissues of the body without the protection of the skin. The patient may also go into **hypovolemic shock** if a lot of blood and fluids were lost through the burned tissue. If the patient was burned in a fire, they may also experience inhalation injuries, in which inhaling smoke caused damage to the lungs, compromising breathing and oxygenation. Patients with severe burns will potentially need intravenous fluids to restore fluid volume, blood products, topical treatments (including antibiotics), and eventually skin grafting. Patients admitted with burns are often admitted to specialized burn units or intensive care units.

Practice Quiz

1. What are the blood vessels called that carry blood back to the heart from the rest of the body?
    a. Capillaries
    b. Arteries
    c. Ventricles
    d. Veins

2. The nursing assistant is taking a manual blood pressure reading from a patient who is seated in an armchair. Which of the following body positions should the nursing assistant ask the patient to change in order to get the most accurate reading?
    a. Crossed legs
    b. Holding remote with hand not getting blood pressure reading
    c. Resting head on head rest
    d. Slouching

3. The nursing assistant heard the doctor telling the patient how he needed to change his diet and get more exercise to better manage his diabetes. The nursing assistant knows that the patient did not want to hear this and that the patient has been vocal in the past about not needing to change anything about his lifestyle. The nurse senses that the patient feels angry and frustrated by his conversation with the doctor. The patient is very agitated when the nursing assistant comes to collect vital signs and tells her that he thinks she is lazy. Which defense mechanism is the patient displaying?
    a. Intellectualization
    b. Undoing
    c. Reaction formation
    d. Displacement

4. The nursing assistant walks into the room where the patient is clutching his chest, sweating, and appears short of breath. The patient reports he is experiencing chest pain that is crushing and severe, with some pain in his left arm as well. The nursing assistant knows that this type of chest pain is most likely associated with which following medical condition?
    a. Myocardial infarction
    b. Gastroesophageal reflux
    c. Pneumonia
    d. Pleuritis

5. The nursing assistant is speaking with a patient who suddenly loses consciousness and is unresponsive to verbal and painful stimuli. The nursing assistant does what immediately?
    a. Applies oxygen
    b. Activates the emergency response system
    c. Performs chest compressions
    d. Checks for a pulse

Answer Explanations

1. D: The blood vessels that carry blood back to the heart are called veins. Capillaries are where arteries and veins meet to exchange oxygen and carbon dioxide at the tissue level. Arteries carry blood away from the heart to the tissues of the body. Ventricles are a type of blood pumping chamber in the heart, although there are also ventricles in the brain that serve a different purpose.

2. A: The nursing assistant should politely ask the patient to uncross her legs to get the most accurate blood pressure reading. Crossed legs can affect the blood pressure reading, since blood vessels can be compressed. Holding a remote, slouching, and resting the head will not compress any major arteries or veins and affect the blood pressure reading, so there is no need for the nursing assistant to correct these positions.

3. D: The patient is displaying displacement, in which he is taking his negative feelings toward the doctor and expressing them toward the nursing assistant, unreasonably. Reaction formation is when a person feels negatively but reacts positively. Intellectualization is when a person focuses on minute details of the situation rather than coping with the negative emotions associated with it. Undoing is when a person has done something wrong and acts excessively in the opposite way to redeem themselves of prior wrongdoing.

4. A: The chest pain described is most likely cardiac in origin, so the patient could be experiencing a myocardial infarction, or heart attack. Chest pain associated with gastroesophageal reflux is more often described as a burning sensation, without the other symptoms described. Pneumonia and pleuritis may both cause the patient to have a different type of chest pain, in which a sharp, stabbing sensation is felt upon breathing.

5. B: The *very first* thing to do when a patient becomes unresponsive is to activate the emergency response system. If the patient has truly experienced cardiac arrest, the patient needs an external defibrillator as soon as possible. Every minute counts, and the nursing assistant will need help to revive this patient. Applying oxygen is outside of the nursing assistant's scope of practice and should be done by the nurse or respiratory therapist. Chest compressions should only be performed after the emergency response team has been activated and there is no pulse detected. Checking for the pulse comes after activating the emergency response team.

Providing Specialized Care for Residents with Changes in Health

Each resident the nursing assistant encounters will have different needs and different health histories upon entering the facility. It is important that the nursing assistant be able to recognize differing health issues and situations and be able to respond appropriately.

Physical Problems

Some issues the resident may have will be physical in nature, affecting their ability to control the body and perform normal tasks of movement and communication. Sometimes, the impairment will be of a psychological nature, affecting mood, behavior, and perception of reality. There will often be combinations of both physical and psychological impairments.

At times, the nursing assistant will care for a resident who has entered into **palliative care**—care focused on improving quality of life for those with life-threatening or life-limiting illness. In the case of the resident who is dying, quality end-of-life care that is respectful of the resident's and family's wishes and is delivered in a timely and mindful manner will make all the difference.

Common physical impairments include issues with sensory impairment, such as hearing or visual deficits. The resident may have a speech impairment, difficulty with mobility, issues related to going to the bathroom, or issues with feeding themselves properly. Residents may also have oxygen delivery devices, skin breakdown, or need assistance with pain management. The health care team, including the nursing assistant, will work together to manage these issues to ensure that quality care is delivered and the best possible resident outcomes are achieved.

Sensory Impairment
Many residents the nursing assistant encounters will have **sensory impairments**. These include hearing, visual, and other impairments.

Care for the Hearing Impaired
There are various causes of hearing loss in the adult resident, but the most common is nerve-related hearing loss, also known as **sensorineural hearing loss**. This type is related to aging, exposure to noise, and/or blood circulation issues in the ear.

The nurse aid should first determine the resident's baseline hearing: whether one ear is more functional than the other and what characteristics of speech, such as louder or deeper, the resident hears. The resident, their family, and the handoff report from the previous shift can all help determine this information.

Different techniques can aid communication between the nursing assistant and the resident with a hearing impairment. The nursing assistant may stand in the resident's line of vision, aim their voice at the resident's less-affected ear, and use written communication when possible. Decreasing unnecessary noise in the room can also be beneficial when communicating, such as turning down the volume on the resident's television or closing the door to outside hallway chatter.

Speaking in the "good" ear of a resident with a hearing impairment.

Care for the Visually-Impaired

A common cause of visual impairment is **cataracts**, which are clouding protein deposits formed on the lens of the eye in old age. Other common causes of visual impairment include glaucoma, age-related macular degeneration, and diabetic retinopathy.

When encountering a resident with a visual impairment, it is important to establish baseline functioning through the resident report, the family report, and/or the health care record. For example, the nursing assistant may determine the severity of the visual impairment, how much assistance the resident needs with daily activities, and how much can be done independently.

The nursing assistant can create a clutter-free environment in the resident's room and orient them to where common objects are located, such as the bedside table. This is true for all resident rooms as the risk of falling and resulting injury is reduced when commonly used items are within reach. When addressing the resident, the nursing assistant should consciously place themselves in the resident's line of vision.

When ambulating the resident, the nursing assistant should alert the resident to their surroundings, making the resident aware of obstacles and changes in environment. Alerting others on the health care team to the visual impairment using appropriate signage is important. The nursing assistant should ensure that the resident's visual impairment is stated, both when the resident leaves the unit for procedures and in the handoff report. **Braille**—tactile communication used by those with visual impairment—can be used when appropriate and available, in order to communicate written information.

Care for the Touch-Impaired

Almost three-fourths of older patients have a diminished sense of touch, meaning they are unable to feel routine tactile sensations such as pressure, vibration, and even pain. Risk factors include malnutrition and neurological disorders. These patients may require extra monitoring for bedsores, nerve damage, and pain, as they may not be able to feel discomfort until an injury progresses significantly. Some patients may also be extra-sensitive to pressure and temperature, and therefore may require particular concern when they are being physically cared for (e.g., gentler touches, layered clothing).

Speech Impairment

A **speech impairment** refers to problems with articulating words. **Articulation** entails the production of sounds, while voice is the characteristics of the sounds produced.

Language impairment refers to an inability to understand the meaning of information conveyed through language. While there may be residents who struggle with speech impairments, such as stuttering and hoarseness, the focus here will be on language disorders caused by brain damage, specifically aphasia.

Aphasia is when a resident has an impaired ability to speak or understand spoken or written language as a result of a brain injury. The most common cause of aphasia is stroke, where part of the brain directing language is damaged and the language function is impaired.

There are two major categories of aphasia: **expressive aphasia**, where the resident is unable to express language coherently, and **receptive aphasia**, where the resident is unable to understand the meaning behind language.

Care for the Speech-Impaired

When interacting with residents who have aphasia, it is important not to rush them. Intelligence is usually unaffected in people with aphasia; thus, the nursing assistant should try not to get frustrated or impatient with them. Helping, encouraging, and praising residents when they do well is important. Body language, such as gestures, can also be helpful. The nursing assistant should encourage independence and provide opportunities for the resident to succeed, such as posing simple questions. Whenever possible, they should also decrease outside distraction and stimulation when communicating with the resident, such as the television, the radio, or crowded rooms, so that the resident may focus on the task of communicating.

Changes in Mobility

A natural part of aging is a decrease in mobility in most adults. **Mobility** refers to the ability to walk, sit down, and get up from sitting or lying. There are different causes for a decrease in mobility, including disease processes, pain, joint problems, weakness, and injuries from falls.

When a resident is admitted to a facility, it is especially important that fall precautions are put in place. An unfamiliar environment and the side effects of illness and medications contribute to increased risk for a fall. A fall can be a devastating event in the life of an older adult. Falls cause injury, worsening of disease, depression, and even death, in some cases.

Common fall precautions include maintaining a clutter-free environment in the resident's room, keeping the call light close at hand for the resident so that they can call for assistance when it is needed, putting socks with tread on the resident, obtaining a bed that is low to the floor in high-risk residents, and other precautions, depending on the facility and each resident's fall risk level.

Paralysis, whether partial or complete, is a major factor affecting mobility. **Paralysis** is when a part of the nervous system is damaged and, as a result, muscle function and/or sensation in a part of the body is lost. The nursing assistant can determine from the health history and report where and how the resident with paralysis is affected. If possible, the nursing assistant should communicate with the resident and family about the resident's level of independence and activities with which assistance is needed. The resident may need assistance with meals, elimination, and/or turning in bed to prevent skin breakdown.

Changes in Elimination

There are many situations in a facility in which the resident is unable to **eliminate**—i.e., defecate and/or urinate—independently. Elimination is a basic and highly personal need for all people, and the nursing assistant needs to be able to assist with this task appropriately and respectfully. Common issues in elimination are incontinence, constipation, and diarrhea. Some residents may have devices to assist with elimination, such as a colostomy, rectal tube, or urinary catheter.

Incontinence is a term meaning the resident cannot control their bladder and/or bowels. Some residents may be said to be incontinent of bowel, incontinent of bladder, or both. This can be for various reasons including neurological impairment, such as paralysis, or a physical impairment, such as a broken hip. In any scenario of incontinence, it is important to monitor the resident's elimination throughout a shift and assist when possible. If the resident is oriented enough to request help before having a bowel or bladder movement, the nursing assistant should be as available as possible to assist. This may entail assisting the resident to the bathroom or providing a bedside commode or a bedpan.

If the resident is incontinent in bed, a partial bath will be needed along with a linen change. Checking for incontinence frequently is important, as a timely cleanup of a resident who has been incontinent is crucial to preventing skin breakdown. Proper hand hygiene needs to be performed before and after any perineal care to prevent spread of disease.

Constipation refers to a condition in which the bowels have slowed down their movement, preventing normal defecation and potentially causing discomfort to the resident. Immobility and medications may cause constipation as a side effect.

Monitoring of output is one way to discover constipation, along with the resident and/or family report of bowel patterns. If constipation is suspected, the nursing assistant should alert the nurse. The health care provider may prescribe a stool softener, a laxative, or—in severe cases—an enema. Soap suds and fleets enemas are commonly used types.

Each institution has individual policies on who can perform enemas on residents. The nursing assistant may or may not be permitted to perform an enema on a resident. Other interventions used to alleviate constipation include encouraging mobility, encouraging intake of fluids when possible, and increasing fiber intake.

When the bowels are overly active and amounts of liquid stool are passed frequently, it is called **diarrhea**. Causes of diarrhea include food intolerance or allergy, infection, a medication side effect, or a reaction to a surgical procedure. A major complication of diarrhea is dehydration. Dehydration can occur

rapidly in a resident with diarrhea due to loss of fluids. Intake and output need to be vigilantly monitored along with encouragement of fluid intake, if appropriate.

A **colostomy** is a surgically-placed opening from the large or small intestines to the abdominal wall as a result of a bowel condition, such as colon cancer. A colostomy bag is attached to the skin around the colostomy to collect stool. Depending on how long the colostomy has been in place and how well developed the colostomy is, the resident may be able to care for their colostomy bag independently or may need varying levels of assistance from the health care team. Most colostomy bags are fairly easy to remove, drain, and replace when necessary. The nursing assistant will not be required to care for the colostomy site itself, but rather take care of emptying the bag and recording output for the medical record.

Another assistive device for elimination of the bowels is called a **rectal tube**. A rectal tube is a tube that is inserted into the rectum to collect stool or relieve gas. At the end of the tube is a balloon that can be inflated to anchor it in place as it collects stool. The rectal tube is used in residents who are incontinent, at risk for or have skin breakdown, and/or have diarrhea. Each facility will have specific policies outlining when a rectal tube is needed. Complications, such as atony (loss of muscle tone) of the rectum and internal tissue breakdown, may arise when rectal tubes are in place for extended periods. The nursing assistant may not insert or remove the rectal tube unless facility policy states otherwise. The rectal tube drains into a bag that the nursing assistant can empty and record as output in the medical record. Perineal care may be required around the site of the rectal tube if any leakage occurs.

The resident may have a urinary catheter for various reasons including immobility and monitoring of output. The catheter has an inflatable balloon at the end filled with normal saline that anchors the catheter in place as it drains urine from the urinary bladder to a collection bag. The nursing assistant can then empty this bag and record the output in the medical record. The nursing assistant may not insert or remove the catheter. The nursing assistant must report to the nurse if the catheter comes out or if there is drainage around the catheter as this may indicate a malfunction.

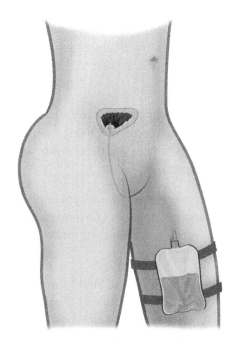

During the resident's daily bath or whenever perineal care is necessary, proper technique must be used to prevent a **urinary tract infection (UTI)**. The nursing assistant must follow the facility's policy regarding proper catheter care, including using warm water around the site to cleanse the urethra and always using a circular motion around the tube moving away from the resident. The nursing assistant should never use a back and forth motion as this could introduce bacteria into the urethra, resulting in a UTI. Signs and symptoms of a UTI include fever, chills, cloudy urine, blood in the urine (hematuria), or a change in mental status. If any of these occur, the nurse should be alerted immediately.

Changes in Nutritional Needs

A resident admitted to a facility will often have specific nutritional needs, such as a diet modification or restriction. Conditions, such as nausea or vomiting, and equipment, such as nasogastric tubes, can further complicate the goal of maintaining adequate nutrition. The nursing assistant should also be familiar with intravenous (IV) accesses and how to monitor them.

There are several different dietary restrictions that a resident may have depending on their condition. A **cardiac diet**, or heart-healthy diet, is for residents with heart conditions. This diet is generally low in sodium, fat, and cholesterol. The nurse will educate the resident about this diet, but it is important for the nursing assistant to ensure the correct meal tray is delivered to the resident. Other dietary restrictions for health reasons include the renal diet—for residents with kidney problems or failure—a diabetic diet, which focuses on controlling carbohydrate intake, and a fluid-restricted diet for residents with heart or kidney failure.

There are cultural and religious considerations to be aware of when it comes to dietary restrictions. Some adherents of the Jewish and Islamic faiths, for example, do not consume pork products. Some Jews also do not consume meat and dairy products in the same meal. Acceptable Jewish meals are referred to as **kosher**, while in the Islamic faith, foods that are acceptable are called **halal**. Some people believe it is wrong to consume any meat and only eat non-animal foods. They are called **vegetarians.** **Vegans** do not consume any animal product of any kind, such as milk or honey.

Some residents may be lactose intolerant. **Lactose** is a sugar found in dairy products that can cause gastrointestinal upset to sensitive individuals. These people may need to abstain from consuming dairy products or take a digestive aid—such as the enzyme lactase—to help them digest the lactose.

There are numerous other dietary restrictions a resident can have for various reasons. The important points for the nursing assistant are to be familiar with the resident's diet order, to ensure the correct tray is delivered, to correct a mistake made by the food service, and to ensure the resident's wishes are respected.

Illness and medications can sometimes bring on side effects of nausea and/or vomiting. The resident experiencing these side effects will likely prefer to abstain from food—called **fasting**—until the nausea and vomiting subsides. If the nausea and vomiting is short-lived, fasting is not a problem. If the fasting is prolonged, however, the resident will experience nutritional deficits and further complications.

The nursing assistant must always assist the health care team in carefully monitoring all of a resident's **intake and output (I&O)** to ensure adequate nutrition and hydration. Any nausea or vomiting must be recorded, as well as the amount of meals eaten. The intake and output record will be tracked by the health care team and interventions based upon it. There are medications, such as Zofran (ondansetron), that can alleviate nausea and prevent vomiting. In the case of a resident receiving chemotherapy

119

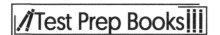

treatments who has constant nausea and trouble eating, there are medicines that can encourage appetite. Whatever the case, it is important that the nursing assistant monitor and record intake and output accurately and report any changes to the nurse immediately.

Patients who are unable to absorb nutrients through typical digestive processes manually receive nutrients though other mechanisms, including intravenously. Placing and monitoring this type of feeding mechanism is complex, as it is an invasive procedure and infection is a serious concern. Intravenous nutrition must be planned by a registered dietitian and prepared by a licensed pharmacist; in critical cases, intravenous feeding mechanisms must be placed and handled by surgeons. In most states, only registered nurses can place or remove intravenous tubes. Nursing aides should monitor physical changes in the patient, such as whether they appear dehydrated or malnourished, and alert a supervising clinical staff member immediately if the intravenous feeding mechanism appears dysfunctional.

Some residents may have a **nasogastric (NG) tube** placed through the nose, down the esophagus and into the stomach for therapeutic or diagnostic purposes. The nursing assistant may not insert or remove the tube. The nursing assistant ensures resident comfort and monitors the tube for dislodgement or displacement. The tube is usually secured in one nostril of the resident's nose with a strip of tape. Any changes in the tube must be reported to the nurse immediately.

The resident who is confused can be even further aggravated by the placement of an NG tube and may need special assistance to prevent disturbing the tube. As a last resort, a method of preserving the tube would be to put physical restraints on the resident, but only if all other options have been exhausted. The nursing assistant will not initiate physical restraints.

The nursing assistant will generally not be required to change the tube feeding bag or administer a tube feeding, but it is important to alert the nurse if the volume remaining in the tube feeding bag is nearly empty or if an alarm is going off. Sometimes there may be a kink in the tubing between the bag and the resident. The nursing assistant can check for these blockages and restore patency to the tube by repositioning if necessary. The nursing assistant should know the facility's policy on NG tube care to ensure they are within the scope of practice.

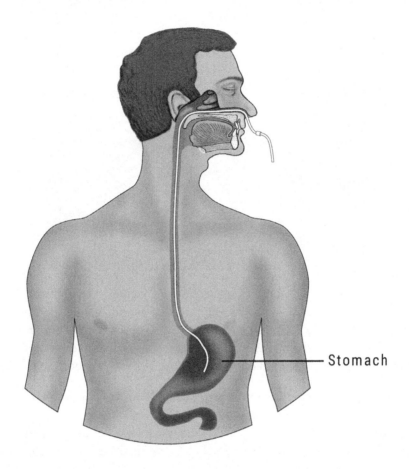

Stomach

Respiratory Problems

Some residents experiencing respiratory issues may receive supplemental oxygen. Oxygen can be administered in several different ways. The most common and minimal administration technique is via **nasal cannula**. The oxygen will flow through the nasal cannula into the resident's nose, and the tubing will be connected into either a mobile oxygen tank or an oxygen supply on the wall of the resident's room. Depending on the facility, there will often be a respiratory therapy team in charge of caring for residents' respiratory issues.

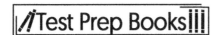
This picture demonstrates oxygen being administered via nasal cannula. The two prongs are placed into the nostrils of the resident.

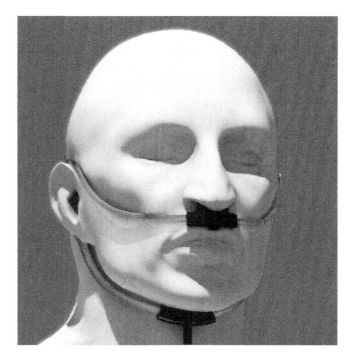

Part of the nursing assistant's normal vital signs collection will include oxygen saturation readings. This is especially important in residents receiving supplemental oxygen and/or with identified respiratory issues. Normal values are generally considered to be 93 to 100 percent, but some residents with COPD may have a baseline saturation in the high 80s. The nursing assistant should not assume this is a resident's normal level; rather, they should confirm with the nurse and report anything abnormal.

It is important that the aide understand the flow rate of supplemental oxygen that the resident is receiving. A typical rate is 2 to 4 liters per minute (LPM). The nursing assistant should look for signs of **hypoxia**—a lack of oxygen in the body. These include decreased level of consciousness, shortness of breath, bluish lips or blueness of the extremities/nail beds (**cyanosis**), or unresponsiveness. Any change in respiratory status or suspected issues with oxygen administration should be reported to the nurse or respiratory therapist immediately.

Finally, the nursing assistant must be familiar with IV (intravenous) accesses. The nursing assistant does not place or remove IVs. IVs are used to administer medicine and fluids. Signs that an IV access is compromised are redness around the site, resident discomfort, bruising, and leakage. Any changes in IV access, IV pump alarms, and resident complaints should be reported to the nurse immediately.

Changes in Skin Integrity

Residents with illness, altered nutrition, decreased mobilization, and/or incontinence of bowel and/or bladder are at high risk for skin breakdown. There are some important steps a nursing assistant can take to help prevent breakdown and promote healthy skin.

Skin health depends on adequate nutrition—especially protein intake—and proper circulation of nutrients, such as oxygen to the capillary beds near the skin's surface. Immobility and side effects of medications may cause the residents to refrain from repositioning themselves as they normally would in bed to redistribute pressure. When this happens, pressure on certain areas of the skin will cut off the supply of blood to that area. As a result, oxygen and other important nutrients will cease to nourish the area, and a pressure ulcer will begin forming.

Some common areas where pressure ulcers occur are the sacral area/lower back/buttocks and the heels. When turning and bathing, these areas need to be checked for redness, skin breakdown, and **blanching**, which occurs when the skin turns white when pressed, then promptly returns to its natural color. Other common areas include the ears, the back of the head, the shoulders, the elbows, and the inner knees.

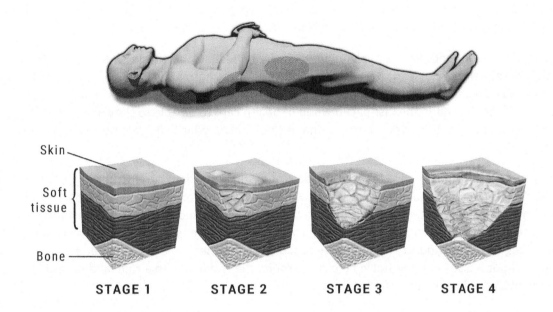

As mentioned in a previous section, there are four main stages of pressure ulcers, ranging from mild pinkness or redness of the skin to severe damage down into the fascia, muscles, and tendons. The nursing assistant does not classify pressure ulcers, but rather observes the skin carefully for changes. Incontinence is a major risk factor for skin breakdown. The nursing assistant may apply lotions or creams to prevent skin breakdown when providing baths and perineal care to the resident. The nursing assistant will also turn and reposition immobile residents every two hours to decrease pressure on bony prominences. Positioning the resident's limbs and back carefully with pillows redistributes pressure.

Any changes in skin such as redness, tearing, or worsening of existing wounds would need to be reported to the nurse immediately. Some facilities may have a skin wound assessment team to oversee the care of the ulcers and recommend interventions.

Pain Management

Pain has been called the **fifth vital sign**. In addition to heart rate, temperature, blood pressure, and respiratory rate, the resident's experience of pain is just as vital for the health care team to assess, monitor, and treat. The nursing assistant assists in this goal by reporting to the nurse when the resident has pain. As an additional and valuable set of eyes and ears to the team, the nursing assistant may be especially receptive to how the resident experiences pain.

The resident may report their pain to the nursing assistant verbally or nonverbally. Nonverbal signs of pain the nursing assistant can look for are facial grimacing, moaning, and tension throughout the body. Behavior that is different for a resident may also be a sign of pain. For example, the nursing assistant may know one resident to normally be very talkative and alert, but they are instead laying silently on the bed for most of the morning and barely acknowledging anyone entering the room. This may be a sign the resident is experiencing pain and should be investigated and reported to the nurse.

Providing for Safety, Care, and Comfort

With all the physical impairments that residents may present with, it is important that the nursing assistant keep their safety, care, and comfort as the primary goal of care. When these principles are at the forefront of care, all other interventions will fall into place naturally.

Resident safety begins with patience, planning, and mindfulness. Rushing tasks, without anticipating potential consequences, can lead to mistakes and even resident harm. Being able to plan ahead in a thoughtful way is a part of critical thinking, which every member of the health care team should actively practice. It can be difficult in the fast-paced world of health care to be able to slow down and give every task the time it deserves to be done well, but that is the ideal for which each member of the team should aim.

The nursing assistant should strive for another ideal of ensuring resident comfort throughout their stay. If the resident is not comfortable physically, this will affect all other aspects of their recovery and care. They will not be able to concentrate on rehabilitation, will likely be more irritable, and may be less receptive to valuable instruction and education from the health care team. Managing the resident's pain and providing the highest quality hygienic care based on the resident's needs are a good start. The nursing assistant is also instrumental in helping surround the resident with a calm and uncluttered environment that will make them feel at home.

Impact of Impairment on Resident Safety, Care, and Comfort

Whether it is a sensory, speech, or other physical impairment, each resident's impairment will impact their safety, care, and comfort.

Resident safety can be negatively impacted by physical impairments in a number of ways. A sensory impairment affects how the external environment is perceived. Issues with elimination and nutrition can affect the ability to care for oneself independently. If not managed properly, these physical impairments can lead to additional complications.

The comfort of the resident is impacted by all of these physical impairments, as they are a major disruption of normal human functioning. Not being able to control one's own bowels and bladder, for example, is a loss of independence. The anxiety associated with loss of independence and lack of control over functions as simple as breathing—for example, in the case of the resident receiving supplemental oxygen—can lead to physical symptoms, such as elevated blood pressure, heart rate, and other physical reactions causing discomfort.

The nursing assistant must recognize each individual resident's physical impairments and the impact these impairments have on their care. Safety and comfort are always the priority in resident care.

Psychological Problems

Many residents who enter a facility will not only have physical problems, but psychological problems as well. **Psychology** involves the mental and emotional processes that go on within a person's mind, dictating behavior and how the environment is perceived. These processes can become unhealthy in ways analogous to the physical body. Caring for the psychological aspect of a resident's health is equally as important as the physical. The two are intertwined and affect each other.

Common Psychological Impairments

Some of the most common psychological impairments the nursing assistant will encounter are depression, anxiety, and confusion. Delirium, phobias, and addiction will also be discussed:

Depression

Depression can be described as a prolonged state of feeling sad, empty, or tearful, and is sometimes characterized by disinterest in one's normal activities. Depression can have a broad range of effects, including disruptions in sleep habits, eating habits, daily activities, and relationships with others. A general lack of motivation and sadness may fill a person's mind, even distorting perception of reality and thwarting any usual enthusiasm, positivity, and motivation.

Depression is a complicated condition and pinpointing the exact cause of one's depression may not be possible. Possible causes of depression include abuse, personal loss, and illness. Physiologically, an imbalance of chemicals in the brain is ultimately what leads to the symptoms of depression. Depression is quite common, and often coexists with physical impairments. Depression can negatively impact one's ability to recover from physical illness and should be recognized, diagnosed, and treated with equal urgency and care. Medications and behavioral therapy are treatments offered to help alleviate symptoms of depression and help the resident return to a healthy state of mind.

Anxiety

Anxiety is a normal human response to stressful situations. It involves hormonal signals affecting different functions of the body including blood pressure, heart rate, breathing, and digestion. These physical reactions help us cope with and work through difficult situations. When the anxiety response is prolonged, extreme, excessive, and/or irrational, however, there may be a clinical psychological problem called an **anxiety disorder**. The cause of an excessive anxiety response is unknown, but contributing factors include a chronic overexposure to stress, genetic predisposition, and/or the inability of the brain to regulate emotions such as fear.

The clinical symptoms associated with anxiety disorders include a feeling of panic, increased heart rate and blood pressure, uncontrolled sweating, shortness of breath, nausea, muscle tension, and an inability to focus or concentrate. An acute exacerbation of these symptoms is termed a **panic attack**, and it can sometimes be so severe as to mimic symptoms of other health emergencies, such as a stroke or heart attack. Treatment of anxiety disorders typically involves medications aimed at soothing the disproportionate panic response to everyday situations. Diet and lifestyle changes may help, such as managing stress, eating a healthy diet, and regular exercise. Psychotherapy and behavioral therapy aim at recognizing one's own stress response and how to manage and cope with stressful situations in a healthy, effective manner.

Delirium

Delirium is an acute state of mental confusion. It is a psychological state that can be brought on by a number of different factors. An infection, medication, fever, metabolic imbalance—such as low sodium—or withdrawal from alcohol or drugs can all contribute to delirium. Symptoms of delirium can either be hyperactive, hypoactive, or both. **Hyperactive delirium** can involve pacing, difficulty focusing on one task or topic, and a general restlessness. **Hypoactive delirium** can have the opposite effect, with a resident becoming lethargic, dull, and sluggish. A **mixed delirium** is considered to be when the resident switches between these states.

Delirium can easily be confused with **dementia**, another mental impairment causing similar behavioral and cognitive problems. The differences between the two are that delirium usually comes on suddenly, is usually treatable, and if the cause is identified and treated in a timely manner, it can usually be resolved. A person with dementia may have periods of delirium from time to time, usually correlated with illness. When the delirium resolves, the person returns to the previous state of dementia. Dementia is slow and progressive, with no possibility of reversing the damage to brain function.

Treatment for delirium starts with identifying the cause and treating it, whether that be an infection, alcohol withdrawal, or a metabolic imbalance. Once the cause is treated, controlling the resident's environment as much as possible is the next intervention. As with dementia, a calm, peaceful environment with familiar objects, such as family photos, can be comforting. The health care staff must take careful measures to be calm and soothing when speaking and working with the resident. Any excess equipment or invasive treatments that can be discontinued should be removed. These can be contributing factors to the delirious resident's irritability. Keeping the resident well rested is also key to preventing and treating delirium. A sleep schedule can be maintained by encouraging regular rest times and providing a restful environment, including appropriate noise level and low lighting.

Phobia

A **phobia** is a type of anxiety disorder, occurring when a person has an unreasonable, unusually-heightened, and/or excessive fear or aversion, typically disproportional to any actual risk. Common phobias include fear of heights, social situations, and specific animals. Causes of phobias are unknown, but there are certain factors that put a person at risk for developing them. Risk factors for developing a phobia include a person's age, temperament, experience of a traumatic event related to the phobia, and environmental conditioning.

When a person is exposed to the object of the phobia, they will experience intense panic and do everything in their power to avoid the object. The person may experience physical reactions similar to a panic attack, including heart palpitations, sweating, and shortness of breath. A feeling of powerlessness and helplessness when confronted with the phobia may also occur. Treatment of an intense phobia may include **exposure therapy**, in which the person is slowly and methodically exposed to the fear in increasing amounts until they become desensitized to it. Medication is an option with anxiety alleviation as the goal; sometimes, anxiolytics, antidepressants, or beta blockers are used to slow down the body's overreaction to the stimulus.

Addiction

Addiction has components of mental illness and behavioral abnormalities. Addiction is both mental and physical. It is often paired with the term **dependence**, implying a person cannot do without a certain substance and compulsively partakes in that substance without self-control. The most common addictions dealt with in the health care environment are alcohol and drug addictions. These are usually characterized by a high tolerance to these substances and severe symptoms of withdrawal when the person stops using them.

Symptoms of withdrawal include tremors, delirium, and a myriad of other physical and psychological symptoms depending on the substance. Care for a resident with an addiction includes group therapy, medications, and rehabilitation programs. Prevention of addiction is the best treatment, but helping the resident cope with the symptoms of withdrawal and managing compulsions to partake in the addiction are of significant value as well.

Safety, Care, and Comfort for Psychological Impairments

In all of these psychological conditions that the nursing assistant encounters, it is of vital importance that the resident's safety, care, and comfort remain at the forefront of care. Psychological conditions such as depression, anxiety, delirium, phobias, and addiction can all be dangerous to the residents and those around them. They can also cause significant discomfort and aggravate existing physical issues.

The nursing assistant can assist in this effort by monitoring the resident's safety. If a resident is going through withdrawal from alcohol, the nursing assistant behaves in a calm, controlled manner around the resident. They maintain a peaceful environment around the resident, decreasing stimulation that could irritate the resident and cause them to inflict harm to self or others.

Comforting a resident with a psychological impairment is similar to comforting a resident with a physical impairment. Listening to the resident carefully and observing body language can go a long way in determining needs. The nursing assistant should report any changes in behavior and thinking to the nurse immediately as this could be a sign of psychological impairment.

Care of the Dying Resident and Post-Mortem Care

In health care, there are two different goals of care: curative and palliative. **Curative care** focuses on restoring the resident back to health after an illness. **Palliative care**, on the other hand, focuses on maximizing quality of life, sometimes when the disease process has reached a point at which a cure is no longer possible. In this case, the goal of care is to comfort the resident, provide pain management, spiritual support, and as high a quality of remaining life as possible.

When caring for the resident who is dying, it is of utmost importance that the health care team respect the wishes of the resident and family. At some point, very difficult decisions regarding care may have to be made by the resident, the family, and the health care team.

The nursing assistant should be a comfort and help to the resident and the family during this difficult time. Sensitivity to the emotional and physical needs of the resident and the family will help guide care. The following will be a discussion of how to properly care for a dying resident, post-mortem care, and dealing with grief in bereaved family members.

Grief Process

Everyone grieves differently after the death of a loved one. Grief, and how it manifests itself, is different in each individual and depends on the relationship with the deceased. For some, grief will be brief, and for others, it will be prolonged. There is a general guideline for the grieving process, but it is descriptive,

not prescriptive. Individuals may experience all stages in order, some stages, but not all, or switch between stages out of order at various points in time.

The **Kubler-Ross grieving model** includes five stages: denial, bargaining, depression, anger, and acceptance. For example, when a terminal diagnosis for a loved one is received, the family members may deny what is happening and not acknowledge reality. After this stage of denial, they may begin to bargain, or try to make deals with whoever they believe has the power to change the circumstances for their loved one. This could include long arguments with the health care team over care or praying to a higher power for a healing miracle. After bargaining, they may fall into a depression, with feelings of helplessness or powerlessness against the forces of the disease. This may be followed by a stage of anger in which they act outwardly or express frustration that they cannot change the circumstances. The last stage of grief is acceptance, and this is considered the stage in which the grieved person is finally at peace with the circumstances and can begin healing.

As mentioned before, these categories of grief are a rough guideline of what a person may experience. Grief varies in intensity from person to person and depends a great deal on the nature of the relationship with the deceased. The nursing assistant need only be familiar with the stages in order to recognize them in family members and/or the dying person, who may go through these stages as well. If one recognizes the grief process is occurring, one is more sensitive to the needs of the grieving.

Emotional Needs of the Resident, Family, and Caregivers

Grief is a highly emotional process. The range of emotions experienced by those grieving the loss of a loved one is vast. The initial reaction of shock and disbelief may morph quickly into anger, then sadness, and even fear. Sometimes the resident or family may feel such intense emotional pain that physical symptoms such as chest pain, gastrointestinal issues, and shortness of breath may occur. The stress of losing a loved one is both physical and emotional. The nursing assistant can recognize this and be of assistance.

The best way to help those who are grieving—whether it is the anticipatory grieving the dying resident may feel or the grief that occurs after the resident passes on—is to be there to support the family.

The role of the nursing assistant is to help in any way possible, but not to offer empty optimistic statements or promises, such as "It'll be okay soon," or "You'll move on before you know it." These statements are not helpful and may aggravate the recipient. Instead, focusing on what can be done in the present to assist them is the best approach.

Grief is a process that is different for each individual and is necessary for healing. The nursing assistant can offer a listening ear, a hug, or a hand to hold if welcomed and appropriate, and can inquire how the resident or the family are doing. Simply asking how they are doing shows that the nursing assistant cares and would like to be of assistance in any way possible.

Providing for the physical comfort of the grieving by offering a cup of coffee, a warm blanket, or a snack is a way to support them. The emotional pain they are going through may have caused them to ignore their own basic physical needs, such as eating and resting. Helping them focus on something besides their emotional pain can be helpful.

The nurse, doctor, and social worker will offer social services, grief counseling, and other resources that will connect the grieving to other forms of support.

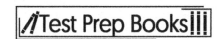

Responses to Grief

Not only will each individual respond differently to grief based on personality and relationship with the deceased, but also the response will differ based on their own spiritual beliefs and cultural influences. These beliefs and influences affect how a person thinks they should act during the mourning period, what to wear, what rituals need to be performed, and what happens after a person dies.

Each individual culture will not be discussed since there are many variations of how different people handle this process. It is not necessary for the nursing assistant to know each and every one, but rather have a general knowledge of differences and be respectful towards them.

Some cultures believe an outward show of emotion is appropriate and necessary. Sometimes, this entails an outward expression of weeping and wailing. Other cultures may be more conservative and think it is appropriate to be stoic, serious, and somber, without crying and losing one's composure. Some have specific rituals before and after the death, involving holy men, priests, or other clergy who prepare the person and/or the body for an afterlife. Some may not have any religious affiliation and may not believe in a life after this one.

Regardless of what cultural and spiritual beliefs are present, the role of the health care team is to respect those wishes as much as possible. It is imperative that the team explore the resident and family's wishes in this respect, rather than overlooking or refusing to allow them. It is always appropriate to politely ask how best to respect the resident and family's wishes when performing tasks for the dying or deceased resident. For example, some family members may prefer to clean the body themselves after death, an important ritual to express grief and ensure proper care in their view.

Each member of the health care team, including the nursing assistant, needs to assess their own beliefs about death and dying. Self-knowledge on the subject is valuable as it may not be something one has consciously acknowledged. This self-assessment also helps reveal any unfair biases and prejudices towards cultures and people whose worldview is different than one's own. Discovering what one's own beliefs and others' beliefs are leads to a better understanding between groups. These groups can then begin to find ways to work together during the difficult end-of-life period.

Physical Changes and Needs as Death Approaches

As the resident approaches death, the nursing assistant will play an important role in ensuring physical comfort. The resident may have increased pain, skin irritability, decreased control over bowel and bladder, decreased mobility, and decreased consciousness. There are concrete steps that the nursing assistant can take to ensure the resident is as comfortable as possible during the last stage of life.

Monitoring the resident's level of pain is important. Pain medicine as necessary will be used to provide adequate comfort. The nursing assistant should watch for nonverbal signs of pain, such as body tension, moaning, and facial grimacing.

Elimination may become difficult if the resident loses consciousness and mobility. The nursing assistant can make elimination easier for the resident by assisting the resident to a bedside commode or bed pan, and/or checking for incontinence in order to perform perineal care to keep the resident clean and dry.

The resident's skin may become dry and brittle. Breathing through the mouth can cause the oral cavity to dry out quickly, sometimes called **cotton mouth**. Applying lotions, balms, and moisturizers to skin and

129

lips, as well as making sure the oral cavity is well moisturized, are all steps that can relieve skin discomfort. Mouth sponges or swabs can be dipped in water to wet the mouth. Some residents find these sponges comforting to chew on or take a few drops of water from.

Preventing pressure ulcers or preventing existing pressure ulcers from worsening at the end of life is a consideration for nursing assistants to keep in mind. These can cause additional pain and discomfort that might be avoided. Using pillows to prop and position at-risk areas, such as heels, buttocks, elbows, and the back of the head will help minimize pressure.

The resident will likely have difficulty regulating body temperature, and may experience periods of feeling hot, cold, or both. The resident may not be able to verbalize these needs, but the nursing assistant can watch for nonverbal cues such as shivering or sweating. It is important to keep the resident comfortably warm or cool, using blankets and fans. Electric blankets should not be used, as the resident may not be able to verbalize if it is too hot, risking burn injuries.

Breathing may become difficult for the resident. They will likely develop increased secretions in the airway. The resident will likely be too weak to clear these secretions, resulting in a rattling or gurgling sound. Turning the resident's head to the side, providing a cool-mist humidifier (if available), and using suction equipment are all interventions that can alleviate the resident of these secretions. Depending on the facility, the nursing assistant may or may not be able to perform the task of suctioning. The resident may be given supplemental oxygen via nasal cannula for comfort. Monitoring to make sure the prongs of the nasal cannula are in place and not causing discomfort to the resident is important.

The resident may not appear to be awake, but still may be able to hear and perceive what is going on around them. Because of this, it is always important for the nursing assistant to identify oneself to the resident when entering the room and tell the resident what they are doing in the room. This courtesy may comfort a resident who is otherwise alone. The nurse aid should talk to the resident, provide quiet music, and keep the lighting low and/or natural. These environmental changes can all soothe the resident and should be guided by the resident and the family's wishes. Some residents may prefer a room full of visitors and others may be more private, preferring only a few close relatives and friends.

The nursing assistant needs to be mindful of the family's needs as well. Again, their grief and emotional response in the moment may cause them to forget their own basic needs, such as eating and getting proper rest. It is important to remind them to rest when they need to, offer them drinks and snacks as appropriate, warm blankets, and any other offering available to comfort them during this difficult time.

The end of life need not be a lonely, miserable experience, lacking warmth, thoughtfulness, and care. The nursing assistant can assist the health care team in providing comfort for the resident's physical needs as well as creating a soothing environment around the resident as they approach death.

Post-Mortem Care Procedures

After the resident has passed, the first step the nursing assistant can take is to determine the family's needs. This is a time when spiritual and cultural considerations need to be respected. Some families may linger and talk over the body for hours before leaving the room, while others may say a brief goodbye and leave. The health care team should determine if there are any specific burial preparations that need to be done. Funeral and/or burial arrangements, such as cremation or embalmment, will be determined.

Once these considerations are determined, the health care team can prepare the body. Generally, the body will need to be cleaned, as bowel and bladder incontinence happens after death. Having an assistant, usually the nurse, is necessary, as the body will be difficult to move by a single person. Any excess tubes or IVs will need to be removed by the nurse or the nursing assistant, depending on facility policy. The body may need to be placed in a body bag, if in a facility with a morgue. This can be done using the same turning and repositioning techniques used to perform bath care.

The nursing assistant should be aware that there are sights and sounds that one might see in a dead body that might be alarming and unexpected. For example, there may be a release of air from the lungs of the body as the nursing assistant is cleaning or turning that may sound like a gasp or cry. The body may also have muscle twitches and slight movements as the neurological and muscular systems shut down. Both of these are normal. If the nurse and/or doctor have confirmed official death, post-mortem care can proceed.

After the body has been bathed and placed in a body bag, the body will be transferred to a gurney or some sort of transport stretcher. The body is then transported to the morgue. A **morgue** refers to the refrigerated room where deceased bodies are held pending funeral and burial arrangements. The cold temperature drastically slows down the decomposition process in the bodies, preserving them for the funeral presentation.

Some nursing assistants may find post-mortem care to be uncomfortable, disturbing, and even depressing. This is an initial reaction, and many adjust to it with time and experience. Dealing with dead bodies is not something that the general public is used to experiencing. The nursing assistant must keep in mind that post-mortem care is a continuation of respecting and caring for the resident. Everyone dies, and their bodies must be taken care of afterwards. Thinking of it as an act of respect and courtesy is perhaps the best perspective. The deceased must be treated with dignity, even in death. The nursing assistant is in the unique position to provide such dignified care to the individual.

The reason that one enters the health care field should stem from an earnest desire to help others and care for them in their time of need. This extends beyond their life to their death by taking care of their remains appropriately and respectfully.

Practice Quiz

1. What is the best approach when dealing with a resident who is withdrawing from alcohol and is quite agitated?
   a. Using soothing therapeutic communication
   b. Ignoring the resident and shutting the door until he or she calms down
   c. Restraining the resident to prevent self-harm
   d. Turning up the TV and turning on all the lights to distract the resident

2. The nursing assistant notices a resident has several bruises on his arms and legs in various stages of healing. The resident suffers from dementia and has had the same caregiver for over a decade. The nursing assistant gets the sense from the caregiver that he is fatigued and stressed out from his care of the resident. What might the nursing assistant suspect is going on here?
   a. Nothing. Caregiver fatigue happens often, and there are rarely any negative side effects.
   b. The resident may be getting physically abused by the over-stressed caregiver.
   c. The caregiver may be emotionally abusing the resident.
   d. The bruises are probably a result of the resident being old and fragile.

3. The resident has been recently diagnosed with terminal cancer and is refusing further treatment. The resident's son has been arguing with the doctor for the past fifteen minutes that there must be more that can be done for his father to prolong his life. What stage of grief does the son appear to be in?
   a. Depression
   b. Acceptance
   c. Denial
   d. Bargaining

4. The resident reports to the nursing assistant that he is feeling constipated and has not had a bowel movement in three days. The nursing assistant reports this finding to the nurse and can anticipate which of the following interventions?

   I. Increased fluids
   II. Bedrest
   III. Stool softener
   IV. Increased dietary fiber

   a. All of the above
   b. Choices I and IV
   c. Choices III and IV
   d. Choices I, III, and IV

5. The resident that the nursing assistant has been caring for at the long-term care facility has lately become disinterested in her daily activities, refuses to take part in group activities, and sits in her room looking out the window all day. The nurse suspects this change may indicate which of the following psychological conditions?
   a. Anxiety
   b. A fear of heights
   c. Depression
   d. Delirium

Answer Explanations

1. A: The nursing assistant should try and calm the resident down using soothing therapeutic communication. Increasing the volume of the TV and visual stimulation with the lights may aggravate withdrawal. Ignoring the resident may worsen the problem. Restraints are a last resort option when all other options have been exhausted. Only the nurse, with a doctor's order, can put the resident in restraints; this is not the best option.

2. B: The caregiver may be physically abusing the resident, and the nursing assistant must report this suspicion to their supervisor. Caregiver fatigue can result in abuse at times, especially in long-term dementia residents. It is true that older adults bruise easily due to fragile blood vessels, but it should not be assumed that this is the cause if there are other factors present.

3. D: The resident's son is attempting to bargain with the doctor to find a treatment that can prolong his father's life. Denial would occur if the son were acting like nothing was wrong with his father. Depression would be decreased interest in what was going on, lack of caring, and sadness. Acceptance is the final stage of grief where the outcome is accepted, and those grieving are at peace with the death.

4. D: Choices I, III, and IV are interventions that help increase bowel motility and relieve constipation. Bed rest does not help constipation.

5. C: The resident seems to be depressed. The nursing assistant should report this change to the nurse immediately. The other three psychological conditions do not match the description.

Practice Test #1

1. Delirium differs from dementia in what way?
   a. Delirium is slow, progressive, and untreatable.
   b. Delirium has an acute onset and is treatable.
   c. Delirium includes increased alertness.
   d. The cause of delirium is unidentifiable.

2. In order to maintain certification, most states require the nurse aide to do which of the following?
   a. Present a special waiver from their facility.
   b. Retake the state certification exam every year.
   c. Show proof of twelve hours of continuing education (CE) credits.
   d. Show proof of twelve hours of community service.

3. What is the typical flow rate for oxygen administered via nasal cannula?
   a. 2-4 LPM
   b. 2-4 mL/s
   c. 10 L/s
   d. 20 mL/hr

4. What resident right allows a resident to make their own health care decisions called?
   a. Self-expression
   b. Confidentiality
   c. Privacy
   d. Self-determination

5. A fax containing resident information and prescriptions is sent from a doctor's office. This is what type of communication?
   a. Verbal
   b. Written
   c. Nonverbal
   d. Non-sequential

6. The nursing assistant is turning a resident in bed when he notices her lower back has some redness to it that he did not notice before. In addition to completing the turn and supporting her back, arms, and heels with pillows to decrease pressure, what should the nursing assistant do?
   a. Nothing. He should just keep an eye on it over the course of the shift.
   b. He should note it in his charting, but not alert the nurse, as the nurse probably already knows.
   c. He should apply lotion to the red spot and hope it goes away.
   d. He should notify the nurse of the new red spot on the lower back so that the nurse can assess.

7. The nursing assistant at a long-term care facility notices that the resident's nephew is always hasty to check the resident's mail before the resident looks at it. The nursing assistant knows that the resident gets her social security check every month in the mail. What might be going on here?
   a. The resident might be at risk for financial abuse. The situation should be investigated and reported to the nurse and escalated if necessary.
   b. This is normal, and the nursing assistant should ignore it.
   c. The nursing assistant should check the mail herself before letting the nephew see it.
   d. The nursing assistant should confront the nephew and accuse him of stealing from his aunt.

8. What is something the nursing assistant can do to alleviate the dry mouth caused by breathing through the mouth in the dying resident?
   a. The aide can encourage the resident to close his mouth, which will help with increasing salivation.
   b. The aide can do nothing. This is a natural end of life occurrence; there is nothing that can be done.
   c. The aide can encourage lots of fluids; that way, the resident will feel better.
   d. The aide can use mouth sponges to wet the mouth cavity.

9. The nursing assistant sees that the resident has a sign on his door that says "NPO." What does this mean?
   a. The sign doesn't have an important meaning.
   b. The sign means that the resident is on a normal diet.
   c. The sign means "nothing by mouth."
   d. The sign means that the resident gets a renal diet.

10. The nursing assistant is asked by the nurse to remove a resident's IV. The nurse says he is very busy, and the resident needs to be discharged. The nursing assistant knows that this is against the facility policy and outside of his scope of practice to remove an IV. What is the appropriate action the nursing assistant should take?
   a. He should tell the nurse that it is outside the nursing assistant's scope of practice and ask if there is anything else he can do to assist the nurse.
   b. He should go ahead and remove the IV; it is easy to do, and the nursing assistant knows other aides who have done it.
   c. He should involve the charge nurse and nurse manager in this conflict before confronting the nurse.
   d. He should take a break and ignore the request.

11. The nursing assistant has been taking on extra shifts at work to buy nice Christmas presents for her children this year. She notices that to cope with the fatigue and stress, she has been drinking alcohol every night of the week and eating a huge fast-food meal in front of the TV after work every day. The nursing assistant recognizes *what* in regards to these actions?
   a. They will probably help energize her for her next shift.
   b. They will help her sleep better and make her happy.
   c. They are perfectly all right; she's earned the right to drink and eat whatever she wants.
   d. They are an example of negative coping with stress and should be corrected.

12. Of the following patients, which one has the highest risk for skin injury?
   a. An elderly woman in an assisted-living facility who ambulates with a cane
   b. An eighty-year-old man in the hospital recovering from hip surgery
   c. A seventy-year-old man hospitalized for pneumonia
   d. An elderly woman who is incontinent of stool and is showing signs of confusion

13. Which of the following is not a preventative measure for pressure-ulcer formation?
   a. Padding bony areas on the body
   b. Repositioning the patient at least every two hours
   c. Keeping the patient in a sitting position while in their bed
   d. Changing soiled linens and clothing promptly

14. An aide is caring for a patient with a known respiratory infection. The patient is on droplet precautions. What is the minimum PPE required when caring for this patient?
   a. Gloves, gown, N-95 respirator
   b. Gown, eyewear, gloves, and a disposable mask
   c. Gloves and a disposable mask
   d. Disposable mask, sterile gloves, and eyewear

15. During lunchtime in the dining area, an aide notices a resident grabbing their throat. What should the aide's first action be?
   a. To call for help
   b. Have the resident stand up
   c. Ask the resident if they are choking
   d. To try to open the resident's mouth

16. Of the following tasks, which one is not considered "dirty"?
   a. Changing a diaper
   b. Assisting with oral care
   c. Changing a wound dressing
   d. Helping a patient get dressed

17. An aide enters a patient's room in response to the call light and sees a fire behind the television. What is the aide's first action?
   a. Activate the fire alarm.
   b. Use the nearest fire extinguisher.
   c. Move the patient to a safer location away from the room.
   d. Smother the fire with a blanket.

18. Which of the following is not a risk factor for falls in the elderly?
   a. Using a cane to walk
   b. Inadequate lighting in a room
   c. Muscle weakness
   d. Slower reflexes

19. Which type of precaution would be used for a patient with a *Clostridium difficile* infection?
   a. Droplet
   b. Airborne
   c. Contact
   d. Standard precautions only

20. Which step in the handwashing process below is incorrect?
   a. Turn on the warm water.
   b. Place soap in the palm of the hand.
   c. Rub hands and wash for at least ten seconds.
   d. Rinse hands with fingers pointing down.

21. From the list of symptoms below, which is a symptom of a systemic infection?
   a. Chills
   b. Redness of the area
   c. Pus
   d. Swelling

22. When placing wrist restraints on a patient, the ties should be secured in what location?
   a. On the side rails of the bed
   b. They should not be secured
   c. To the bed frame
   d. Somewhere behind the patient

23. A nursing assistant is assisting a diabetic resident with breakfast. The resident is scheduled for heart surgery in the afternoon. Which breakfast tray is appropriate for this resident?
   a. Coffee, apple juice, lime gelatin, and clear broth
   b. Coffee with sugar substitute, oatmeal, scrambled eggs, and bacon
   c. Coffee with sugar, grits, egg white omelet, and a cup of fresh fruit
   d. This resident should not receive a breakfast tray.

24. A resident's orders state that they should remain in the Semi-Fowler's position. What does this mean?
   a. The resident should remain on their stomach.
   b. The resident should remain flat on their back.
   c. The resident should remain on their back with the head of their bed raised between thirty and forty-five degrees.
   d. The resident should remain on their back with the head of their bed raised above sixty degrees.

25. A resident is experiencing diarrhea and complaining of lightheadedness when standing. The resident is normally able to ambulate to the bathroom without assistance. What's the first action a nursing assistant should take?
   a. Encourage the resident to drink lots of fluids to prevent dehydration.
   b. Immediately find the nurse on duty and report the findings.
   c. Provide the resident with additional washcloths, soap, and towels for perineal care.
   d. Place the call bell within reach, and instruct the resident to call for assistance before getting out of bed.

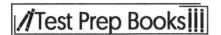

26. A nursing assistant is providing AM care to a comatose resident. The resident has been immobile for several weeks and is at risk for muscle atrophy and contractures. What action should the nursing assistant take in caring for the resident?
   a. Passive range of motion exercises should be done with the resident.
   b. Perineal care should be provided, but a full bed bath should be avoided due to the resident's risk for pressure sores.
   c. Before providing oral care, the head of the resident's bed should be flat and the resident's head should be turned to the side to prevent aspiration.
   d. The resident should be encouraged to do active range of motion exercises while lying in bed.

27. During HS care, a nursing assistant notices that a resident has new, onset bilateral ankle and pedal edema. What's the first action the nursing assistant should take?
   a. Assist the resident in ambulating around the room.
   b. Encourage the resident to consume additional fluids.
   c. Immediately report the findings to the nurse.
   d. Massage the resident's ankles and feet.

28. During hourly rounds, a post-surgical patient complains of pain in their right calf. What action(s) should the nursing assistant take?
   a. Encourage the patient to ambulate up and down the hall as often as able.
   b. Apply lotion and massage the calf to lessen the pain.
   c. Encourage the patient to do active range of motion exercises with the leg.
   d. Report the findings to the nurse on duty.

29. When using a gait belt to help a resident to ambulate, where should the nursing assistant be in relation to the resident?
   a. To the side and slightly behind the resident
   b. Directly behind the resident
   c. Directly to the side of the resident
   d. Facing the resident

30. A nursing assistant is planning the daily care schedule for an older resident with limited mobility. The resident has physical therapy at 10:00 am and occupational therapy at 2:00 pm. Which schedule is most appropriate?
   a. The nursing assistant will provide AM care at 8:00 am and afternoon care at 3:00 pm.
   b. The nursing assistant will provide AM care at 8:00 am and afternoon care at 4:00 pm.
   c. The nursing assistant will provide AM care at 9:00 am and afternoon care at 4:00 pm.
   d. The nursing assistant will provide AM care at 9:00 am and afternoon care at 3:00 pm.

31. A nursing assistant is caring for a resident who doesn't have pressure sores but is at risk for them due to immobility. How often should the resident be repositioned?
   a. Because the resident doesn't have pressure sores, it's not necessary to reposition them.
   b. The resident only needs to be repositioned when they express discomfort.
   c. The resident should be repositioned at least once every two hours.
   d. The resident should be repositioned each time perineal care is provided.

32. During AM care, an older resident who is experiencing cognitive changes tells the nursing assistant, "I don't want to pick out what I'm going to wear today because it takes me too long to decide. It would be easier if you could just do it for me." What's the most appropriate response from the nursing assistant?

    a. "Thank you. I'm in a hurry today, so I'll pick out your outfit."
    b. "I'm not in a hurry. Would you like me to help you decide?"
    c. "I can pick out your outfits from now on if you'd like?"
    d. "You must pick out your own outfits. I'm not allowed to choose them for you."

33. Which of the following is not an expected age-related change?

    a. Decreased lung elasticity
    b. Increased circulation
    c. Dry skin
    d. Constipation

34. Which of the following is an example of a physiological need?

    a. Sleep
    b. Family
    c. Employment
    d. Status

35. A nursing assistant is assisting a new resident with care when the resident says, "I hate being here. I don't have any friends, and I never know what's going on." What's the most appropriate response from the nursing assistant?

    a. "You'll get used to it soon enough. Just give it more time, and you'll become adjusted to living here eventually."
    b. "This is what's best for you, so you should accept it."
    c. "I know what you mean. I would hate to live in a place like this, but it is what it is."
    d. "I'm sorry you feel that way. Is there anything I can do to help? I can give you a daily schedule so you'll have a better idea of what's going on and introduce you to some of the other residents, if you'd like."

36. While performing passive range of motion exercises on a resident's shoulder, the nursing assistant grasps the resident's arm and moves it away from the midline of the body, being careful not to stress the joint. This is an example of which of the following motions?

    a. Adduction
    b. Abduction
    c. Flexion
    d. Extension

37. The nursing assistant takes a pulse oximeter reading on a patient who was admitted for COPD exacerbation. The reading says 82 percent. What should the nursing assistant do next?

    a. Chart this as a normal finding.
    b. Call a code blue.
    c. Notify the nurse.
    d. Check the amount of oxygen the patient is getting via nasal cannula.

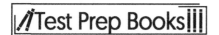

38. While feeding a patient her dinner, the nursing assistant notes that she is sleepier than usual as she eats. The patient takes a sip of her drink from a straw and begins to choke and cough. The nursing assistant suspects aspiration and should do which of the following after alerting the nurse?

    a. Try to sweep his finger in the patient's mouth to remove the foreign object

    b. Take away all food and drink from the patient's reach for the time being

    c. Lower the head of the bed all the way down so the patient can rest

    d. Allow the patient a few more drinks from the cup to clear her throat

39. A patient is admitted with prolonged vomiting, greater than three days. The nursing assistant knows this patient will need what type of therapy to counteract a dangerous result of prolonged vomiting?

    a. Intravenous (IV) fluids

    b. Antibacterial medications

    c. Anti-nausea medications

    d. Physical therapy

40. The nursing assistant walks into a patient's room and witnesses the patient violently convulsing with rigid muscles. The patient is completely unconscious. The nursing assistant notifies the nurse immediately and recognizes this is what type of seizure?

    a. Myoclonic

    b. Absence

    c. Grand Mal

    d. Tonic

41. The nursing assistant is speaking with a patient when she notices that the patient is having trouble forming thoughts into sentences and one side of his face appears to be drooping. What emergency condition is likely occurring in the patient?

    a. Meningitis

    b. Migraine

    c. Seizure

    d. Stroke

42. A patient with diabetes has been off the unit all morning for a test and returns just as the lunch trays are being picked up. The patient was not able to eat or drink for the test, so did not receive his breakfast. The nursing assistant recognizes this patient is at risk for what condition?

    a. Hypoglycemia

    b. Diabetic ketoacidosis

    c. Diabetic coma

    d. Hyperglycemia

43. What is the difference between delirium and dementia?

    a. Delirium is chronic and dementia is acute.

    b. Dementia has to do with attention and delirium has to do with memory.

    c. Delirium has no known cause.

    d. Delirium is acute and dementia is chronic.

44. If a patient can be described as sleepy yet arousable to verbal stimuli, the nursing assistant knows the term for this altered level of consciousness is what?
    a. Coma
    b. Delirium
    c. Somnolent
    d. Stupor

45. A patient who has been admitted with tuberculosis begins to cough up blood in his sputum, as noted by the nursing assistant. The nursing assistant knows the medical term for this condition is which of the following?
    a. Hematopoiesis
    b. Hemoptysis
    c. Hematemesis
    d. Hematochezia

46. Which of the following are precautions the nursing assistant can take to help prevent a patient from falling?
    a. Lay down a familiar rug by the patient's bed to remind the patient of home.
    b. Turn off all the lights and close the patient's curtains at night so the patient's sleep is not disturbed.
    c. Place the call light within the patient's reach so it is easy to call for assistance when needed.
    d. Keep the patient's glasses and hearing aid in the closet so the bed table does not get cluttered.

47. The following risks are associated with prolonged immobility EXCEPT:
    a. Skin breakdown
    b. Constipation
    c. Muscle deterioration
    d. Heart attack

48. A patient is on an 1800 cc fluid restriction. This is equal to how many ounces?
    a. 60
    b. 180
    c. 100
    d. 540

49. A newly admitted patient has fallen three times at home in the past six months. The nursing assistant has given them nonslip footwear and notified the RN of their falls. What else should the nursing assistant do to ensure the patient's safety?
    a. Check on the patient every six hours.
    b. Turn on the bed alarm.
    c. Leave the patient alone because the steps already taken are sufficient.
    d. Stay in the patient's room for the remainder of the shift.

50. HIPAA is a law designed to protect the patient's:
    a. Dignity
    b. Identity
    c. Physician
    d. Family

51. A patient with advanced COPD has an oxygenation saturation level of 88%. The nursing assistant should:
    a. Notify the RN.
    b. Administer oxygen.
    c. Expect this result.
    d. Check their pulse.

52. A patient who recently had a stroke is slurring their speech. The nursing assistant can help them communicate by doing which of the following?
    a. Ask the family to communicate with the patient.
    b. Get the patient a pen and paper.
    c. Ask the nurse to communicate with the patient.
    d. Speak loudly.

53. The nursing assistant is performing perineal care on a female resident who has an indwelling urinary catheter. What is the appropriate technique for cleaning the catheter?
    a. Clean the catheter every hour.
    b. Wipe the catheter with a bleach sanitary wipe.
    c. Using a circular motion, wipe the catheter moving away from the resident's body.
    d. Using a back and forth motion, wipe the tube while moving towards the resident's body.

54. The nursing assistant is caring for a resident who is hearing impaired. What is one step the nursing assistant can take to aid in communication with the resident?
    a. Talk to the resident while his back is turned.
    b. Stay in the resident's line of vision while speaking with him.
    c. Talk quietly so as to maintain a calm environment.
    d. Use Braille to communicate with the resident.

55. The nursing assistant is performing post-mortem care. While repositioning the body to place in the body bag, the body lets out a sound that sounds like a gasp. The nurse assures the aide that this a natural body process where air is released from the lungs after death and that death has been verified. What are some other possible characteristics a deceased body may display?
    I. Twitching of muscles
    II. Release of bowel and bladder
    III. Deep tendon reflexes
    IV. Eyes remain open

    a. All of the above
    b. Choices I, II, and III
    c. Choices II and IV
    d. Choices I, II, and IV

56. A patient has hearing loss that was caused by aging, exposure to noise, and decreased blood circulation. This patient has which type of hearing loss?
    a. Conductive hearing loss
    b. Sensorineural hearing loss
    c. Mixed hearing loss
    d. Auditory neuropathy hearing loss

57. Which of the following actions is most effective when communicating with a patient who suffers from hearing loss?
    a. Use written communication when possible
    b. Speak in a louder, higher voice
    c. Speak into the patient's more affected ear
    d. Stand at the head of the bed when speaking

58. The nursing assistant is caring for a patient with complete vision loss. Which of the following actions would NOT be appropriate while caring for this patient?
    a. Orient the patient to the layout of their room
    b. Establish the baseline functioning of their vision upon admission
    c. Allow the patient to hold onto the nursing assistant's arm when ambulating
    d. Only explain the plan of care to the patient's wife who has no vision loss

59. A patient has difficulty producing language coherently but can properly comprehend what is being said to them. The patient has which type of speech impairment?
    a. Receptive aphasia
    b. Wernicke's aphasia
    c. Expressive aphasia
    d. Global aphasia

60. The nursing assistant is caring for a patient with a colostomy. Which action would be most appropriate while caring for this patient?
    a. Clean and change the colostomy bag twice daily
    b. Report loose stool to the nurse immediately
    c. Palpate the stoma to assess for swelling
    d. Empty the bag regularly and record stool output

Answer Explanations #1

1. B: Delirium has an acute (sudden) onset and is usually treatable. Dementia has a slow onset and is irreversible. Delirium and dementia are both characterized by decreased alertness, and the cause is usually identifiable.

2. C: The nursing assistant must provide proof of twelve hours of continuing education (CE) credits. Community service and re-taking the exam are not required for maintaining certification. There is no waiver a facility can produce that exempts the nursing assistant from continuing their education.

3. A: The normal flow rate is 2-4 LPM; the other answers are incorrect.

4. D: The right of the resident to make their own, informed health care decisions is the right of self-determination. The other terms refer to other resident rights.

5. B: This type of communication is called written. Verbal communication is spoken, nonverbal communication does not use words (either spoken or written), and the other term does not refer to communication types.

6. D: The nursing assistant should report any changes in skin integrity immediately to the nurse to prevent skin breakdown. The nursing assistant can apply lotion whenever needed, but this does not address the change in skin integrity. The nursing assistant should not only notify the nurse, but also document the finding and any following interventions.

7. A: This resident may be at risk for financial abuse. The nursing assistant must report any suspicion of abuse to the supervisor to be investigated. It is illegal to open other people's mail, so that option is incorrect. Confronting the nephew and accusing him of stealing is inappropriate; the situation must be appropriately reported and investigated before accusations are made.

8. D: Mouth sponges are available to help alleviate dry mouth in residents with a low level of consciousness. Encouraging fluids may cause the resident to aspirate (choke). Ignoring the problem is not part of proper end of life care. Encouraging the resident to close the mouth is incorrect; the resident is not alert enough to follow such a command.

9. C: The sign means "nothing by mouth" and may mean the resident is scheduled for a procedure today. The nursing assistant should make sure that the resident does not eat or drink anything. The other options are incorrect.

10. A: The nursing assistant should address this conflict with the nurse and see if there is another way to help that is within his scope of practice. Involving the charge nurse and supervisor is not necessary if the problem can be solved between the nurse and the nursing assistant. Ignoring the problem is not proactive and could lead to bigger problems and conflict later on. The IV should not be removed if it is outside the nursing assistant's scope of practice; doing so could lead to resident harm and nursing assistant liability.

11. D: Binge eating and abusing substances are examples of negative coping with stress. The nursing assistant should adjust her coping mechanism or decrease the stress in her life in order to remain focused and energized at work. The other options are incorrect.

12. D: An elderly woman who is incontinent of stool will need frequent linen changes and cleansing of her bottom. The constant moisture has a very high potential for causing skin breakdown. She is also showing signs of confusion, which means she may become agitated and unaware of her surroundings, leading to potential bruises or tears on her extremities. The other patient scenarios described are also at risk for skin injury. However, with the information given, *D* is the patient with the highest risk.

13. C: Keeping a patient in a sitting position in their bed puts extra pressure on their coccyx and bottom due to gravity; therefore, this option is not a preventative measure for pressure-ulcer formation. Choices *A*, *B*, and *D* are interventions that should be done to help prevent pressure ulcers.

14. C: Gloves and a disposable mask are all that are required for droplet precaution; however, additional PPE may be used if desiring extra protection. The key word in this question is *minimum.* Choice *A* is not correct because an N-95 mask is not required. Choice *D* is not correct because sterile gloves are not needed and eyewear is optional. Choice *B* would give the most coverage for protection but it is not the minimum PPE required.

15. C: The first thing to do is to check to see if the patient is choking. They may nod their head if they are asked about choking, and they will not be able to talk. If the person is choking, help them stand up so that the Heimlich maneuver can be started. Choice *A*, calling for help, would not be necessary unless the person becomes unconscious or if help is needed with the Heimlich. Choice *D* is incorrect because it is not appropriate to look in the person's mouth for a lodged piece of food as the nursing assistant could make the obstruction worse, as well as waste precious time.

16. D: Helping a patient get dressed is not considered a dirty task unless the clothing is soiled with any bodily fluid. Choices *A*, *B*, and *C* are all tasks that involve bodily fluids and are considered dirty. Clean tasks should be performed first, followed by dirty tasks.

17. C: Use the acronym RACE to answer this question. The information given in the question leads to the fact that the patient is in the room, and that there is probably an electrical fire. The first action should be to rescue the patient by removing them from the room. Next, activate the fire alarm and then contain the fire by closing the door to the room. Extinguish the fire with the appropriate extinguisher if available. Choice *D*, smothering the fire, is not appropriate for an electrical fire.

18. A: Use of a cane is not a risk factor for falls in the elderly. A cane would actually benefit a person by giving them extra stability when walking. Poor lighting is a risk factor because it could cause someone to stumble over items on the floor or cause an imbalance by bumping into unseen furniture. Muscle weakness and slower reflexes are also risk factors for falls in the elderly.

19. C: Contact precautions are used for a patient with a *Clostridium difficile* infection. Contact precautions include wearing a gown and gloves to keep the infectious bacteria from spreading to clothing and hands.

20. C: When performing proper handwashing, the hands should be rubbed together for at least twenty seconds, not ten seconds. The other answer choices are correct steps in the handwashing process.

21. A: Of the symptoms listed, chills are a symptom that could be caused by a systemic infection. Choices *B*, *C*, and *D* are all symptoms of a localized infection.

22. C: Restraint ties should be secured to a nonmoveable part of the bed, such as the bed frame. The side rails are movable, "somewhere behind the bed" is too vague, and, of course, the restraints must be secured in order to be effective.

23. D: A resident scheduled for surgery in the afternoon would be NPO (nothing by mouth) status, so they would not be allowed to have any food or beverage. Choice *A* is an example of a clear liquid diet, which would not be appropriate for a resident with an upcoming surgery. This diet is more appropriate for a resident post-surgery, before progressing to a regular diet. Choice *B* is an appropriate diet for a diabetic resident, but this resident is scheduled for surgery in the afternoon and should be NPO. Finally, Choice *C* is an example of a heart-healthy diet, which may be appropriate for the resident after being cleared to eat solid foods post-surgery.

24. C: Semi-Fowler's position means the head of the bed is raised thirty to forty-five degrees. Choice *A* is a description of prone positioning. Choice *B* is a description of supine positioning. Choice *D* is a description of High-Fowler's positioning.

25. D: The *first* action the nursing assistant should take is to give the call bell to the resident and instruct them to call for assistance. If a resident is experiencing lightheadedness, they're at risk for a fall. Resident safety is the number one priority. In Choice *A*, if not contraindicated, the resident should be encouraged to drink lots of fluids, but this is not the first action the nursing assistant should take. In Choice *B*, the findings should be reported to the nurse; however, the nursing assistant should not leave the room before placing the call bell within reach of the resident and instructing them to call for assistance before getting out of bed. In Choice *C*, the resident might require additional supplies for perineal care, but this isn't the first action the nursing assistant should take.

26. A: "Muscle atrophy" is the weakening of a muscle, and a "contracture" is the shortening of a muscle. Both conditions are due to immobility. Therefore, passive range of motion exercises (unless contraindicated) should be done with the resident. In Choice *B*, residents at risk for pressure sores can have full bed baths, but the nursing assistant must thoroughly dry the resident's skin to prevent breakdown. For Choice *C*, the nursing assistant would be expected to provide oral care to the resident, and the resident's head should be turned to the side (if possible) to prevent aspiration. However, unless contraindicated, the head of the resident's bed should be elevated for oral care. For Choice *D*, active range of motion exercises are those performed by the resident independently. A comatose resident is unable to perform active range of motion exercises, so passive range of motion exercises must be performed by the nursing assistant.

27. C: Sudden, new onset edema can be indicative of a developing or worsening medical condition. While it's expected to see edema in a resident, any new onset of edema should be assessed by the nurse. Therefore, the nursing assistant should report the finding to the nurse immediately. In Choice *A*, ambulation can be helpful for a resident experiencing edema due to limited mobility, but it's not yet clear what the cause of the edema is. For Choice *B*, increased fluids can help with edema in some situations, but again it's still unclear what the cause of the edema is. If, for example, the edema is due to fluid overload related to congestive heart failure, increasing fluids could be harmful to the resident. In Choice *D*, massage can help with edema in some situations, but it can be harmful in other cases (such as a DVT). Before providing any interventions, the nursing assistant must first report the finding to the nurse.

28. D: Calf pain (especially in only one leg) in a post-surgical patient can be a sign of DVT and should be reported to the nurse immediately. In Choice *A*, encouraging ambulation in a post-surgical patient might be appropriate, but because of the patient's complaint, the nurse must first be notified so the patient can be assessed immediately. For Choice *B*, if the patient is suffering from DVT, the calf must never be massaged, as this could put the patient at risk for a pulmonary embolism. In Choice *C*, encouraging active range of motion exercises in a post-surgical patient can be appropriate, but because of the patient's complaint, again the nurse must be notified first so the patient can be assessed immediately.

29. A: The nursing assistant should ambulate with the resident by standing to the side and slightly behind them while holding the gait belt with both hands. For Choice *B*, walking directly behind the resident doesn't give the nursing assistant enough control if the resident falls. In Choice *C*, walking directly to the side of the resident again doesn't give the nursing assistant enough control if the resident should fall. For Choice *D*, the nursing assistant should face the resident when assisting them with standing from a seated position but, when assisting with ambulating, the nursing assistant should be positioned to the side and slightly behind the resident.

30. B: Older residents need time to rest between activities, so adequate rest intervals should be allotted when planning a resident's schedule. Providing AM care at 8:00 am would give the resident time to rest before going to physical therapy and providing afternoon care at 4:00 pm would give the resident time to rest after returning from occupational therapy. In Choice *A*, providing afternoon care at 3:00 pm doesn't give the resident an adequate rest period after occupational therapy. For Choice *C*, providing AM care at 9:00 am doesn't give the resident time to rest before physical therapy. In Choice *D*, providing afternoon care at 3:00 pm again doesn't give the resident an adequate rest period after occupational therapy.

31. C: Even if no pressure sores are present, all immobile residents should be repositioned at least once every two hours. For Choice *A*, the resident should be repositioned at least once every two hours to prevent pressure sores from developing. Again, in Choice *B*, an immobile resident should be repositioned at least once every two hours. However, if the resident expresses discomfort, the nursing assistant can reposition the resident even if they were repositioned less than two hours ago. For Choice *D*, while it might be appropriate to coordinate care in this manner, the resident should still be repositioned at least once every two hours whether or not any other care is being provided.

32. B: This is the most appropriate response because the nursing assistant should let the resident know that there's no rush. The resident might be embarrassed about being unable to make a quick decision. Offering to help the resident is a good way for the nursing assistant to acknowledge the resident's needs without causing further embarrassment. Choice *A* is inappropriate and doesn't promote emotional support or autonomy. Choice *C* might be an appropriate response for a later time but, for now, the nursing assistant should try to keep the resident participating in ADLs. Choice *D* is again an inappropriate response. While it's appropriate to encourage the resident to pick out their own outfit, this response isn't emotionally supportive.

33. B: Decreased, not increased, circulation is an expected age-related change. Choice *A*, decreased lung elasticity, is an expected age-related change. In Choice *C*, decreased skin moisture and elasticity are also expected age-related changes. Choice *D*, constipation due to slowed digestion, is another expected age-related change.

34. A: Physiological needs are the most basic needs and include food, water, clothing, shelter, sex, and sleep. Choice *B*, family, is a social need. Choice *C*, employment, is a safety need. Choice *D*, status, is an esteem need.

35. D: Acknowledging the resident's feelings and giving them a chance to talk openly is the appropriate response. Offering a new resident some suggestions for integration is also appropriate. Choice *A* is inappropriate because it's unsupportive. Choice *B* is also inappropriate, as it doesn't acknowledge the resident's feelings and is condescending. Choice *C* acknowledges the resident's feelings but is not supportive or helpful in any way.

36. B: Abduction is the movement of a limb away from the midline of the body. Choice *A*, adduction, is the movement of a limb towards the midline of the body. Choice *C*, flexion, is the bending of a limb at the joint. Choice *D*, extension, is the straightening of a limb at the joint.

37. C: The nursing assistant should notify the nurse of this abnormal finding. A code blue is not appropriate if the patient is still responsive. The amount of oxygen the patient is receiving may be noted but is not the most important factor in this situation.

38. B: All food and drink should be removed from the patient's reach until swallowing function is assessed to prevent further aspiration. Never sweep one's finger in a patient's mouth to try and remove a foreign object, since it could push the object farther down the throat or result in a bite wound. The head of the bed should be at least forty-five degrees or higher to promote effective swallowing. The patient should not have any further drinks at this time.

39. A: One of the most serious side effects of prolonged vomiting is dehydration, thus the patient needs fluids to restore him back to a more normal, hydrated status. Antibiotics may be used in a case of severe bacterial infection, but not likely in this case. Anti-nausea medication will likely be used to stop the vomiting but will do nothing to fix the resulting dehydration. Physical therapy is not typically necessary for such a case unless the patient was bedridden for a long time, which does not seem to be the case here.

40. C: This type of seizure with muscle rigidity, convulsions, and unconsciousness is called a grand mal seizure. An absence seizure involves a brief loss of consciousness where the patient may stare into space. A myoclonic seizure involves the body making jerking movements. A tonic seizure is characterized by rigidity and stiffness of the muscles.

41. D: The patient is most likely experiencing a stroke, as evidenced by the difficulty with speech and facial drooping. A migraine is a severe headache that can sometimes mimic stroke symptoms but is less severe. A stroke should be suspected until it is proven otherwise in order to get the patient timely and effective treatment. A seizure is characterized by muscle rigidity, convulsions, and loss of consciousness. Meningitis is an inflammation of the meninges and does not fit the description of symptoms here.

42. A: This patient is at risk for hypoglycemia, or a blood sugar less than 70 milligrams per deciliter due to the missed meals and perhaps missed regular insulin and anti-diabetic medication dosages. A disruption in a diabetic patient's schedule can lead to hypoglycemia, and the nursing assistant should be vigilant in monitoring the patient's intake. Diabetic ketoacidosis is a result of too much blood sugar, or hyperglycemia. The patient is still conscious, so therefore is not in a diabetic coma. Hyperglycemia is a blood sugar level greater than 200 mg/dL, but this condition is not likely because the patient has not had any oral intake.

This material is provided for exam preparation purposes only and does not indicate an endorsement of any specific scientific, political, or religious point of view. © TPB Publishing. You have been licensed one copy of this document for personal use only. Any other reproduction or redistribution is strictly prohibited. All rights reserved.

43. D: Delirium is an acute situation while dementia is a long-term, chronic situation. Symptoms of delirium and dementia are similar in that the patient will be confused and agitated. Delirium can be brought on by a number of factors such as an infection, medication, fever, metabolic imbalance or withdrawal from alcohol or drugs. Dementia is a chronic problem and does not come on suddenly.

44. C: A patient who is somnolent can be described as sleepy, only arousing to verbal stimuli but returning to sleep when the stimuli is stopped. Stupor refers to someone who is sleeping and only arouses to painful stimuli. Delirium is characterized by confusion and agitation. Coma is a state in which the patient cannot be aroused at all, either by verbal or painful stimuli.

45. B: The medical term for coughing up blood in the sputum is hemoptysis. Hematemesis is when there is blood in the vomitus. Hematopoiesis is the process of creating new blood cells in the body. Hematochezia refers to rectal bleeding.

46. C: Keeping the call light within the patient's reach and encouraging the patient to use it is a good way to prevent falls. Rugs should not be placed in a patient's room, since they can be tripped on. A nightlight is a good way to keep the room dimly lit during the night without disturbing a patient's sleep. A completely dark room may be especially disorienting to a hospitalized patient. If the patient frequently uses glasses and a hearing aid, those should be placed within the patient's reach to help the patient hear and see the environment.

47. D: Heart attack is not necessarily associated with prolonged immobility. The patient's skin and muscles can break down if they are immobile. Immobilization can also slow the GI tract, predisposing the patient to constipation.

48. A: 1800 cc is equal to 60 ounces. 30 cc is equal to 1 ounce, so $1800 \div 30 = 60$.

49. B: Turning on the bed alarm is an effective way to prevent falls. The bed alarm notifies staff as soon as a patient begins to exit the bed. Checking on a patient every six hours is not enough. While it would be unsafe to leave the patient completely alone, it is not necessary or practical to stay with the patient for the whole shift. The bed alarm provides an extra measure of safety when no one else is in the room.

50. B: HIPAA is a law that protects a patient's identity. It prevents disclosure of information without the patient's knowledge and consent.

51. C: Because it is normal for people with advanced COPD to have an oxygen saturation level below 90%, the nursing assistant can expect this result. It is not necessary to notify the RN. Even if administration of oxygen were necessary in this situation, it is beyond the scope of practice for the nursing assistant. Checking the patient's pulse is not necessary because their oxygen level is normal for a patient with COPD.

52. B: Providing the patient with a pen and paper can facilitate their communication by allowing them to write while they are having difficulty speaking. Speaking loudly is not necessary, as there is no mention of hardness of hearing. It is also not necessary to rely on the RN or the family to communicate with the patient.

53. C: Care should be taken to clean the catheter while moving away from the resident's body, so as to not introduce disease-causing bacteria into the urethra. It is not necessary to clean the catheter every hour. Using a bleach wipe may break down the catheter and/or cause irritation and should not be used.

54. B: The nursing assistant should stay in the resident's line of vision while speaking with him so that the resident can see that the nursing assistant is speaking and can receive nonverbal cues. Talking with one's back to the resident and talking quietly both make it difficult for the resident to hear the nursing assistant. Braille is used for visually impaired residents.

55. D: The resident may display all of these examples of the body shutting down. Deep tendon reflexes are present in a person who is alive.

56. B: Hearing loss that is caused by regular aging, exposure to noise, and decreased blood circulation to the ear is sensorineural, or nerve-related, hearing loss. This is the most common type of hearing loss in aging patients. Choice A is incorrect because conductive hearing loss is when there is a physical blockage in the external or middle ear that does not allow sound to travel. Choice C is incorrect because mixed hearing loss is when someone has hearing loss due to both nerve-related loss and physical blockage of the ear. Choice D is incorrect because auditory neuropathy is a rare type of hearing loss that affects the nerve impulses in the brain related to hearing.

57. A: When caring for a patient with hearing loss, it is best to use written communication when possible. Patients with hearing loss may pretend to hear or understand out of shame or embarrassment and therefore may not get adequate care or communication. Using written communication helps to eliminate opportunity for miscommunication. Choice B is incorrect because the nursing assistant should speak clearly in a normal volume and tone. Choice C is incorrect because the nursing assistant should direct their head and voice towards the patient's unaffected ear. Choice D is incorrect because the nursing assistant should stand directly in the patient's eyeline, allowing them to read lips more easily.

58. D: When caring for a patient who suffers from vision loss but has no cognitive issues, the nursing assistant should communicate directly with the patient as opposed to going through a family member. The remaining choices are correct actions the nursing assistant should take when caring for a patient with vision loss.

59. C: Patients with expressive aphasia can think clearly and know what they want to say, but they have difficulty communicating language coherently. Choice A is incorrect because a patient with receptive aphasia may be able to speak clearly, but they have difficulty understanding the meaning of words. Choice B is incorrect because Wernicke's aphasia is another name for receptive aphasia. Choice D is incorrect because a patient with global aphasia can neither comprehend words nor articulate them.

60. D: The nursing assistant can and should regularly empty the colostomy bag and record the output for stool. Choice A is incorrect because it is outside of the scope of practice of the nursing assistant to change the colostomy bag; however, they should notify the nurse if the outside of the bag is becoming loose or dirty. Choice B is incorrect because it is common for patients with colostomy bags to have loose or unformed stool. Choice C is incorrect because the nursing assistant should take care not to touch the stomas when providing care as this can cause irritation, infection, or prolapse of the stoma.

Practice Test #2

1. The nursing assistant enters the resident room and notices that there is a puddle of tube feeding on the floor, and the resident's nasogastric (NG) tube is lying beside the resident, who is calmly watching TV in bed. What is the appropriate action for the nursing assistant to take first?
   a. She should empty the resident's Foley catheter and record the output.
   b. She should check the resident's vital signs.
   c. She should turn off the tube feeding and report the dislodgement of the NG tube to the nurse immediately.
   d. She should clean up the tube feeding and throw the NG tube in the trash.

2. The nursing assistant must be able to prioritize time wisely. Which of the following situations would take the highest priority on the nursing assistant's to-do list?
   a. Delivering a meal tray to a resident
   b. Checking routine vital signs on a resident
   c. Turning and repositioning a resident who is due to be turned in fifteen minutes
   d. Assisting a nurse with a resident who has just fallen

3. The nursing assistant took a picture of an unconscious resident's foot that he thought was especially grotesque and posted it to his social media page. Which of the following may occur?
   a. Everyone who sees it will agree that the foot is grotesque and tell the nursing assistant what a hard job he has.
   b. Nothing; this is within his rights to do so.
   c. If the nursing assistant adjusts his privacy setting so that only his friends can see this, it is perfectly acceptable.
   d. The nursing assistant will be subject to disciplinary action and possible revocation of his certification for violation of resident's rights and unethical behavior.

4. The nursing assistant needs to assist the resident from his bed to the chair. The nursing assistant sees a gait belt on the resident's sink but chooses not to use it because she is in a hurry. Which of the following may occur as a result of her rushing this task?
   I. The nurse strains her back trying to lift the resident.
   II. The resident falls because he is too heavy for the nursing assistant to lift.
   III. Nothing; gait belts are not really necessary and are a hassle to use.
   IV. The tasks take longer and require more effort without the help of the gait belt.

   a. Choices I, II, and IV
   b. Choices I, III, and IV
   c. Choices II, III, and IV
   d. Choices I and IV

151

5. The nursing assistant notices there is a doctor who wears a small, round hat on the back of his head every day. She makes fun of it when talking with other nursing assistants. Her supervisor finds out and takes her aside and likely talks to her about what?
   a. Prioritizing tasks over conversation with coworkers
   b. Cultural diversity in the workplace
   c. Respecting resident's rights
   d. Proper body mechanics

6. The nursing assistant finds that the resident has a temperature of 101 °F while taking vital signs in the morning. The resident has also just asked the nursing assistant for help ambulating to the bathroom before breakfast. What action should the nursing assistant take?
   a. Give the resident a bed bath to cool off and then recheck the temperature.
   b. Administer Tylenol (acetaminophen) for the resident's temperature, open the windows in the resident's room, then assist the resident to the bathroom.
   c. Assist the resident to the bathroom, and then notify the nurse of the resident's temperature.
   d. Tell the resident to try to use the bathroom on his own and immediately leave the room to notify the nurse of the resident's temperature.

7. What does SBAR stand for?
   a. Situation, background, assessment, and recommendation
   b. Situation, background, allergies, and results
   c. Situation, breathing, assessment, and results
   d. Situation, breathing, allergies, recommendation

8. Which measurement is NOT an example of something that a nursing assistant would record if they were charting by exception?
   a. Respiratory rate of 30
   b. BP 170/95
   c. Blood glucose 50
   d. Oxygenation saturation 97%

9. A patient has a sign on their door that says NPO. What would be an appropriate meal tray for the nursing assistant to bring them?
   a. A vegetarian meal with spaghetti and juice
   b. A low carb meal with shrimp, asparagus, and water
   c. A low sodium meal with grilled chicken, sweet potatoes, and diet soda
   d. No meal tray

10. A nursing assistant has a patient with DM II, and the nurse needs to check their blood glucose TID. How many times a day should the nursing assistant check this patient's blood glucose?
   a. Four times a day
   b. As needed
   c. Three times a day
   d. Every morning

11. Which patient condition listed below needs to be urgently reported?
    a. A patient with COPD is sitting in bed coughing occasionally.
    b. A patient who was previously alert and oriented has started asking where they are.
    c. A newly admitted patient is asking to speak with the doctor.
    d. A patient has a blood pressure of 135/75.

12. There is a tornado in the area of the facility, and an aide is responsible for moving a bedridden patient to safety. The patient's room has a window and is located on the first floor. Which answer is most appropriate?
    a. Stay with the patient but do not move them.
    b. Push the bed into the doorway.
    c. Push the bed into a room in the interior of the building.
    d. Carry the patient to an interior room.

13. In the event of a fire emergency in a nursing home, which residents should be evacuated first?
    a. Bedridden residents in an area adjacent to the fire
    b. Any residents in the direct location of the fire
    c. Residents who are able to ambulate without assistance
    d. No residents should be evacuated until the fire department arrives

14. What is the number one cause of traumatic brain injuries?
    a. Falls
    b. Motor-vehicle accidents
    c. Being struck by something
    d. Assault

15. A nursing assistant enters a patient's room and finds the patient unresponsive, with no pulse. After activating the emergency response system, what should his next action be?
    a. Begin rescue breaths.
    b. Begin chest compressions with a rate of thirty compressions to two breaths.
    c. Recheck the pulse in a different artery.
    d. Roll the patient onto their left side.

16. Which of the following is an ergonomic workplace hazard?
    a. An electrical cord running across the floor of the patient's doorway
    b. Turning and repositioning a patient with the side rails raised
    c. A patient's dressing that is soaked through with blood
    d. Spilled bleach on the workspace

17. The nursing assistant is attempting to move a heavy box of equipment. Which of the following represents incorrect lifting techniques?
    a. Keeping the box far away from their body and center of gravity
    b. Avoiding the twisting of back muscles when turning
    c. Pushing the box rather than pulling it
    d. Maintaining the box between waist and shoulder height

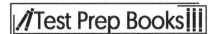

18. The nursing assistant is caring for an elderly patient who is immobile due to a previous stroke. The patient often soils the sheets and must sit in their urine or feces until the nursing assistant can clean them, change the sheets, and reposition them. This patient is at most risk for which type of injury?
   a. Skin tears
   b. Hip and shoulder dislocations
   c. Falls
   d. Pressure ulcers

19. Which of the following patients would NOT have increased risk for burn injury?
   a. A patient with a decreased sense of smell
   b. A patient with Parkinson's disease
   c. An elderly patient living with their adult children
   d. A patient with drug or alcohol intoxication

20. When repositioning a patient in the supine position, it is important for the nursing assistant to make sure which areas of the body have additional padding underneath them?
   a. Calves
   b. Middle of the back
   c. Heels
   d. Upper thigh

21. The nursing assistant is attempting to move a patient up in their bed to help make the patient more comfortable. Which of the following is a correct step to move the patient up safely and easily?
   a. Adjust the bed to the Trendelenburg position
   b. Raise the side rails of the bed for safety
   c. Maintain a firm grasp on the patient's gown when moving
   d. Instruct the patient to keep their arms down by their side

22. What is the primary cause of injury and leading cause of death due to injury in the elderly?
   a. Burns
   b. Falls
   c. Pressure ulcers
   d. Skin tears

23. A nursing assistant is providing perineal care for a female resident with an indwelling urinary catheter. Which of the following techniques is appropriate?
   a. The nursing assistant should first clean the perineum, making sure to clean from front to back. With a fresh washcloth, the nursing assistant should then clean the exposed tubing of the catheter starting with the part closest to the resident and wiping away from the resident.
   b. The nursing assistant should only clean the exposed tubing of the catheter, starting with the part closest to the resident and wiping away from the resident. The resident doesn't need perineal care because she has an indwelling catheter.
   c. The nursing assistant should first clean the perineum, making sure to clean from back to front. With a fresh washcloth, the nursing assistant should then clean the exposed tubing of the catheter starting with the part closest to the resident and wiping away from the resident.
   d. The nursing assistant should clean the perineum, making sure to clean from front to back. The catheter tubing should not be cleaned as this can put the resident at risk for infection.

24. A patient with heart failure is placed on a low sodium diet. Their dinner tray includes fried chicken, fries, and green beans. What is the most appropriate action for the nursing assistant to take?
   a. Instruct the patient to eat only half of the meal.
   b. Remove the patient's tray and notify the nurse so the correct meal tray can be sent.
   c. Instruct the patient to eat only the green beans and ensure that their next meal is low sodium.
   d. Allow the patient to eat the meal, but make sure their breakfast order is a low sodium meal.

25. The nursing assistant is caring for a patient with dysphagia who is at high risk for aspiration. What is a correct step to take while feeding this patient?
   a. Check that the patient completely swallowed their food after each bite.
   b. Encourage the patient to wash down each bite of food with a drink.
   c. Ensure that liquids are thin to reduce risk of choking.
   d. Have the patient remain sitting upright for at least ten minutes after eating.

26. The nursing assistant is completing a bed bath for an incontinent patient who is unable to ambulate due to left-sided weakness. Which of the following scenarios should be reported to the patient's nurse?
   a. The patient had difficulty turning from one side to another.
   b. The patient insisted on washing their face and hands without assistance.
   c. The patient had a bowel movement in the bed.
   d. The patient has redness and irritation around their sacrum.

27. Which of the following is a correct step when providing perineal care on a patient with an indwelling urinary catheter?
   a. Wipe the tubing from the end closest to the bag and progress back towards the patient.
   b. Hang the catheter bag at the head of the bed or on a separate IV pole.
   c. Ensure that the catheter tubing is securely attached to the patient's leg.
   d. Wait until the catheter bag is full before emptying.

28. The nursing assistant is cutting the toenails of a patient. They should take extra care when doing this for a patient with which condition?
   a. Hip dislocation
   b. Pneumonia
   c. Diabetes
   d. Congestive heart failure

29. Which of the following tasks should the nursing assistant NOT do during mouth care?
   a. Report odor or discoloration to the nurse.
   b. Dampen the patient's lips with a washcloth for moisture at the end of care.
   c. Provide mouth care during AM/HS care and after meals.
   d. Perform routine oral care for intubated patients.

30. Which of the following actions can help prevent skin breakdown for patients?
   a. Frequent perineal care for incontinent patients
   b. Using powder routinely for damp skin
   c. Leaving skin damp after bathing
   d. Ensuring that heels, sacrum, and elbows are resting firmly and securely on the bed

31. The nursing assistant is caring for a patient with Parkinson's disease who requests help with shaving their face. The nursing assistant looks at the patient's chart and sees that they are on anticoagulation medication. Which measure should the nursing assistant take during grooming to help reduce risk of bleeding?
    a. Do not shave their face since they are a bleeding risk.
    b. Allow the patient to shave themselves while supervised.
    c. Use a razor with a new blade.
    d. Use an electric razor to shave their face.

32. The nursing assistant is helping a patient with full right-side paralysis put on a shirt. Which is a correct technique to help safely dress this patient?
    a. Remove the soiled shirt from the left side first.
    b. Understand that some force may be needed to get their arms through the shirt.
    c. Assist the patient to a standing position before changing.
    d. Place the new shirt on from the left side first.

33. The nursing assistant is providing mouth care for an unconscious patient. Which action should they take to promote the patient's safety?
    a. Use their fingers to help open the mouth and move the gums.
    b. Place the head of the bed flat for better visualization of their mouth.
    c. Keep the patient's head facing forward so they cannot turn to the side during care.
    d. Dry the outside of the patient's mouth after completing care.

34. Which of the following is a way to help prevent edema?
    a. Keep the feet of the bed lowered or have the patient in a sitting position.
    b. Encourage bed rest.
    c. Perform range-of-motion exercise while in bed.
    d. Wear loose clothing on the extremities.

35. The nursing assistant is caring for an elderly patient who has weakness on both sides and difficulty ambulating. They place an egg-crate mattress topper on the bed and use wedges and cushions to position the patient. These actions help prevent what condition in patients?
    a. Joint dislocation
    b. Pressure sores
    c. Localized infection
    d. Hypothermia

36. The nursing assistant is caring for a patient who has only eaten two meals each day over the past three days. When weighing the patient in the morning, the nursing assistant notes that the patient has gained four pounds since yesterday. This finding would be most concerning for which patient?
    a. A patient with breast cancer
    b. A patient who is one day post-op from an appendectomy
    c. A patient with congestive heart failure
    d. A patient with diabetes mellitus II

37. The nursing assistant is taking care of a patient who is about to undergo an arm amputation. The patient will neither discuss nor acknowledge their upcoming surgery. This is a defense mechanism known as:
    a. Denial
    b. Regression
    c. Acting out
    d. Projection

38. The lungs are part of which body system?
    a. Pulmonary
    b. Cardiovascular
    c. Musculoskeletal
    d. Neurological

39. Which gland secretes growth hormones?
    a. Thyroid
    b. Pancreas
    c. Ovaries
    d. Pituitary

40. What is the acronym for stroke symptoms?
    a. ARM
    b. STROKE
    c. FAST
    d. TIME

41. Which term describes a patient who is tired but can be easily aroused?
    a. Somnolence
    b. Lethargy
    c. Delirium
    d. Coma

42. The nursing assistant is taking care of a postpartum woman who is bleeding uncontrollably. The uncontrollable bleeding could be:
    a. A stroke
    b. A hemorrhage
    c. An episode of hematemesis
    d. A normal effect of giving birth

43. The "rule of nines" is a way to classify burns based on the amount of skin involved. According to this rule, the anterior trunk accounts for what percentage of the body?
    a. 9%
    b. 1%
    c. 27%
    d. 18%

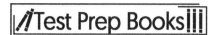

44. The nursing assistant is helping a patient with their meal, and they start to choke. This patient is at risk of:
    a. Malnutrition
    b. Dehydration
    c. Aspiration pneumonia
    d. Bronchitis

45. While taking a patient's vitals, the nursing assistant records a heart rate of 140. What should the nursing assistant do considering this finding?
    a. Stay with the patient.
    b. Move on to the next patient.
    c. Notify the RN.
    d. Yell for help.

46. A 10-year-old child has started wetting the bed. Which of the following might cause this behavior?
    a. Coping mechanisms
    b. Grief
    c. Acting out
    d. Regression

47. If a patient's axillary temperature is 101.2 degrees Fahrenheit, what is their body temperature?
    a. 100.2 degrees Fahrenheit
    b. 98.6 degrees Fahrenheit
    c. 102.2 degrees Fahrenheit
    d. 101.2 degrees Fahrenheit

48. Which organ system is the largest?
    a. Cardiovascular
    b. Integumentary
    c. Musculoskeletal
    d. Pulmonary

49. Difficulty breathing that can be caused by asthma is called:
    a. Apnea
    b. Orthopnea
    c. Dyspnea
    d. Pneumonia

50. Severe anxiety may cause which of the following?
    a. Panic attacks
    b. Regression
    c. Depression
    d. Violence

51. Epilepsy is a disease which causes:
    a. Abnormal glucose
    b. Seizures
    c. Abnormal sodium
    d. A heart attack

52. A patient had a heart attack one month ago. His wife tells the nursing assistant privately that he doesn't remember having it. This is a defense mechanism known as:
    a. Denial
    b. Repression
    c. Dissociation
    d. Grief

53. While caring for a patient with an indwelling urinary catheter, which of the following actions could cause complications for the patient?
    a. Using warm water to cleanse the urethra where the tubing enters
    b. Wiping the catheter tubing in a back-and-forth motion
    c. Reporting any drainage around the catheter to the nurse immediately
    d. Attaching the catheter tubing securely to the patient's leg

54. The nursing assistant is caring for a patient who recently had a heart attack and has been placed on a cardiac diet. How would the nursing assistant most accurately describe this diet to the patient?
    a. High in sodium, low in cholesterol and fat
    b. Increased carbohydrate and water intake, low in sodium and fat
    c. Low in sodium, fat, and cholesterol
    d. Increased carbohydrate intake, decreased water intake, low in cholesterol

55. The nursing assistant is caring for a patient with a nasogastric (NG) tube. When they enter the patient's room, they see that the tape holding the tubing to the nose came off, and the tube is out three inches further than it was previously. What is the most appropriate action for the nursing assistant to take?
    a. Do not touch the NG tube and notify the nurse
    b. Remove the NG tube completely
    c. Reinsert the NG tube to the same length and reapply tape
    d. Flush the NG tube with sterile water and notify the nurse

56. The nursing assistant would be most concerned about NG tube displacement or removal in which of the following patients?
    a. An 80-year-old patient with dementia
    b. A 35-year-old homeless patient
    c. A 60-year-old patient who is 2 days post-op cholecystectomy
    d. A 70-year-old patient with pneumonia

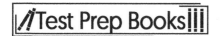

57. A patient is receiving supplemental oxygen at 4 LPM. The nursing assistant notices that the patient is harder to wake up and that their lips and nail beds have a bluish color. The patient is most likely suffering from which condition?
   a. Stroke
   b. Pneumonia
   c. Hypoxia
   d. Hypothermia

58. A patient with an IV in their arm complains of pain around the IV site. The nursing assistant notes redness around the site as well. What is the most appropriate action for the nursing assistant to take?
   a. Flush the IV with 10cc of saline
   b. Clean and change the dressing around the IV site
   c. Remove the IV from the patient's arm
   d. Do not touch the IV and notify the patient's nurse of the findings

59. While giving a patient a bed bath, the nursing assistant notices that the patient's left hip is non-blanchable. This means the patient is at risk for which condition?
   a. Bruising
   b. Pressure ulcer
   c. Skin tear
   d. Hip dislocation

60. What are the five vital signs?
   a. Heart rate, temperature, blood pressure, respiratory rate, pain
   b. Temperature, urinary output, heart rate, blood pressure, respiratory rate
   c. Blood pressure, heart rate, blood glucose, respiratory rate, urinary output
   d. Blood pressure, lung sounds, blood glucose, heart rate, pain

Answer Explanations #2

1. C: The nursing assistant should turn off the tube feeding so no further mess is made and notify the nurse immediately. The resident is not in distress, so checking vital signs most likely is not necessary unless the nurse requests. Cleaning up the tube feeding and NG tube can occur once the nurse has been notified and has assessed the situation.

2. D: The nursing assistant needs to assist the nurse with the resident who has just fallen as he or she may have sustained serious injury and need further interventions. The other situations can wait and are not as urgent.

3. D: The nursing assistant has violated a resident's rights in a major way and is at risk for disciplinary action, loss of job, and even revocation of certification. The nursing assistant has behaved unethically and needs to correct this error of judgment immediately before further consequences occur.

4. A: The nursing assistant risks straining her back, the resident falling, or the task taking longer as a result of not using the gait belt. The gait belt is an assistive device used to help with lifts; not using it in situations such as this one risks both the resident and the nursing assistant.

5. B: The nursing assistant's behavior reflects lack of cultural awareness. The doctor is likely Jewish, and the hat he is wearing is called a kippah or yarmulke. The nursing assistant making fun of it shows a lack of cultural awareness and also great disrespect for his religious beliefs. Choice *A* is somewhat relevant, but the question does not indicate that the nursing assistant was talking to coworkers at inappropriate times. The other topics would not be pertinent to her behavior.

6. C: The nursing assistant should assist the resident to the bathroom and then notify the nurse of the resident's temperature. Choice *A* is incorrect because if the resident has a fever, the nurse needs to be notified. Choice *B* is incorrect because administering medication is outside of the nursing assistant's scope of practice. Choice *D* is incorrect because if the resident needs help walking but tries to do it on his own, he is at risk for falling.

7. A: *Situation, background, assessment, and recommendation* is the correct meaning of the acronym SBAR, which is used in patient handoff reports.

8. D: An oxygen saturation of 97% is within normal limits and would not be included in charting by exception. In charting by exception, only abnormal findings are included. The other answer choices are all findings that are outside of expected normal ranges and would therefore be included when charting by exception.

9. D: NPO means *nothing by mouth*, so the patient should not be given a meal tray. Patients may be put on NPO precautions if they are aspiration risks or have an upcoming surgery.

10. C: The abbreviation TID means three times a day, so the patient with DM II (diabetes mellitus II) should have their blood glucose checked at that frequency.

11. B: A patient who was previously alert and now does not know their location is newly confused. This represents a change in level of consciousness and can be indicative of a medical emergency that should be reported to the patient's nurse urgently. Occasional coughing would be an expected finding in a

patient with COPD, so Choice A is incorrect. The nursing assistant should let the nurse know if the patient would like to speak with the doctor; however, it does not need to be reported urgently, so Choice C is incorrect. Although Choice D represents a blood pressure that is outside of normal range, it is not a dangerously high blood pressure that needs to be urgently reported. Regardless, the nurse should still be made aware of the value.

12. C: The safest place to be during a tornado is a basement or an interior room away from windows. Because the patient's room has a window, the patient must be moved out of the room. Choices A and B are not safe or appropriate. Choice D, carrying the patient out, is also not safe because an injury could occur when attempting to carry the patient.

13. B: In a fire emergency, people in the immediate area of the fire should be evacuated first, followed by people in adjacent areas. Choice B is first, and then A. Choice D is not correct because an evacuation should occur as soon as possible. In Choice C, residents who are able to walk independently can evacuate to a designated area at the same time that other residents are being assisted out.

14. A: Falls are the number one cause of traumatic brain injuries, accounting for 40 percent of all traumatic brain injuries. Choice C, being struck by something, accounts for 15.5 percent. Motor-vehicle accidents account for 14.3 percent, followed by D, assault, at 10.7 percent.

15. B: When a patient becomes unresponsive, the nursing assistant should activate the emergency response system immediately and CPR should be started immediately after, beginning with effective chest compressions. Choice C, rechecking the pulse, takes time away from initiating CPR, and should only be rechecked for ten seconds, after a few minutes of CPR. Choice A, rescue breaths, should be started if the patient is not breathing but has a pulse. Choice D is the recovery position, which is used when the patient has regained a pulse and is recovering. Depending on facility protocol and if an emergency response team is available, the nursing assistant may only need to perform chest compressions while waiting for emergency response to restore perfusion to vital organs, especially if a respiratory team is available to insert an oral airway, which is more effective than administering rescue breaths.

16. B: An ergonomic hazard is one that affects how a person works in their environment. This includes using proper and safe body mechanics for repositioning patients or lifting heavy equipment. Attempting to move a patient with the side rails still raised does not allow use for proper body mechanics. Choice A is incorrect because an electrical cord on the floor is an example of a physical hazard that could cause someone to trip. Choice C is incorrect because possible exposure to bodily fluids that can cause infection is an example of a biological hazard. Choice D is incorrect because unsafe exposure to toxic cleaning products, vapors, fumes, or gases is an example of a chemical hazard.

17. A: Keeping a heavy object further away can put greater strain on the body and make it more difficult to carry. For proper lifting technique, the nursing assistant should keep the object as close to their body as possible. The remaining choices are all examples of good lifting techniques.

18. D: Bodily fluids, such as feces and urine, can be very damaging to the skin and can lead to breakdown that causes pressure ulcers. Additionally, immobile patients may be more prone to pressure ulcers because they are not able to move or turn themselves, and they have decreased blood flow with increased pressure on bony areas. The remaining choices can be common injuries for patients; however, the patient described in the scenario is at highest risk for pressure ulcers.

19. C: An elderly patient living with family members does not have increased risk for burn injury since they are living with other adults who can decrease fire risks and help assist the elderly individual in case of a fire. Choice A is incorrect because a patient with a decreased sense of smell may not be able to smell smoke from a fire. Choice B is incorrect because a patient with Parkinson's may experience hand tremors when handling hot or flammable items that can lead to burns. Choice D is incorrect because someone who is impaired due to drugs or alcohol may be disoriented, clumsy, and have altered judgment, therefore being more likely to burn themselves.

20. C: When a patient is lying flat on their back in the supine position, it is important to pad bony prominences such as the heels, tailbone, elbows, shoulder blades, and head. The remaining choices naturally have more padding and may be uncomfortable to the patient if additional padding is added.

21. A: Placing the patient in the Trendelenburg position, with the head of their bed at a downward angle, allows the nursing assistant to use gravity to help move the patient up in bed. Choice B is incorrect because the patient's bed rails should be lowered so the nursing assistant can have easier access to reposition the patient safely. Choice C is incorrect because the nursing assistant should grasp the draw sheet underneath the patient to reposition, not the patient's gown. Choice D is incorrect because having the patient's arms down at their sides can cause injury and make it more difficult to reposition the patient. The nursing assistant should instruct the patient to cross their arms over their chest.

22. B: The primary cause of injury and leading cause of death due to injury among elderly residents is falls. The nursing assistant should take fall-prevention interventions with all patients, but especially with those who are high fall risks. While the other choices describe injuries that can happen to elderly patients, they are not the most common.

23. A: The nursing assistant should clean the perineum from front to back, and then clean the exposed catheter tubing. Before cleaning the catheter tubing, the nursing assistant should make sure it's secured to the resident's leg to avoid dislodging it. In Choice B, perineal care should be provided to all residents, whether they have an indwelling catheter or not. For Choice C, the perineal area of a female must always be cleaned from front to back to avoid introducing harmful bacteria into the vaginal area. Finally, in Choice D, when providing perineal care to a resident with an indwelling catheter, it's appropriate to clean the exposed tubing of the catheter as well.

24. B: A meal tray with fried foods would be high in sodium and not an appropriate meal for this patient. If the patient is not given the correct meal tray according to their diet, the nursing assistant should remove the tray so the patient does not eat it and then notify the nurse so they can get a new one. The remaining choices would either allow the patient to eat high sodium foods or prevent them from having a complete meal, both of which are unsafe for the patient.

25. A: A patient with dysphagia is at increased risk of choking and aspirating. The nursing assistant should ensure that each bite of food is completely chewed and swallowed to help avoid choking. Choice B is incorrect because patients with dysphagia should not try to drink while they are eating, as it can increase their chance of choking. Eating and drinking should be done slowly and separately to reduce aspiration. Choice C is incorrect because liquids should be thickened, not thinned, per orders to help reduce choking. Choice D is incorrect because patients should remain sitting upright for at least 30 minutes after eating to help reduce risk of aspiration.

26. D: Redness and irritation around a patient's sacrum should be reported to a nurse, as this could be a sign of skin breakdown or a pressure ulcer. Choice A is incorrect because a patient who has left-sided weakness would be expected to have difficulty turning. The nursing assistant should help the patient reposition. Choice B is incorrect because the patient should be encouraged to perform appropriate tasks independently. Choice C is incorrect because it may be expected for a patient who is incontinent and immobile to have a bowel movement in the bed.

27. C: The tubing of the indwelling catheter should be securely attached to the patient's leg. This prevents the tubing from tugging or being dislodged from the inside of the bladder. Choice A is incorrect because the tubing should be cleaned from the end closest to the patient then down towards the bag to prevent bacteria going inside the urethra. Choice B is incorrect because the catheter bag should be placed below the level of the patient's bladder to promote draining of urine. Choice D is incorrect because the bag should not be almost full before emptying. The bag should be checked regularly and emptied before it gets to about three-quarters full.

28. C: The nursing assistant providing foot care to a patient with diabetes should take extra care during their tasks to not cause any irritation or breaks in the skin. People with diabetes are at higher risk of infection due to poor wound healing. Additionally, people with diabetes can often develop peripheral neuropathy that makes it more difficult to tell if an injury was sustained by the foot care. The remaining choices are conditions that would not require extra care when cutting a patient's toenails.

29. B: At the end of performing mouth care, the nursing assistant should ensure that the patient's lips are dry, since moisture from water can cause their lips to dry further. The nursing assistant can also apply lip balm if appropriate. The remaining choices are all correct actions the nursing assistant should perform when providing mouth care.

30. A: Incontinent patients often have feces and urine on their skin, which can cause skin irritation and breakdown. These patients should have frequent perineal care and skin assessments done to help reduce the amount of time these irritants are on their skin and assess for any new signs of irritation and skin breakdown. Choice B is incorrect because powder can cake in the folds of the skin and contribute to skin breakdown. Choice C is incorrect because leaving the skin damp after bathing can lead to dryness and skin breakdown. The nursing assistant should ensure that the patient is completely dry after bathing. Choice D is incorrect because pressure points, such as heels, sacrum, and elbows, should have extra cushioning. Having these points rest firmly on the bed can lead to skin breakdown and pressure ulcers.

31. D: An electric razor can help reduce risk of skin irritation or bleeding and should be used when shaving a patient on anticoagulants or for those with bleeding disorders. Choice A is incorrect because the nursing assistant should still provide safe care to make sure that the patient is comfortable and has their needs met. Choice B is incorrect because a patient with Parkinson's disease may have hand tremors, making them more likely to accidentally cut their face while shaving themselves. Choice C is incorrect because a regular razor should not be used if an electric razor is available, since it is more likely to cause bleeding or irritation.

32. A: For a patient with right-sided paralysis or weakness, the soiled shirt should be removed from the left side, their stronger side, before removing the right side. Choice B is incorrect because patient's limbs should not be forced through their clothing when dressing them, as it can cause injury. A patient with paralysis may also not be able to tell if an injury has occurred while dressing. Choice C is incorrect

164

because it would be unsafe to have a patient with paralysis stand while changing their shirt, since it would unnecessarily increase risk of falling. Choice *D* is incorrect because when putting on a new shirt, the patient should put the right side, their weaker side, through the shirt first before putting on the left side.

33. D: The nursing assistant should ensure that the outside of the patient's mouth is dry after completing oral care. Leaving the patient's mouth damp with water can cause the skin to dry further and leave them more susceptible to skin breakdown and infection. Choice *A* is incorrect because the nursing assistant should never place their fingers inside the mouth of an unconscious patient. Choice *B* is incorrect because the patient should be kept upright to help prevent aspiration and choking during mouth care. Choice *C* is incorrect because a patient's head should be turned to the side, if possible, to help prevent aspiration and choking.

34. C: Edema is the buildup of fluid in the body tissue that may be caused from immobility or conditions that cause fluid retention. For a patient who is bedbound or may not be able to ambulate easily, performing range-of-motion exercises in bed can help promote circulation and prevent edema. Choice *A* is incorrect because patients should have their legs elevated while in bed to prevent fluid from pooling at their extremities. If they are able, patients should get out of bed and move around to increase their circulation and decrease edema; therefore, Choice *B* is incorrect. Choice *D* is incorrect because wearing tighter clothing, such as compression socks, can help reduce edema and prevent fluid from pooling in the body tissue.

35. B: Using an egg-crate mattress topper on the bed can help eliminate pressure points and prevent pressure sores. Using wedges and cushions also helps keep weight off these pressure points and keeps the patients positioned properly to prevent pressure sores. The remaining choices are not prevented by using these devices.

36. C: The patient has not been eating their full meals, which means the weight gain is not likely from nutrition intake and may be from excess fluid retention. A patient with congestive heart failure who has gained over two pounds in a one-day period may be experiencing fluid overload, which should be reported to the nurse. Any patient that has gained or lost more than two pounds in a one-day period may be a cause for concern; however, this weight fluctuation in a patient with congestive heart failure would be more concerning than the remaining choices.

37. A: Denial occurs when a patient refuses to acknowledge something that is painful. Regression is reverting to an earlier stage of development. Acting out occurs when a patient engages in a behavior that is unusual for that person. Projection occurs when a patient attributes their own negative feelings or characteristics to another person.

38. A: The lungs are part of the pulmonary system, which also includes the airways and diaphragm. The cardiovascular system includes the heart and blood vessels. The musculoskeletal system includes muscles, bones, and soft tissues such as cartilage and tendons. The neurological system is composed of the brain and spinal cord.

39. D: The pituitary gland secretes growth hormones. The thyroid secretes thyroid hormones, which help to regulate metabolism and contribute to brain development. The pancreas secretes insulin and digestive enzymes. Ovaries secrete the sex hormones progesterone and estrogen.

40. C: FAST is the acronym for stroke symptoms. It stands for *face*, *arms*, *speech*, and *time*. *Face* refers to facial droop on one side of the face. *Arms* refers to sudden weakness or inability to move the arm, usually just on one side. *Speech* refers to the slurring of words, and *time* refers to the importance of getting the patient to a hospital in a timely manner because the risk for significant brain damage increases the longer the patient goes untreated.

41. A: Somnolence is a state of drowsiness in which a patient can be easily aroused from sleep. If a patient is lethargic, it is more difficult for them to be aroused, and they are likely to fall right back to sleep if left alone. Delirium is a state of confusion in which the patient is not usually drowsy. If a patient is in a coma, they cannot be aroused.

42. B: A hemorrhage is an episode of uncontrolled bleeding. A stroke is caused by lack of oxygen to the brain. Hematemesis is when a patient vomits blood. Hemorrhaging is not normal during childbirth; it is a rare and abnormal complication.

43. D: The anterior trunk accounts for 18% per the rule of nines, which is a burn classification system in which the body's surface area is separated into areas by multiples of 9. The head and arms each comprise 9%; the anterior trunk, posterior trunk, and legs each comprise 18%; and the perineum accounts for 1%.

44. C: The patient is at risk of aspiration pneumonia, which can occur if a patient chokes and aspirates food into the lungs. Malnutrition occurs if the patient does not get adequate nutrition for a long period of time. Dehydration occurs if the patient does not take in enough water. Bronchitis is an infection of the lungs, but it is not caused by aspirating food.

45. C: The nursing assistant should notify the RN because a heart rate of 140 is abnormally fast and therefore would be considered tachycardia. The patient can be left alone briefly to notify the RN; it is not necessary to yell for help if this is the only abnormal finding. Moving on to the next patient would not be appropriate at this time, as the patient may become unstable.

46. D: Regression occurs when a patient reverts to a previous developmental stage. A 10-year-old child would not be expected to wet the bed according to their developmental stage. Coping mechanisms include many different strategies to deal with unpleasant circumstances, but wetting the bed is not likely to be one. Grief involves many stages and is a reaction to significant loss. Acting out involves unusual, radical, or rebellious behavior.

47. C: The patient's body temperature is 102.2 degrees Fahrenheit. One degree Fahrenheit is added to the axillary temperature to obtain a patient's body temperature.

48. B: The integumentary system is the largest body system. It includes the skin, hair, nails, and some exocrine glands.

49. C: Dyspnea is defined as shortness of breath. Apnea is the cessation of breathing. Orthopnea is shortness of breath while lying flat. Pneumonia is an infection in the lungs.

50. A: Severe anxiety may (but does not always) cause panic attacks. Severe anxiety does not directly cause regression (a defense mechanism) or depression (a mood disorder). It is common for depression and anxiety to coexist in the same patient, however. Anxiety is also not likely to cause someone to act out in violence.

51. B: Epilepsy causes seizures. Abnormal glucose and abnormal sodium can cause seizures, but these conditions are not caused by epilepsy. Epilepsy does not cause heart attacks.

52. B: Repression is a coping mechanism in which a patient forgets a traumatic event that has happened to them. Denial is a coping mechanism in which a patient refuses to acknowledge something that has happened. Dissociation occurs when a patient separates from reality. Grief is a general term that describes a series of stages someone goes through after a significant loss.

53. B: Wiping the catheter tubing in a back-and-forth motion can introduce more bacteria into the urethra and lead to a urinary tract infection (UTI). The nursing assistant should wipe in circular motions going away from the patient. The remaining choices are incorrect because they are all appropriate steps when caring for a patient with an indwelling catheter.

54. C: A cardiac diet consists of food that is low in sodium, fat, and cholesterol. Patients with cardiac conditions such as heart disease, recent cardiac events, high cholesterol, and high blood pressure are often placed on his diet. Choice *A* is incorrect because a diet that is high in sodium would cause a patient to retain more water, which can increase blood pressure and put more stress on the heart. Choices *B* and *D* are incorrect because increased carbohydrate and water intake can also raise blood pressure and cause weight gain, which would put more stress on the heart. Water intake should be monitored and only restricted if specifically indicated.

55. A: If a nasogastric (NG) tube is partially removed, the nursing assistant should immediately notify the patient's nurse and not attempt to remove or reinsert it. Choice *B* is incorrect because the nursing assistant should not remove the tubing; the nurse should be notified to assess the situation. Choice *D* is incorrect because it is outside of the scope of practice for the nursing assistant to reinsert the tube and reinsertion could cause injury to the patient. Choice *D* is incorrect because the nursing assistant should not flush an NG tube. Additionally, flushing an NG tube that is not in proper position could be an aspiration or injury risk.

56. A: A patient who has dementia may be confused or not remember having the NG tube placed and would be more likely to self-remove the tube. A patient with any condition that causes confusion may be at risk of removing their NG tube. Measures should be taken to help prevent a patient from doing this; however, the least restrictive methods should be used before escalating to physical restraints. The remaining choices are incorrect because these conditions would not put a patient at increased risk of removing their NG tube.

57. C: A patient with a decreased level of consciousness and blue skin tones around their mouth, extremities, or nail beds is likely hypoxic. Hypoxia is caused by lack of oxygen in the body. A patient with hypoxia may also be completely unresponsive or short of breath. A patient who is already on supplemental oxygen may have an underlying respiratory condition that puts them at higher risk of becoming hypoxic. Although these symptoms may have a similar presentation to hypothermia, it is far less likely that a patient in a hospital or other care facility has hypothermia as opposed to hypoxia; therefore, Choice *D* is incorrect. Choice *A* is incorrect because a patient having a stroke may have weakness or numbness on one side, confusion, headache, dizziness, and vision changes. Choice *B* is incorrect because a patient with pneumonia may have difficulty breathing, fever, increased cough, and sharp or stabbing chest pain.

58. D: Changes in the patient's IV site such as redness, swelling, leakage, and bruising, or a patient reporting of pain should be reported to the nurse immediately. The nursing assistant should not attempt to interfere with the IV itself. The remaining choices are incorrect because they are outside the regular scope of practice of the nursing assistant. The nurse should be notified to assess the IV before attempting to remove, flush, or change the IV or dressing.

59. B: Normal, healthy skin should be blanchable, meaning that it should turn white when pressed, but color should return immediately upon release of pressure. If a patient's skin is non-blanchable, that means the color does not return to the skin. This is a sign of poor circulation, which puts the patient at higher risk of developing a pressure ulcer. Since the hip is a bony prominence, it has greater risk for a pressure ulcer. The remaining choices are incorrect because the observations described do not match with those medical conditions.

60. A: The five vital signs are heart rate, temperature, blood pressure, respiratory rate, and pain. Pain was recently recognized as the fifth vital sign and should be checked regularly. Although it may be important to measure the other options listed, they are not considered to be main vital signs.

Practice Test #3

1. Which technique represents safe lifting when moving patients or heavy objects?
   a. Lift using your back.
   b. Keep the patient or object at the farthest distance from you.
   c. Keep your back straight.
   d. Relax your stomach muscles.

2. Which activity below is an example of self-care that could help alleviate a nursing assistant's job stress?
   a. Picking up extra shifts to save for a personal gift
   b. Joining an adult kickball league
   c. Getting fast food after a difficult shift
   d. Driving quickly to get home as soon as possible after a shift

3. Daily exercise, meditation, healthy eating, and spending time with friends and family are examples of which of the following?
   a. Progressive coping mechanisms
   b. Neutral coping mechanisms
   c. Negative coping mechanisms
   d. Positive coping mechanisms

4. Which example of communication below protects resident rights and is HIPAA-compliant?
   a. The nursing assistant talking with the patient's nurse about recent MRI results
   b. The nursing assistant talking to their friend, an NA on another unit, about their patient's recent complaints
   c. The nursing assistant looking up the medical record of a friend who is admitted on a unit on another floor
   d. The nursing assistant letting their friend know they are taking care of their uncle and discussing his care

5. The nursing assistant comes to bring a patient their lunch and help them eat. The patient refuses to eat and says they are not hungry right now. The nursing assistant explains that it is important for them to keep their body nourished, but they continue to refuse. What is this an example of?
   a. Right to fair treatment
   b. Right to not accept abuse
   c. Right to self-determination
   d. Right to non-discrimination

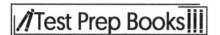

6. The nursing assistant is caring for a patient who was admitted for pneumonia. The patient's partner comes to visit during the day. After the partner leaves, the nursing assistant notices the patient grimacing when they go to sit down and sees new bleeding on the perineal area when helping them change gowns. The nursing assistant is concerned that the patient may be experiencing what kind of abuse?
   a. Physical abuse
   b. Sexual abuse
   c. Emotional abuse
   d. Financial abuse

7. The nursing assistant is helping to admit a new patient from a local nursing home and notices bruising around the patient's wrists. The patient also appears nervous when approached quickly by medical staff. What would be the most appropriate response to take first?
   a. Report possible signs of abuse to the nurse or charge nurse for appropriate next steps to be taken.
   b. Get ice for the bruises and let the nurse know if they get worse.
   c. Confront the patient ask why they do not want to cooperate with the medical team.
   d. Call the nursing home they came from to ask if they were abusing the patient.

8. A patient's family member is observed being verbally threatening to the patient and regularly causing them to feel fearful and worthless. This is an example of what kind of abuse?
   a. Physical abuse
   b. Sexual abuse
   c. Emotional/mental abuse
   d. Financial abuse

9. The nursing assistant is working a shift while a new nurse, who is wearing a hijab, is being oriented to the unit. What is a culturally appropriate response that reflects being supportive in a diverse workplace?
   a. Say nothing, but internally feel bad that her culture makes her wear a hijab.
   b. Compliment the nurse on the color of their hijab and ask if they can help turn a patient.
   c. Try to avoid interaction because the nursing assistant doesn't know much about their culture.
   d. Wear a hijab to work on the next shift in solidarity with the new nurse.

10. What is the correct order of the chain of command for reporting information?
   a. Nursing assistant, nurse, charge nurse, nurse manager, nurse director
   b. Nurse manager, charge nurse, nurse, nursing assistant, nurse director
   c. Nursing assistant, nurse manager, nurse, charge nurse, nurse director
   d. Nursing assistant, nurse, charge nurse, nurse director, nurse manager

11. The nursing assistant and a nurse get into an argument during a day shift about one of them having to answer more call lights than the other. They bring this issue to the charge nurse, who is unable to resolve the conflict. The nursing assistant and the nurse are now refusing to work together on their next shift. Who is the most appropriate person to escalate this conflict to next?
   a. The night shift charge nurse
   b. The nurse manager
   c. The nurse director
   d. The nurse who witnessed the initial argument

12. The nursing assistant is helping a patient who is alert and oriented transfer from their bed to a wheelchair. What should be the nursing assistant's first step?
   a. Lower the side rails of the bed
   b. Explain the procedure for transferring to the patient
   c. Place a gait belt around the patient's waist
   d. Put nonslip footwear on the patient

13. The nursing assistant is helping a patient, who is a high risk for falls, get out of bed to ambulate in the hallway. Which of the following interventions could decrease a patient's risk of falling?
   a. Placing rugs on the floor to prevent slipping
   b. Using low lighting in rooms so patients do not strain their eyes
   c. Encouraging the patient to walk independently to help strengthen their muscles
   d. Wearing rubber-soled shoes for grip

14. A patient is ambulating in the hallway while the nursing assistant walks alongside them and holds onto their gait belt. The nursing assistance is offering what kind of assistance for ambulation?
   a. Minimum assistance (MIN)
   b. Maximum assistance (MAX)
   c. Stand by assistance (SBA)
   d. Contact-guard assistance (CGA)

15. The nursing assistant is instructing a patient with weakness in both legs on how to use a walker without wheels. Which of the following instructions should the nursing assistant give to the patient?
   a. Stand one arm's-length behind the walker
   b. Use the arms to push the walker forward on the ground with each step
   c. Keep their weight on the stronger leg and take a step with the weaker leg
   d. Step to the front end of the walker when taking a step

16. A patient has a tibia fracture in their left leg and was told that they cannot bear any weight on that side. Which crutch gait would be most appropriate to educate the patient on?
   a. Two-point crutch gait
   b. Swing-through crutch gait
   c. Swing-to crutch gait
   d. Three-point crutch gait

17. Which of the following is NOT a type of patient restraint?
   a. Having someone sit with and watch the patient
   b. Giving the patient a medication to reduce anxiety
   c. Raising the side rails of the bed
   d. Coercing the patient to act a certain way

18. A patient with dementia is becoming aggressive with the staff and keeps trying to remove their foley catheter. Which of the following actions is appropriate to take when using restraints correctly?
   a. Apply the restraints quickly without explaining to the patient what is happening since they are confused.
   b. Check the positioning of the restraints every hour and remove them every four hours for range of motion.
   c. Notify the physician or medical practitioner that restraints were applied first thing in the morning.
   d. Ensure that a wrist restraint is tied with a knot that allows for quick release.

19. Which patient is at highest risk for elopement?
   a. A disoriented patient who recently had a stroke and currently has full left-sided paralysis
   b. A patient with dementia who was recently using their walker to open the exit door of the facility
   c. A patient with Alzheimer's who was seen recently pacing anxiously in their room
   d. A patient who is in active drug withdrawal after a motor vehicle accident resulting in a BKA

20. Which patient would be considered immunocompromised and at highest risk for infection?
   a. A patient who has recently given birth to twins
   b. A patient who is one week post lung transplant
   c. A patient who is two days post cardiac stent placement
   d. A patient undergoing severe drug withdrawal

21. The nursing assistant is using their stethoscope to check a patient's blood pressure manually and wants to determine the best way to clean the stethoscope afterward. The stethoscope is considered to be at what level of risk for infection?
   a. Low-risk
   b. Medium-risk
   c. Moderate-risk
   d. High-risk

22. What is the best way to prevent the spread of germs?
   a. Wear a properly fitted mask when around patients
   b. Wear gloves and a gown during each patient interaction
   c. Handwash with soap and water frequently
   d. Wipe down work areas with disinfectant at regular intervals

23. The nursing assistant is caring for a patient who has not been drinking an adequate amount of fluid over the past week. Which of the following symptoms might indicate dehydration?
   a. Constipation
   b. Blood pressure of 165/95
   c. Heart rate of 55 bpm
   d. Diaphoresis

24. The nursing assistant is caring for a patient who follows a Kosher diet. Which of the following trays would be appropriate to give them?
   a. Eggs, bacon, and toast
   b. Ham and cheese sandwich
   c. Cheeseburger with fries
   d. Steak with green beans

25. The nursing assistant is caring for a patient who is missing their back molars. Would they expect the patient be on a specific diet modification, and why?
   a. The patient does not need to be on a specific diet because they can eat using their remaining teeth.
   b. The patient should be on a softened diet to make chewing food easier.
   c. The patient should be on a diet with thickened liquids to prevent aspiration.
   d. The patient does not need to be on a specific diet because they can dice their food to chew more easily.

26. The nursing assistant gives the patient a meal tray with creamed spinach, brown rice with gravy, and diced meatloaf. This patient is likely on which therapeutic diet?
   a. Mechanical soft diet
   b. Full liquid diet
   c. Regular diet
   d. Clear liquid diet

27. Which of the following actions does NOT promote healthy sleep and rest for a patient?
   a. Assisting with ambulation during the day, if able
   b. Keeping the blinds closed during the day
   c. Grouping care activities together for the patient
   d. Discouraging the patient from excessive napping during the day

28. Which of the following bodily fluids should be counted towards a patient's output?
   a. Urine output only
   b. Urine and stool
   c. Urine, stool, and emesis
   d. Urine, stool, emesis, and saliva

29. The nursing assistant is helping a patient use the restroom during evening care. The nursing assistant should report which finding to the patient's nurse?
   a. The patient just had their third bowel movement of the day
   b. The patient's urine is clear and light yellow
   c. The patient's stool is formed and light brown
   d. The patient's urine has a fruity odor

30. The nursing assistant raises the head of a patient's bed to 40 degrees. In which position is the bed?
   a. Prone
   b. Semi-Fowler's
   c. Fowler's
   d. High Fowler's

31. The nursing assistant is caring for a patient with a prosthetic leg. Which finding should be reported to the nurse?
    a. Redness or irritation on the skin where the prosthesis attaches
    b. Phantom limb pain
    c. Muscle atrophy in the residual limb
    d. Request to use a walker while ambulating with their prosthesis

32. Which of the following represents proper technique for assisting a patient out of bed and into a chair?
    a. Adjust the bed's height so that the patient's feet are just above the floor when sitting up.
    b. Stand directly to the side of the patient.
    c. Firmly grasp the patient's forearms to help lift them up.
    d. Ensure that the back of the resident's knees are touching the front of the chair before they sit.

33. The nursing assistant is using a gait belt to walk with a patient who has been unsteady on their feet. If the patient begins to fall, which action should the nursing assistant take?
    a. Attempt to catch the patient around the waist before they fall.
    b. Fall with the patient to help cushion them and prevent injury.
    c. Hold the gait belt and slowly lower the resident to the ground.
    d. Attempt to cradle and cushion their head as they fall.

34. The nursing assistant is instructing a patient to pump their legs and arms independently throughout the day while in bed to keep their joints healthy and flexible. This is an example of which movement technique?
    a. Passive range of motion
    b. Active assisted range of motion
    c. Passive assisted range of motion
    d. Active range of motion

35. The nursing assistant is performing range of motion exercises with a patient who is in bed. They move the patient's arm laterally up towards their shoulder. This is an example of which kind of movement?
    a. Flexion
    b. Extension
    c. Abduction
    d. Adduction

36. What is the primary underlying cause of pressure ulcers?
    a. Bilateral weakness
    b. Poor circulation
    c. Compromised immune system
    d. Incontinence

37. The nursing assistant goes into a patient's room to measure their vital signs. Their vital signs are normal, but the patient complains of chest pain. What should the nursing assistant do?
   a. Notify the RN.
   b. Yell for help.
   c. Administer oxygen.
   d. Stay with the patient.

38. Which term means low blood pressure when moving from a sitting position to a standing position?
   a. Hypotension
   b. Hypertension
   c. Orthostatic hypotension
   d. Orthostatic hypertension

39. Working efficiently and correctly exemplifies which of the following?
   a. Time management
   b. Work ethic
   c. Health promotion
   d. Safety practices

40. The RN asks the nursing assistant to scan and administer a patient's medications. This action would be illegal in accordance with the CNA's:
   a. Job responsibilities
   b. Job requirements
   c. Scope of practice
   d. Ethics

41. Providing perineal care to a patient with a foley catheter is important for the prevention of:
   a. Kidney stones
   b. Urinary incontinence
   c. Dehydration
   d. Urinary tract infections

42. A newly admitted patient wears dentures, but his family hasn't brought them in yet. The patient may need which of the following?
   a. Mechanical soft diet
   b. Speech therapy evaluation
   c. A swallow study
   d. NPO until they have their dentures

43. When taking a patient's blood pressure on the upper arm, the arrow should be aligned with which of the following?
   a. The radial artery
   b. The brachial artery
   c. The femoral artery
   d. The popliteal artery

44. Which of the following is NOT a factor that contributes to patient falls?
    a. Gait
    b. Age
    c. Medications
    d. Height

45. Which of the following is equivalent to sleep apnea?
    a. Cardiac arrest
    b. Sleepwalking
    c. Breathing briefly stops
    d. Tachycardia

46. What is the most important action to protect patients from infection?
    a. Bathe patients daily.
    b. Wash hands frequently.
    c. Check vital signs.
    d. Give antibiotics.

47. A patient becomes combative and starts hitting staff members. The patient cannot legally be restrained unless there is:
    a. A doctor's order
    b. The nurse's permission
    c. A facility administrator's permission
    d. The patient's family's permission

48. The nursing assistant is the first to discover unusual bruising on a newly admitted patient. When asked what happened, the patient states that their daughter struck them while she was drunk. It is your legal obligation to notify which of the following?
    a. Coworkers
    b. Adult Protective Services
    c. The MD
    d. The patient's family

49. Which of the following requires only a gown and gloves?
    a. Reverse Isolation
    b. Advanced Droplet Precautions
    c. Airborne Precautions
    d. Standard Precautions

50. Skin tearing can cause all of the following EXCEPT:
    a. Infection
    b. Fractures
    c. Pressure ulcers
    d. Prolonged hospital stay

51. Common psychological disturbances in patients can include each of the following EXCEPT:
   a. Depression
   b. Attachment
   c. Anxiety
   d. Fear

52. Repositioning a quadriplegic patient is important to prevent pressure ulcers on which part of their body?
   a. Hands
   b. Legs
   c. Bony prominences
   d. Head

53. The nursing assistant is caring for a patient who is one day post-op from a lung resection. Which of the following signs would NOT indicate that the patient is in pain?
   a. The patient is sleeping with a grimace on their face
   b. The patient has turned onto their non-affected side
   c. The patient is less talkative than usual
   d. The patient has tensed the muscles in their body

54. Which of the following patients would be at highest risk of skin breakdown?
   a. A patient who is admitted for COPD exacerbation
   b. A patient who is three days post-op from a bowel resection
   c. A patient who is sedated and intubated
   d. A patient who has an indwelling urinary catheter

55. The nursing assistant is caring for a newly admitted patient with COPD who is on 2 LPM of supplemental oxygen via nasal cannula. During the initial assessment, the patient's oxygen saturation is found to be 89%. What is the most appropriate action for the nursing assistant to take first?
   a. Record the finding since this is normal for a patient with COPD
   b. Increase the oxygen to 3 LPM and recheck the oxygen saturation
   c. Replace the nasal cannula with a new one and set it back to 2 LPM
   d. Notify the patient's nurse of the oxygen saturation

56. The nursing assistant is performing a bed bath and morning care on an immobile patient with a sacral pressure ulcer, indwelling urinary catheter, and a colostomy bag. They know they need to complete bed baths and care for four other patients this morning. Which of the following actions by the nursing assistant could put the patient's care and comfort at risk?
   a. Emptying the colostomy bag completely at the start of care
   b. Completing the first bed bath within ten minutes to stay on schedule for the morning
   c. Repositioning the patient on their right-side using wedges
   d. Cleaning the catheter tubing in a circular motion

57. Which of the following is NOT a manifestation or symptom of depression in an adult?
   a. Hyperactivity
   b. Binge eating
   c. Distortion of reality
   d. Insomnia

58. The nursing assistant is caring for a patient with an anxiety disorder. Which of the following should they incorporate into care of this patient?
   a. Exposure therapy
   b. Avoidance of sedative medication
   c. A controlled environment
   d. Regular exercise

59. A patient in an acute state of mental confusion is seen lying in bed all day and appears to be sluggish and dull. This patient likely has which psychological disorder?
   a. Hyperactive delirium
   b. Dementia
   c. Hypoactive delirium
   d. Mixed delirium

60. The nursing assistant is caring for a 65-year-old patient who was admitted to a mental health unit after a panic attack. They see the nurse give the patient a beta blocker, but the patient does not have any history of cardiac conditions. Should the nursing assistant take action?
   a. Yes, immediately notify the nurse of a possible medication error
   b. No, a beta blocker is given to all patients over 60 years old
   c. No, a beta blocker is often used in treatments for anxiety
   d. Yes, instruct the patient not to take the medication and notify the charge nurse

Answer Explanations #3

1. C: Keeping your back straight when lifting heavy objects and moving patients is part of proper body mechanics. The other choices represent poor body mechanics that can be dangerous.

2. B: Joining an activity that promotes exercise is an example of positive self-care. Although the remaining examples may be common ways that a nursing assistant can cope with the stress of the job, these are negative coping mechanisms that can be damaging in the long term.

3. D: These are all examples of positive coping mechanisms that can help nursing assistants deal with the daily stress of their jobs. Self-care can help nursing assistants cope with physical, mental, and emotional stress.

4. A: The Health Insurance Portability and Accountability Act (HIPAA) protects the resident's rights to privacy with their health information. Choice A is a proper discussion of patient care as the nurse and nursing assistant are both directly caring for the patient and may discuss relevant results. The remaining choices are incorrect and not HIPAA-compliant because private medical information about a patient is being discussed with individuals who are not involved in the patient's medical care.

5. C: Although the nursing assistant should encourage their patients to stay well-nourished, patients have the right to make their own decisions regarding their care. This is an example of the patient's right to self-determination. The remaining choices are rights of the patient that the nursing assistant should be familiar with; however, they are not the rights described in this question.

6. B: A patient who has new, unexplained pain when sitting and new bleeding in the perineal area may be experiencing sexual abuse. The patient was also recently visited by their partner, who could likely be the abuser. Physical, emotional, and financial abuse are other types of abuse that the nursing assistant should be aware can happen in the hospital. Physical abuse involves bodily injury from kicking, punching, or hitting that may cause bruising, bleeding, or cuts. Sexual abuse is similar, as it can be physical in nature; however, this type of abuse specifically involves sexual acts, rape, coercion, fondling of genitalia, or any other sexual contact without consent. Emotional abuse is often less noticeable, but it is usually caused by verbal assaults intended to make the victim feel fearful, ashamed, worthless, and insecure. Financial abuse involves limiting an individual's access to their money, stealing directly from the victim, or accessing a vulnerable person's financial information.

7. A: Bruising on wrists as well as apparently fearful reactions to medical staff can be indicative of abuse; this concern should be reported to the nurse manager or charge nurse. Additionally, there are hotlines that can be called to report suspected abuse. Although it is important to treat the bruises for the patient's comfort, Choice B ignores the signs of abuse. Choice C may be seen as intimidating or confrontational to the patient and may cause them to not trust the medical team. Choice D is incorrect because the first step should be to notify the nurse manager or charge nurse, and the nursing assistant should not confront the suspected abuser.

8. C: Verbally assaulting, criticizing, and using language to make a victim feel worthless, insecure, fearful, and belittled are examples of emotional/mental abuse. This abuse should be monitored, investigated, and reported through proper channels.

9. B: Asking for assistance in a professional situation and complimenting the new nurse in a non-offensive manner are proper ways for the nursing assistant to help create a welcoming environment and honor diversity in the workplace. The other choices may alienate the employee, make false assumptions about their culture, make them feel unwelcome, or appropriate their culture.

10. A: The correct chain of command for reporting information is nursing assistant, nurse involved in the patient's care, charge nurse, nurse manager, nurse director or chief nursing officer (CNO). Following the proper chain of command for reporting helps assure that the issue is resolved quickly by the person most equipped to handle it.

11. B: If a conflict with coworkers cannot be mitigated and resolved by the charge nurse on shift, the conflict should follow the chain of command. Therefore, the nurse manager should be notified next.

12. B: The first step of any patient transfer should be to explain to the patient what you will be doing and the steps they will need to take. The remaining choices are all part of a transfer from bed to wheelchair, but these steps should occur after a patient is educated on what they will be doing.

13. D: Wearing rubber-soled shoes can help patients have better grip and reduce slipping, which will decrease the likelihood of falling. Choice *A* is incorrect because having rugs on the floor may be a tripping hazard. Choice *B* is incorrect because low lighting may make it more difficult for a patient to see objects in the room that could cause them to trip or fall. Although it is important for patients to ambulate when appropriate to build strength, Choice *C* is incorrect because patients who are fall risks should walk with assistance and not independently in case of a fall.

14. A: This patient is receiving minimum assistance because they need some support when moving about and require a gait belt, an additional ambulation device. Choice *B* is incorrect because maximum assistance is when a patient cannot walk or stand independently at all and would require two or more staff members for assistance. Choice *C* is incorrect because standby assistance is when a patient can independently move or walk without the need of a gait belt or ambulatory device, but still requires someone to stand by in case they need assistance. Choice *D* is incorrect because contact-guard assistance is when a patient can independently walk but is at high risk for falls and needs an assistant to be within reach in case the patient becomes unsteady or falls.

15. C: Proper technique for using a walker without wheels is to keep the weight on the stronger leg and take a step forward with the weaker leg while holding onto the walker. Choice *A* is incorrect because the patient should stand inside the walker, not behind it. Choice *B* is incorrect because a walker without wheels should be lifted and moved forward with each step, not pushed on the ground. Choice *D* is incorrect because the patient should step to the center of the space in the walker when taking a step.

16. D: A patient who is unable to bear weight on one leg, either due to fractures, pain, or amputation, should use a three-point crutch gait. Choice *A* is incorrect because a two-point crutch gait is used for poor coordination and weakness in both legs. Choice *B* is incorrect because a swing-through crutch gait is used for inability for both legs to bear weight. Choice *C* is incorrect because a swing-to crutch gait is used for weakness in both legs.

17. A: Having a staff member sit with and watch a patient is not considered a type of restraint and is a technique that can be utilized before having to escalate to restraint use. Giving patients medication to alter their behavior is considered a chemical restraint, so Choice *B* is incorrect. Raising the side rails on a patient's bed is considered a physical restraint, so Choice *C* is incorrect. Using verbal or emotional cues

to coerce a patient into acting a certain way is considered an emotional restraint, so Choice *D* is incorrect.

18. D: Any physical restraint, such as a wrist, ankle, or vest restraint, must be tied with a quick-release knot in case of any potential injury or danger. Choice *A* is incorrect because regardless of medical condition, mental state, or a patient's perceived or actual ability to understand, an explanation for what is being done to a patient with restraints is required. Choice *B* is incorrect because positioning of restraints should be checked every thirty minutes and restraints should be removed for range of motion every two hours. Choice *C* is incorrect because restraints need an order from a physician or medical practitioner to be applied. In some cases, restraints can be applied without an order in an emergency; however, the physician or medical practitioner should be notified immediately after.

19. C: A patient who is confused or has an altered mental status and can ambulate without any assistive devices is at highest risk of elopement. The patient in Choice *C* has Alzheimer's, which can cause confusion, and was seen ambulating in his room. Although the remaining choices have situations where patients have some level of mental confusion, they are not able to walk independently or may have to use assistive ambulatory devices and therefore have a lesser chance of elopement.

20. B: A patient who has had a recent tissue transplant, including a lung transplant, would be considered immunocompromised and most susceptible to infection. Other conditions that may cause a person to be immunocompromised include AIDS, cancer, immune system disorders, and old age. The conditions described in the remaining choices would not make a patient immunocompromised.

21. A: Stethoscopes and high-contact surfaces such as tabletops and doorknobs are considered low-risk items and can be cleaned with regular detergent. Choice *B* is incorrect because medium-risk items are those that come into contact with the mucous membrane, such as oral thermometers or respiratory equipment. Choice *C* is incorrect because moderate-risk is not one of the risk levels for infection. Choice *D* is incorrect because high-risk items come into contact with broken or open skin, such as instruments used in surgeries and procedures.

22. C: The best way to prevent the spread of germs is regular handwashing with soap and water, including before and after seeing patients and when hands are visibly dirty. The remaining choices may be appropriate to help reduce infection depending on the patient's condition, but they are not the best way to prevent spread of germs.

23. A: Constipation may be a common sign of dehydration because there is less water in the stool, making it harder to pass. Choice *B* is incorrect because this blood pressure is considered elevated, and low blood pressure is a sign of dehydration. Choice *C* is incorrect because this is a low heart rate, and a rapid heart rate is a sign of dehydration. Choice *D* is incorrect because *diaphoretic* means having sweaty and damp skin, but dry skin is a sign of dehydration.

24. D: Steak and green beans would be appropriate for a patient on a Kosher diet. Patients on Kosher diets cannot eat pork, shellfish, certain birds, or meat and dairy together. The remaining choices would not be appropriate because they do not follow the Kosher diet guidelines.

25. B: A patient who is missing teeth may have difficulty chewing and should be given a softened diet that makes it easier for them to chew and safer to swallow. Choice *A* is incorrect because this patient should be on a modified diet and may not be able to chew comfortably or properly with their remaining teeth. Choice *C* is incorrect because a patient who is missing teeth does not require thickened liquids, as

they can still swallow properly. Although cutting food up into finer pieces may make it easier to eat, the patient still cannot effectively chew their food before swallowing and could choke; therefore, Choice *D* is incorrect.

26. A: These foods all have a puree-like consistency and would therefore be part of a mechanical soft diet. Choice *B* is incorrect because a full liquid diet consists of any clear liquid or liquid that can be consumed through a straw, such as soups or meal replacement shakes. Choice *C* is incorrect because a regular diet would mean there were no dietary restrictions or modifications. Choice *D* is incorrect because a clear liquid diet consists of any clear liquids such as water, coffee, clear broth, and tea without any added milk or cream.

27. B: Keeping the blinds closed during the day can cause the patient to become disoriented as to whether it is day or night, therefore making restful sleep during the night more difficult. The remaining choices are all examples of how to help promote healthy and restful sleep.

28. C: The nursing assistant should count urine, stool, and emesis for a patient's bodily fluid output. Properly tracking input and output can help see if there is any imbalance that may be of concern. It is not necessary to track saliva output.

29. D: Urine with fruity odor could be a sign that there is glucose in the urine, which means that the patient could have a very elevated blood glucose level. This should be reported to the nurse. The remaining choice are all normal findings with elimination.

30. B: Semi-Fowler's position is when the head of the bed is between 30 and 45 degrees. Prone position is when the patient is lying on their stomach with their head turned to the side, so Choice *A* is incorrect. Fowler's position is when the head of the bed is between 45 to 60 degrees, so Choice *C* is incorrect. High Fowler's position is when the head of the bed is 60 to 90 degrees, so Choice *D* is incorrect.

31. A: The nursing assistant should report any redness or irritation that is found where the prosthetic limb contacts the patient's skin. This can be a sign that the limb does not fit properly and can lead to skin breakdown, discomfort, and infection. Choices *B* and *C* are incorrect because phantom limb pain and muscle atrophy in the residual limb are expected findings. Choice *D* is incorrect because many patients with prosthetic legs prefer or require use of additional assistive devices to ambulate safely and comfortably.

32. D: The nursing assistant should make sure that the back of the patient's knees are touching the front of the chair. This ensures that the patient knows where the chair is and will not accidentally miss the chair when sitting down. Choice *A* is incorrect because the height of the bed should be lowered completely so the patient's feet are firmly planted on the ground. Choice *B* is incorrect because the nursing assistant should stand directly in front of the patient with their knees on the outside of the patient's knees. Choice *C* is incorrect because the nursing assistant should grasp the patient underneath the arms when lifting. Attempting to lift the patient by their elbows, forearms, or wrists can cause injury to the patient and will not be as effective.

33. C: If a patient begins to fall while wearing a gait belt, the nursing assistant should retain a firm grasp of the belt and help slowly lower the patient to the ground. This ensures the safety of both the patient and the nursing assistant. The remaining choices are incorrect because those methods could cause further injury to the patient and/or the nursing assistant.

34. D: A patient who is independently performing exercises in bed to help maintain the health and flexibility of their joints is doing active range of motion exercises. Choice *A* is incorrect because passive range of motion are exercises for patients who cannot move their limbs independently; therefore, the nursing assistant moves their limbs for them. Choice *B* is incorrect because active assisted range of motion is when the patient can partially move their limbs but needs additional help from the nursing assistant. Choice *C* is incorrect because passive assisted range of motion is not a type of exercise.

35. C: The movement of a limb away from the body's midline is called abduction. Choice *A* is incorrect because flexion is the bending of a limb at the joint. Choice *B* is incorrect because extension is straightening of a limb at the joint. Choice *D* is incorrect because adduction is the movement of a limb towards the midline of the body.

36. B: The main underlying cause of pressure ulcers or bed sores is poor circulation. When blood cannot adequately perfuse areas of the body, especially bony prominences, the skin is unable to receive the proper nutrients and blood flow needed to keep the skin alive and healthy. The remaining choices can make a person more susceptible to pressure ulcers but are not the underlying cause.

37. A: The nursing assistant should notify the RN. Because the patient's vital signs are stable, the nursing assistant has time to leave the room to do so. The CNA may not start oxygen therapy; only the nurse or respiratory therapist can. The nursing assistant does not need to stay with the patient once the RN is notified.

38. C: Orthostatic hypotension is low blood pressure that results from moving from a seated to a standing position.

39. A: Working efficiently but correctly is an effective means of time management. Work ethic refers to the quality of one's work as well as one's diligence. Health promotion is a strategy to prevent illness. Safety practices are interventions that can be utilized to keep patients free from harm.

40. C: The scope of practice for licensed individuals has lists of duties which they are legally permitted to do. The CNA may not administer medications, even if an RN requests it.

41. D: Perineal care is important to prevent a urinary tract infection, especially for patients with a foley catheter, because bacteria can get on the catheter and cause infection. Perineal care will not prevent incontinence; in fact, the catheter is necessary to manage incontinence to begin with. Perineal care also does not prevent kidney stones or dehydration. Kidney stone prevention requires drinking plenty of water and avoiding certain foods. Dehydration can also be prevented by increased water intake through food and drink.

42. A: The patient may need a mechanical soft diet if they do not have their dentures. A mechanical soft diet is made up of foods that are easier to swallow, therefore making it easier for the patient to eat safely. Neither speech therapy nor a swallow study is necessary unless there is evidence that the patient has choked or aspirated. The patient does not need to be NPO without their dentures because they can still safely eat foods with soft textures.

43. B: The brachial artery should be aligned with the arrow on the blood pressure cuff. The radial artery is in the wrist, the femoral artery is in the groin, and the popliteal artery is in the foot/ankle region.

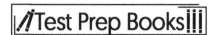

44. D: Height is not considered to be a risk factor for falls. Gait, or the patient's walking pattern, and advanced age are risk factors. Additionally, some medications can make patients prone to falls.

45. C: Sleep apnea is when a patient briefly stops breathing while they are asleep.

46. B: Handwashing is the best way to prevent infection from passing from caregiver to patient. Bathing a patient daily can help to reduce bacteria, but it is not as effective as handwashing. Checking a patient's vital signs does not help to prevent infection. Giving antibiotics can help heal an infection, not prevent one.

47. A: A patient may not be restrained without a doctor's order, even if the family, the administration, or the RN state that the patient should be restrained.

48. B: Nursing assistants have a duty to report suspected abuse to state authorities, or Adult Protective Services.

49. D: Standard Precautions require only a gown and gloves. In Reverse Isolation, gowns, gloves, and medical masks must be worn. Droplet Precautions require surgical masks, gloves, and gowns. Airborne Precautions require an N95 mask, eye protection, a gown, and gloves.

50. B: Fractures are not caused by skin tears. Skin tears can cause infection through the opening of the skin or through pressure ulcers if the skin tears happen on bony prominences. Skin tears could also potentially prolong hospitalization if wound care is needed or becomes complicated.

51. B: Attachment is not a psychological disturbance.

52. C: Bony prominences are the most likely areas to have skin breakdown because there is more pressure on these locations, and they are more likely to be immobilized. The hands, legs, and head are less likely to form pressure ulcers because there is less pressure on these locations, and they are usually more mobile.

53. B: A patient repositioning themselves would not indicate that they are in pain. It may be a positive sign that the patient can reposition themselves without assistance. The remaining examples are incorrect because they are all indications that a patient may be in pain, even if they are observed while the patient is sleeping or are not outrightly expressed by the patient. Pain can present very differently in patients, so it is important that the nursing assistant can recognize uncommon or non-verbal signs.

54. C: A sedated patient is bedbound and unable to reposition themselves. Immobile patients are at a higher risk of skin breakdown because they may be laying on pressure points for longer periods of time and have poor circulation throughout their bodies. The remaining choices describe scenarios that would not alone put a patient at higher risk of skin breakdown.

55. D: The normal oxygen saturation for a patient is 93-100%. 89% is an abnormal finding and should be reported to the nurse immediately. Choice *A* is incorrect because although patients with COPD may have their baseline oxygen saturation in the high 80s, this is a newly admitted patient who has not had a baseline established. This finding should still be reported immediately to the nurse. Choice *B* is incorrect because it is outside of the scope of practice to increase or decrease a patient's supplemental oxygen flow rate. Choice *C* is incorrect because the nurse should be notified first of the abnormal oxygen saturation reading before attempting to change the nasal cannula.

56. B: Attempting to rush through activities or care can make the nursing assistant more likely to make a mistake and cause harm to a patient. The nursing assistant should still work efficiently, but make sure not to rush and give themselves the time to complete each task properly and safely. The remaining choices are examples of proper care techniques and exhibit ways that the nursing assistant can help promote the care, safety, and comfort of patients.

57. A: Hyperactivity is not an expected manifestation of depression in adults; in fact, most adults with depression may experience hypoactivity and lethargy instead. The remaining choices are incorrect because they are common manifestations and symptoms of depression. Some additional signs and symptoms of depression are sleep disturbance, loss of appetite, loss of interest in daily habits, poor hygiene, lack of motivation, and sadness.

58. D: A patient with anxiety is often recommended to have regular exercise and adopt healthy eating habits. Choice *A* is incorrect because exposure therapy is often used in the treatment of certain phobias. Choice *B* is incorrect because a patient with severe anxiety or panic attacks may benefit from sedative medication. Choice *C* is incorrect because controlling a patient's environment is more useful in the treatment of delirium or dementia and may not be beneficial for the patient with anxiety.

59. C: A patient in a sudden or acute state of mental confusion that is lethargic, dull, or sluggish is considered to have hypoactive delirium. Choice *A* is incorrect because hyperactive delirium is a sudden or acute state of mental confusion, but the patient is restless, has difficulty staying focused on one task, and may be up and pacing. Choice *B* is incorrect because dementia is a state of mental confusion that comes on slowly and is progressive in nature. Choice *D* is incorrect because mixed delirium is sudden or acute mental confusion, but the patient may go through episodes of being hypoactive and hyperactive.

60. C: Although beta blockers are commonly used for cardiac conditions, they can also be used when treating the physical manifestations of anxiety. Choices *A* and *D* are incorrect because the nursing assistant does not need to take any immediate action. If the nursing assistant does have any concern about medications, it can still be brought to the attention of the nurse; in this scenario, it does not need to be done urgently. Choice *B* is incorrect because beta blockers are not given to all patients over 60; they are given to patients who have certain medical conditions, such as anxiety.

Practice Test #4

1. A patient was admitted to the emergency room after a motor vehicle accident. They were asked to change into a gown, take off their jewelry for an MRI, and place their belongings in a designated bag. Where is the most appropriate location to store the patient's belongings?
   a. Nurse's mobile cart
   b. Staff breakroom
   c. Behind the receptionist's desk
   d. Closet of the patient's room

2. A nursing assistant is frustrated with her hospital system's new policy on PTO. She posts a status update on a social media account that explains her frustrations, in which she states that the hospital system does not care about their employees. Which of the following best describes this action?
   a. This is unethical behavior because the nursing assistant should abide by a standard of professionalism that includes avoiding social media posts that may slander her work organization.
   b. This is ethical behavior because the nursing assistant has right to voice her concerns how she sees fit.
   c. This is ethical behavior because most of the nursing assistant's followers on social media also work for the same healthcare system.
   d. This is unethical behavior because the nursing assistant should not share details of her pay or PTO to the public.

3. Prior to employment, what must a nursing assistant have as proof of their licensure?
   a. A copy of their nursing assistant program's certificate signifying completion
   b. A copy of their full transcript from their nursing assistant program
   c. Enrollment in the Nurse Aide Registry
   d. Enrollment in the state Board of Nursing

4. What infraction would NOT cause a hiring organization to further review or deny a nursing assistant's job application?
   a. Previous incident of neglecting a patient
   b. A DUI when the nursing assistant was twenty-two years old
   c. Failed first attempt of CNA exam
   d. A previous employer showing proof of the nursing assistant's poor work ethic and attitude

5. Which task is appropriate for the nursing assistant to complete without additional training?
   a. Taking blood pressure measurements q4h
   b. Insertion of a foley catheter
   c. Removal of an IV
   d. Giving an anti-nausea medication as instructed by the nurse

6. The nursing assistant is asked by the nurse to give blood pressure medication to one of their patients while they deal with another patient's emergency. The nurse tells the nursing assistant that they will just chart that the nurse gave the medication in the computer. What is the most appropriate action for the nursing assistant to take?
   a. Give the medication exactly as the nurse instructed them to since it was already charted.
   b. Contact their supervisor to clarify their policy on medication administration and do not give the medication.
   c. Give the medication exactly as the nurse instructed but also let the charge nurse know.
   d. Dispose of the medication because the patient's recent blood pressure reading was within normal limits.

7. One of the interdisciplinary team members you encounter is seen teaching your patient, who had a tracheostomy, different techniques for safe eating and swallowing. Based on this description, you can assume that this team member most likely has which role?
   a. Physical therapist
   b. Respiratory therapist
   c. Occupational therapist
   d. Speech therapist

8. The nursing assistant is caring for a patient who is an aspiration risk and was recently coughing while eating and drinking. Which intervention is appropriate for the nursing assistant to provide as part of their plan of care?
   a. Perform a swallow study to see if the patient is still aspirating food and drink.
   b. Report to the nurse that the patient's coughing after eating is worsening.
   c. Lower the head of the bed when the patient is eating and drinking.
   d. Give the patient medication to help suppress their cough.

9. What are the three main components of basic communication?
   a. Tone, message, receiver
   b. Sender, tone, context
   c. Sender, message, receiver
   d. Context, sender, receiver

10. Which is NOT an example of a physical barrier that may negatively affect therapeutic communication?
   a. Using a phone to call the hospital's medical translator to explain a procedure to a patient who only speaks French
   b. Confirming DNR status with a patient who has had a recent change in their level of consciousness
   c. Giving written discharge instructions to a patient with cataracts
   d. Getting verbal consent for an upcoming surgery from a patient who recently had a stroke with aphasia

11. Which of the following is a good example of using therapeutic communication with patients?
   a. Avoid asking personal questions that might make the patient feel uncomfortable
   b. Ask simple "yes" or "no" questions
   c. Ask "why" questions to get more information from the patient
   d. Use silence to get clarification from a patient

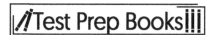

12. The nursing assistant just finished cleaning up a patient with Clostridium difficile after they had a bowel movement in their bed. What is the best way for the nursing assistant to ensure that they are properly disinfected after completing this task?
   a. Use the hand sanitizer as they leave the room
   b. Don a clean surgical mask
   c. Use bleach wipes on their hands as they leave
   d. Wash their hands with soap and water after leaving

13. Which of the following would indicate to a nursing assistant that their patient may have a systemic infection?
   a. Drainage from a wound
   b. Nausea and vomiting
   c. Redness and swelling around a wound
   d. Localized pain

14. The nursing assistant is taking care of a patient who has a serious head injury. Which symptoms would they NOT expect the patient to have?
   a. Unequal pupils
   b. Shortness of breath
   c. Persistent vomiting
   d. Restlessness and irritability

15. The nursing assistant is taking care of a patient who has influenza. Which transmission-based precaution should they take?
   a. Airborne precaution
   b. Contact precaution
   c. Standard precaution
   d. Droplet precaution

16. Which of the following shows the correct order for removing PPE?
   a. Mask, goggles, gown, gloves
   b. Gloves, gown, mask, goggles
   c. Gloves, goggles, gown, mask
   d. Goggles, mask, gown, gloves

17. When caring for a patient, the nursing assistant is trying to perform their tasks in order from clean to dirty. Which of the following is an example of a dirty task that should be completed last?
   a. Providing oral care
   b. Boosting a patient in their bed
   c. Feeding a patient
   d. Checking urine output on a continent patient

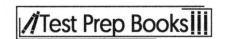

18. The nursing assistant is alerted that a severe thunderstorm is approaching their facility. Which of the following is an important task for the nursing assistant to complete that will ensure safety of the staff, residents, and visitors?
    a. Instruct a few staff members to watch at the windows for signs of the storm approaching
    b. Place the landline phone in each room next to the patient so they can call for an emergency
    c. Ensure that no patients are currently taking baths or showers
    d. Try to finish charting on the computer as quickly as possible in case the power goes out

19. After lunch trays are served, a nursing assistant sees a patient grasping at their throat, unable to speak. The nursing assistant asks if they are choking, and the patient nods their head yes. What would NOT be an appropriate action to take at this time?
    a. Shout for help and begin CPR
    b. Assist the patient to a standing position
    c. Stand behind patient and place hands above the patient's belly button
    d. Thrust upward quickly on the patient's stomach

20. The nursing assistant comes upon a patient in a nursing home who appears to have cut their wrist accidentally on a piece of broken glass. What is a correct action to take?
    a. Assist the patient to a standing position
    b. Talk to the patient to monitor consciousness
    c. Loosely apply gauze around the wound
    d. Have the patient hold their wrist down at their side

21. A nursing assistant is helping take care of a newly admitted patient who was started on an antibiotic for pneumonia. The patient is having difficulty breathing, feels nauseous, and states that their tongue feels swollen. After taking a set of vitals, the nursing assistant sees that the patient's heart rate is 120 bpm, and their blood pressure is 85/50. Based on these symptoms, the nursing assistant suspects that the patient is experiencing which of the following medical emergencies?
    a. Poisoning
    b. Cardiac Arrest
    c. Respiratory Arrest
    d. Allergic reaction

22. Which of the following is NOT a correct step to follow in the case of a fire?
    a. Rescue yourself and others from the fire
    b. Activate the fire alarm
    c. Attempt to extinguish the fire
    d. Open windows in the area surrounding the fire

23. The nursing assistant is caring for a patient with a pressure ulcer. Which action should they NOT take when providing care?
    a. Massage bony prominences.
    b. Keep the skin dry.
    c. Reposition every two hours.
    d. Use wedges to reposition.

24. A patient has a bedsore that has caused partial thickness skin loss through several layers of skin. The bedsore has blistering and abrasions around the borders. This bedsore is at which stage?
   a. Stage I
   b. Stage II
   c. Stage III
   d. Stage IV

25. The nursing assistant is caring for a patient who complains of pain in their calf. They observe redness and swelling in the calf as well. What is the most appropriate action for the nursing assistant to take?
   a. Encourage bed rest.
   b. Massage the affected calf gently.
   c. Notify the nurse of the new findings.
   d. Reposition the patient every two hours.

26. A patient with limited mobility who is at risk for deep vein thrombosis (DVT) should be given which medical device to help reduce risk?
   a. Walker
   b. Trapeze bar
   c. Wedge and cushions
   d. Sequential compression devices

27. An immobile patient is reluctant to increase their fluid intake because they cannot use the toilet by themselves. They express concern that they will become incontinent and make a mess. What is the best initial response from the nursing assistant?
   a. Reassure the patient that they will be available for their toileting needs.
   b. Always have them on a bedpan so they can use it freely.
   c. Suggest to the nurse that they may benefit from an indwelling catheter.
   d. Understand that it is the patient's right to refuse fluids.

28. The nursing assistant is caring for an immobile patient. While performing passive range of motion exercises, the patient says that their elbow feels very stiff to movement. This observation indicates that the patient may have which medical condition?
   a. Contractures
   b. Atrophy
   c. Localized infection
   d. Pressure sore

29. The nursing assistant helps reposition a patient every hour at their request, using wedges and cushions. These actions help promote which aspect of care for the patient?
   a. Self-image
   b. Activity tolerance
   c. Comfort
   d. Strength and endurance

30. During morning care, a patient tells the nursing assistant a story about their grandkid's birthday party from a few years ago and recounted the gifts they received. The nursing assistant comes a few hours later to serve the lunch tray and asks to hear more stories about the patient's grandchildren. The patient now has difficulty remembering their names and is slurring their words as they speak. What is the most appropriate action for the nursing assistant to take?
   a. Don't rush the patient and allow them time to speak at their pace.
   b. Tell the patient they will come back again once they are more rested.
   c. Reassure the patient that they are experiencing normal cognitive changes.
   d. Notify the nurse of the changes in the patient's cognition.

31. An elderly patient in a long-term care facility expresses frustration that they are having difficulty with their memory, can no longer move around independently, and cannot see their family members as frequently. What can the nurse do to help the patient adjust to the psychosocial changes they are experiencing?
   a. Assist the patient with regular ambulation and daily exercise.
   b. Help the patient print pictures of his family to have in his room.
   c. Play games with them that help improve their memory.
   d. Encourage the patient to use a walker when ambulating to promote independence.

32. The nursing assistant is explaining common physical changes that a patient may experience as they age. Which of the following is NOT an expected physical change for an elderly patient?
   a. Urinary retention
   b. Increased digestion
   c. Decreased skin moisture
   d. Decrease sense of smell

33. In Maslow's Hierarchy of Needs, what is considered the second most basic need?
   a. Safety
   b. Physiological needs
   c. Self-actualization
   d. Esteem

34. Feeling a sense of responsibility to work and being able to build a positive reputation is an example of which need from Maslow's Hierarchy?
   a. Social need
   b. Safety need
   c. Self-actualization need
   d. Esteem need

35. A patient expresses frustration to the nursing assistant, stating that they feel like they've lost independence and control since living in a long-term care facility. What is the most appropriate response from the nursing assistant?
   a. Explain that this is a normal change to experience.
   b. Suggest to the nurse that the patient may need medication for anxiety.
   c. Encourage them to participate in planning their daily routine.
   d. Allow them to start ambulating independently.

36. The nursing assistant is caring for an elderly patient whose health has been declining over the past few weeks. They notice that the patient's muscles have been shrinking and they no longer have the strength to assist with turning. This is an example of what health condition?
   a. Paralysis
   b. Muscular dystrophy
   c. Atrophy
   d. Contractures

37. Which of the following is a strategy that the nursing assistant can use to help prevent falls?
   a. Checking on the patient every two hours
   b. Asking the family to check on the patient
   c. Restraining the patient
   d. Turning down the lights

38. What is an effective alternative to using restraints?
   a. Sitting with the patient
   b. Calling security
   c. Sedating the patient
   d. Encouraging the patient to leave the facility

39. The nursing assistant is assessing a patient's level of orientation. The patient states her name, that it is 1948, that she is in the hospital, and that she is there because she forgot her car. Her level of orientation should be charted as:
   a. Alert and oriented x 1
   b. Alert and oriented x 2
   c. Alert and oriented x 3
   d. Alert and oriented x 4

40. Which of the following is an assistive device for mobility?
   a. Physical therapy
   b. Occupational therapy
   c. Crutches
   d. Restraints

41. Which of the following does NOT describe working together as part of a healthcare team?
   a. Initiative
   b. Collaboration
   c. Cooperation
   d. Interdependence

42. The nursing assistant is helping a patient with ambulation. The patient is designated as a 1 assist, meaning they can get up and move around with the assistance of one person, but they are slightly unsteady on their feet. What can be utilized to assist them?
   a. A bed alarm
   b. A Hoyer lift
   c. A gait belt
   d. A wheelchair

43. Which of the following can the nursing assistant avoid by using proper body mechanics when assisting patients?
    a. Back and neck injuries
    b. Falls
    c. Infection
    d. Conflict

44. A patient's blood pressure is 70/40. Earlier, it was 130/80. When should the nursing assistant report this to the RN?
    a. When they are finished taking all their patients' vital signs
    b. Immediately
    c. Not at all; the patient is acting normal
    d. Not at all; they should notify the MD

45. Which of the following conditions would cause a low blood pressure reading?
    a. Hypertension
    b. Hyperglycemia
    c. Hypotension
    d. Hypoglycemia

46. Which of the following is NOT a cause of chest pain?
    a. GERD
    b. Coronary Artery Disease (CAD)
    c. Kidney failure
    d. Pleurisy

47. What is another word for long-term conditions or illnesses?
    a. Emergent
    b. Chronic
    c. Acute
    d. Urgent

48. A patient who wanders away from a nursing home or hospital has engaged in:
    a. Refusing treatment
    b. Leaving AMA
    c. Confusion
    d. Elopement

49. A patient scratches and hits the nursing assistant. What should the nursing assistant do?
    a. Restrain the patient.
    b. Ask the nurse to sedate the patient.
    c. Notify the MD.
    d. Notify the supervisor.

50. TED hose help to prevent which of the following?
   a. Blood clots
   b. Circulation
   c. Difficulty breathing
   d. Falls

51. A patient has a pressure ulcer on their sacrum. The nursing assistant should suggest that the patient receive which of the following?
   a. A bath
   b. Routine repositioning
   c. Pain medicine
   d. A specialty mattress

52. At the beginning of a shift, the nursing assistant receives a report that one patient had a blood pressure of 80/40 and was lethargic. What should the ongoing nursing assistant do?
   a. Begin assessing their patients in order of room number.
   b. Check on the patient immediately.
   c. Do nothing; the RN is already aware.
   d. Save this patient for last since they will probably need the most care.

53. A patient is admitted to the hospital following a car crash while drinking and driving. On the second day of admission, the patient is noted to have tremors, delirium, anxiety, and increased heart rate. This patient's symptoms are most likely related to which condition?
   a. Dementia
   b. Myocardial infarction (MI)
   c. PTSD
   d. Alcohol withdrawal

54. Maximizing quality of life and long-term comfort for a patient with a life-limiting disease is the focus of which kind of care?
   a. Curative care
   b. Palliative care
   c. Urgent care
   d. Long-term care

55. Which of the following represents the proper order for the five stages of grief according to the Kubler-Ross model?
   a. Denial, bargaining, depression, anger, acceptance
   b. Bargaining, denial, anger, depression, acceptance
   c. Denial, depression, bargaining, acceptance, depression
   d. Depression, anger, bargaining, denial, acceptance

56. The nursing assistant is caring for a patient who just received a diagnosis of terminal cancer. Which of the following is an appropriate therapeutic response to tell this patient?
   a. "Everything will be okay soon."
   b. "Tell me about how you're feeling with this new diagnosis."
   c. "I will try to help you avoid any grief."
   d. "I'm sure you will beat this."

57. The nursing assistant is planning to start post-mortem care after a Hindu patient has passed away. The family requests to clean their family member's body themselves. What is the most appropriate response from the nursing assistant?
   a. Explain that it is preferred for the nursing assistant to complete this care.
   b. Allow only one family member to assist the nursing assistant.
   c. Allow the patient's family member to provide care and wash the patient.
   d. Notify the charge nurse that the family does not want you to complete care for the patient.

58. A nursing assistant is caring for a patient who is expected to pass within the next few days. The patient has been asleep for most of the day and is more difficult to arouse. What is the most appropriate action to take when coming to provide perineal care?
   a. Continue to let the patient know what they are doing even if the patient is still asleep.
   b. Try to stay as quiet as possible, allowing the patient to continue sleeping.
   c. Turn the lights on and speak in a loud, clear voice to wake the patient up.
   d. Come back later when the patient is awake.

59. The nursing assistant is providing post-mortem care for a patient who recently passed. During care, the patient sounds like they gasp, and their arm twitches. What is the best action for the nursing assistant to take in response?
   a. Initiate CPR and call a code.
   b. Immediately notify the nurse.
   c. Obtain a set of vitals and notify the nurse.
   d. Continue post-mortem care as instructed.

60. A patient who is in the process of dying is having increased secretions and is heard gurgling as they try to breath. Which of the following is NOT an appropriate action for the nursing assistant to take?
   a. Turn the resident's head to the side.
   b. Use equipment to suction secretions.
   c. Recommend a reduction in fluid intake.
   d. Use a dehumidifier in the patient's room.

Answer Explanations #4

1. D: The safest place for a patient's belongings would be in the closet of their room so that they have easy access to it. Patients often have personal items with them, and it is important that the nursing assistant is compliant with the hospital's policies to help protect these items. The other choices are in areas that could not be secured or watched by the patient.

2. A: Posting slander or information that may reflect badly on the organization in a public domain can harm an organization and is considered unethical behavior. Additionally, hospitals may have policies restricting what can be posted on employees' social media. If the nursing assistant has any grievances with their organization, these should be handled through Human Resources department.

3. C: Nursing assistants must be registered in their state's Nurse Aide Registry. Employers will use this registry to verify eligibility and employment. Choices *A* and *B* may be required to complete the nursing assistant program but are not needed to verify eligibility if they are part of the registry. Choice *D* is incorrect because nursing assistants utilize the Nurse Aide Registry; RNs and LPNs utilize the state Board of Nursing.

4. C: Having a failed attempt on the CNA exam would not preclude an organization from hiring a nursing assistant if they passed the exam on a subsequent attempt. The remaining choices are examples of abuse, criminal charges, and references from previous employers that may stop a candidate from being hired or cause further review of the application.

5. A: Taking routine blood pressure measurements every four hours is within the scope of practice for the nursing assistant. Choices *B* and *C* are incorrect because they are not within the nursing assistant's scope of practice unless they have additional training. Choice *D* is incorrect because giving medication is not within the nursing assistant's scope of practice, regardless of additional training.

6. B: Giving medication is not within the nursing assistant's scope of practice, even if directed by the nurse. The most appropriate action is to not give the medication and report this to the supervisor to make sure proper policy is followed. Choice *A* and *C* are incorrect because even though the nurse already charted the medication as given and the charge nurse was notified, it is still not within the nurse assistant's scope of practice to give the medication. Choice *D* is incorrect because it would be a nurse's decision to make if it was appropriate to give or hold a blood pressure medication.

7. D: The speech therapist's role is to help evaluate swallowing, speech, and language. Speech therapists are commonly consulted for patients who have tracheostomies due to swallowing and speech difficulties. Choice *A* is incorrect because a physical therapist works with patients to improve their physical mobility through various assessments and exercises. Choice *B* is incorrect because a respiratory therapist focuses on respiratory treatment, airway clearance, and various supplemental oxygenation devices. Choice *C* is incorrect because an occupational therapist helps patients do regular activities of daily living, such as brushing their teeth, buttoning their shirt, and combing their hair.

8. B: It is part of the nursing assistant's role to be involved in the care plan and report any changes or updates to the nurse, such as any worsening conditions like increased coughing that could indicate aspiration. Choice *A* is incorrect because this is often completed by a speech therapist. Choice *C* is incorrect because lowering the head of the bed down when the patient is eating and drinking can increase risk of aspiration, coughing, and choking. Choice *D* is incorrect because medication

administration should be completed by the nurse and is outside of the scope of practice of the nursing assistant.

9. C: The three main components of communication are the sender, the message, and the receiver. Although tone and context are important aspects of communication, they are not among the main components of communication.

10. A: Using a medically trained translator to speak with a patient who does not speak or understand English helps reduce communication barriers and provides better education and understanding to patients. Choice *B* is incorrect because a patient who has had a recent change in level of consciousness should not make medical decision regarding code status. Choice *C* is incorrect because a patient with cataracts has a visual impairment, and written instructions rely on eyesight. Choice *D* is incorrect because a patient who has had a stroke and has aphasia may have difficulty speaking, understanding speech, or communicating properly. Therefore, they cannot give verbal consent.

11. D: Using silence when talking with patients can help prompt them to clarify what they are saying and offer the space to add more information. Choice *A* is incorrect because asking personal questions can be an important aspect of therapeutic communication that helps a patient open up and discuss their feelings and concerns. Choice *B* is incorrect because "yes" or "no" questions are close-ended and do not offer the opportunity for the patient to add more information; instead, ask open-ended questions. Choice *C* is incorrect because "why" questions can come off as interrogating or demanding.

12. D: After caring for this patient, the best way to prevent the spread of infection is for the nursing assistant to wash their hands thoroughly with soap and water since Clostridium difficile (C. diff) can only be killed through this method. Hand sanitizer does not kill C. diff and would be ineffective in disinfecting after caring for this patient; therefore, Choice *A* is incorrect. Choice *B* is incorrect because it is not required to wear a surgical mask with a patient who has C. diff. Choice *C* is incorrect because bleach wipes should not be used on the skin.

13. B: Nausea and vomiting are signs that an infection may be systemic and infecting the entire body. Other signs of a systemic infection can include weakness, fatigue, change in mental status, increased respiratory rate, and weight loss. The remaining choices are signs that the patient may have a localized infection.

14. B: Shortness of breath is not an expected symptom associated with a traumatic brain injury. The remaining choices of unequal pupils, persistent vomiting, restlessness, and irritability are all examples of symptoms commonly associated with a brain injury. Other symptoms that may indicate a serious head injury are convulsion, facial or skull fracture, inability to move limbs, severe headaches, loss of consciousness, slurred speech, distorted vision, and clear fluid from the ears, nose, or mouth.

15. D: Patients with influenza should be placed on droplet precautions. The nursing assistant should wear at least a mask and gloves. Choice *A* is incorrect because airborne precautions are used for infections such as Tuberculosis, measles, and chickenpox. Choice B is incorrect because contact precautions are used for conditions such as C. diff, norovirus, or with patients who are incontinent or have ostomy bags. Choice *C* is incorrect because standard precautions are used to prevent contact by blood, bodily fluids, broken skin, rashes, and mucous membranes that do not have additional known infectious agents.

197

16. C: The correct order to remove PPE is gloves, goggles, gown, and then mask. When removing the equipment, make sure to remove equipment by holding onto the non-contaminated parts and properly disposing of the equipment. The remaining choices do not show PPE removal in the correct order.

17. A: Providing oral care is a type of dirty task that should be completed last to lower the chance of contamination and infection. Other dirty tasks include changing dirty linens, bathing a patient, emptying a bedpan, and wound care. The remaining choices are clean tasks that should be performed first. Other clean tasks include taking vitals, assessing a patient, and transferring a patient from bed to chair.

18. C: Being around water, such as baths, showers, or pools, can increase the likelihood of being struck by lightning during a thunderstorm. Choice *A* is incorrect because patients, staff, and visitors should be instructed to stand away from any windows during a thunderstorm. Choice *B* and *D* are incorrect because electrical equipment should not be used or kept near people during a thunderstorm due to risk of electrocution.

19. A: Since the patient was able to nod their head and show consciousness, the nursing assistant should not start CPR. CPR should only be started if the patient goes unconscious. The remaining choices are all correct steps the nursing assistant should take if a patient is choking and conscious.

20. B: In the case of excessive bleeding, the nursing assistant should continue to speak with the patient to monitor their responsiveness until additional help or EMS arrives. Choice *A* is incorrect because a patient with excessive bleeding should be instructed to sit or lie down. Choice *C* is incorrect because gauze, a towel, or a shirt should be held tightly on the wound with continuous pressure to help slow and stop the bleeding. Choice *D* is incorrect because the patient should hold the injured area above the level of their heart to help slow bleeding.

21. D: This patient is most likely having an allergic reaction because they are experiencing difficulty breathing, nausea, tongue swelling, rapid heart rate, and low blood pressure. Additionally, they were started on a new medication which could be the cause of the allergic reaction. Patients experiencing allergic reactions may also experience wheezing, fainting, dizziness, sense of impending doom, or chest pain. Although the remaining choices may share some of the same symptoms, this scenario most closely describes a patient experiencing an allergic reaction.

22. D: In the case of a fire, the nursing assistant should not open windows in the area surrounding the fire because this can cause the fire to spread. Instead, doors and windows surrounding the fire should be closed. The remaining choices are correct steps to take in a fire emergency. Remember the acronym RACE: *Rescue* yourself and others from the fire, *Activate* the fire alarm or call 911, *Contain* the fire, *Extinguish* the fire.

23. A: For a patient who has pressure ulcers (or is at high risk of developing them), massaging bony prominences can cause further skin breakdown and thin the layers of the skin. The nursing assistant should avoid massaging bony prominences such as heels, ankles, coccyx, elbows, knees, or hips. The remaining choices are all actions the nursing assistant should take to help prevent a patient from developing or aggravating a pressure ulcer.

24. B: A pressure ulcer that has damage or skin loss through several layers and causes shallow ulceration, abrasion, or blistering is considered a Stage II pressure ulcer. Choice *A* is incorrect because a Stage I pressure ulcer is when the skin is painful, red, and warm to the touch, but is still unbroken. Choice *C* is incorrect because a Stage III pressure ulcer is full thickness loss of skin that is deep enough to

198

show fatty tissue and may cause tunneling. Stage IV pressure ulcers are the same as Stage III except there is deeper ulceration that exposes muscle, bone, or tendon; therefore, Choice *D* is incorrect.

25. C: A patient with redness, swelling, and pain in their calf is exhibiting signs of a blood clot called deep vein thrombosis (DVT). The nursing assistant should immediately notify the nurse so they can further assess the situation. Patients with a known blood clot or who are at risk of developing one should be encouraged to ambulate as appropriate every two hours to help promote circulation, so Choice *A* is incorrect. Massaging an affected limb with DVT could cause the clot to break off and travel to the lungs, causing a pulmonary embolism that can be life-threatening, so Choice *B* is incorrect. It is important to reposition a patient at least every two hours if they are unable to do so independently, but the nurse should be notified of these findings first before resuming regular care, so Choice *D* is incorrect.

26. D: A patient who is at risk of developing a DVT should be given sequential compression devices (SCDs) to help promote blood flow and circulation, especially in patients who are confined to their beds. Patients who are more mobile can be given anti-embolism stockings to help reduce risk of developing a DVT. The remaining choices are not devices that help reduce the risk of developing a DVT.

27. A: Patients who are immobile and cannot independently use the toilet may experience fear or anxiety over toileting needs. They are also at higher risk of becoming incontinent. It is important for the nursing assistant to be available for frequent toileting and for reassurance. Choice *B* is incorrect because leaving a patient on a bedpan for prolonged periods of time can cause discomfort and skin breakdown. Choice *C* is incorrect because an indwelling catheter for a patient who can eliminate completely with assistance would be inappropriate and put them at unnecessary risk for infection. Choice *D* is incorrect because although patients have the right to refuse, the nursing assistant's initial response should be to encourage fluid intake and reassure the patient that they will be present for toileting needs.

28. A: Stiffening of the joints is an example of contractures that can be common in immobile patients. Although an immobile patient may be at higher risk for the remaining choices, they do not match the symptoms described.

29. C: Repositioning a patient at least every two hours and using devices to help support spinal alignment and reduce pressure points are all examples of comfort measures for a patient. Choice *A* is incorrect because self-image relates to how patient's view themselves. Patients who are immobile may experience a lower self-image due to loss of independence. Choice *B* is incorrect because activity tolerance is the extent to which a patient can actively participate in activities of daily living. Choice *D* is incorrect because strength and endurance refers to the patient's ability to use their muscle strength to perform activities for prolonged periods of time.

30. D: The patient in this scenario experienced a rapid change in cognition, speech, and memory over just a few hours. This is not an expected finding and could be the sign of a medical emergency; therefore, the nursing assistant should notify the nurse right away. Patients may experience cognitive changes; however, these changes are only normal if they happen gradually. The remaining choices are not appropriate for a rapid change in cognition, though they would be appropriate actions to take with a patient who was experiencing expected, gradual changes in cognition.

31. B: To help support a patient who is experiencing psychosocial changes related to not being able to see family members, the nursing assistant can help them put out photos or personal items that reminds the patient of their family. This can help provide comfort to the patient and make them feel more

199

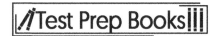

welcome in a new environment. Choices *A* and *D* are incorrect because these actions support a physical change, not a psychosocial change. Physical changes refer to changes in a patient's body system such as decreased circulation, lung capacity, healing capacity, strength, and endurance. Choice *C* is incorrect because this action is supporting a cognitive change, not a psychosocial change. Cognitive change refers to changes in a patient's memory, attention, decision-making, speech, and language.

32. B: As a patient ages, it is expected that they may have decreased digestion, not increased. The remaining choices are all examples of expected physical changes for an elderly patient. Additionally, patients may experience decreased circulation, decreased lung capacity, decreased healing capacity, decreased skin elasticity, constipation, incontinence, and decrease or loss of other senses.

33. A: In Maslow's Hierarchy of Needs, the second most basic need is safety. Starting with the most basic need, the order of Maslow's Hierarchy is physiological needs, safety, love/belonging, esteem, and self-actualization; therefore, the remaining choices are incorrect.

34. D: Having a sense of responsibility, achievement, and reputation are examples of the need for esteem in Maslow's Hierarchy. Choice *A* is incorrect because social need refers to family and relationships. Choice *B* is incorrect because the need for safety refers to a person's physical safety as well as job security and stability. Choice *C* is incorrect because self-actualization refers to the feeling of creativity, authenticity, and reaching one's full potential.

35. C: A patient who is experiencing a loss of independence and control should be given opportunities to help reclaim their autonomy. These include having them plan their daily routines and encouraging them to participate within their environment and build relationships with other residents. Choice *A* is incorrect because although it may be common for patients to feel this in a long-term care facility, their concerns should be addressed, and the nursing assistant should help them regain their independence. Choice *B* is incorrect because only suggesting medication may mask the underlying problem and does not directly address the patient's concerns. Choice *D* is incorrect because this may be an unsafe activity for the patient, and their independence can be promoted through safer activities.

36. C: Atrophy is the loss of muscle mass and muscle strength. Atrophy is often related to immobility and poorer health status. Although the remaining choices are related to a patient's muscle health and strength, they are incorrect because they are not the health condition that is described.

37. A: Checking on the patient every two hours is part of standardized fall precautions. Although the nursing assistant can ask the family for their participation in keeping the patient safe, they should still check on the patient themselves. A patient should not be restrained as a strategy to reduce falls. Lights should be on to help the patient visualize their environment.

38. A: Sitting with the patient is an effective alternative to restraints, as the nursing assistant can provide reorientation and a safe environment. If necessary, security could be notified while the nursing assistant remains with the patient. A patient should not be sedated if they can be kept safe by having someone sit with them. A patient should not be encouraged to leave the hospital or nursing home, even if they are combative.

39. B: The patient would be considered alert and oriented x 2. She knows her name and her location, but she is not oriented to the date or situation. *Alert* refers to being awake and responsive. *Orientation* refers to the patient's awareness of their name and the time, place, and situation.

40. C: Crutches are an example of an assistive device for mobility. Physical and occupational therapies assist with mobility but are not devices. Restraints do not assist with mobility.

41. A: Collaboration, cooperation, and interdependence all describe teamwork. Initiative typically describes individual action.

42. C: A gait belt is the most appropriate choice because one person would be able to assist them. A bed alarm does not provide additional ambulation assistance. A Hoyer lift and a wheelchair are not necessary with a 1 assist patient.

43. A: Back and neck injuries can be avoided by using proper body mechanics.

44. B: The nursing assistant should report this significant change in the patient's blood pressure to the RN immediately. The nursing assistant should not wait until they are finished with their other patients because this could signify a medical emergency. A nursing assistant does not call the MD. Even if the patient is acting normal, the change in blood pressure is still very significant.

45. C: Low blood pressure is called hypotension. High blood pressure is called hypertension. Hypoglycemia is low blood glucose, and hyperglycemia is high blood glucose.

46. C: Kidney failure does not cause chest pain. GERD, or gastroesophageal reflux disease, causes heartburn, which can cause chest pain. Coronary artery disease can cause a lack of oxygen to the heart muscle, which can also cause chest pain. Pleurisy, or inflammation of the lining around the lungs, can also cause chest pain.

47. B: Chronic illnesses or conditions are long-term. Emergent refers to conditions that are immediately life threatening. Acute illnesses are present but usually short-term, and urgent conditions require help as soon as possible.

48. D: Elopement means wandering away from a treatment facility. Leaving AMA, or against medical advice, implies that the patient is aware of the risks and benefits of leaving and chooses to leave a treatment facility. A person who elopes is not necessarily refusing treatment. A patient may be confused, but the act of leaving or wandering away is elopement.

49. D: The nursing assistant should notify the supervisor if they are scratched, hit, or otherwise abused by a patient. That way, the appropriate measures can be executed to take care of the patient as well as the nursing assistant. The nursing assistant may not restrain the patient without a doctor's order. The MD must be notified by the RN, not the nursing assistant. Sedation and restraints are used as last resorts, and only with a doctor's order.

50. A: TED hose help to prevent blood clots. They are used to promote, not prevent, circulation. They do not prevent breathing difficulties or falls.

51. D: A specialty mattress is appropriate for this patient. The nursing assistant can suggest this as a measure to prevent further skin breakdown. Routine repositioning should be done on every patient, even if there is no skin breakdown already present. The patient may not be in pain. A bath would not necessarily help with the skin breakdown.

52. B: The nursing assistant should check on this patient immediately because of the patient's hypotension and lethargy. The nursing assistant should not assume that the RN is already aware. This patient takes priority over other patients and should be seen sooner rather than later.

53. D: Tremors, delirium, anxiety, and increased heart rate are all symptoms of alcohol withdrawal. Additionally, the patient has a known history of drinking which should indicate to the nursing assistant that these symptoms may be related to withdrawal. Choice *A* is incorrect because symptoms of dementia would include a slow progression of cognitive difficulty and confusion. Choice *B* is incorrect because an MI would present as shortness of breath, fatigue, dizziness, nausea, cold sweats, and pressure or pain on the chest, shoulder, back, or jaw. Choice *C* is incorrect because common symptoms of PTSD are having trouble sleeping, being easily frightened, engaging in self-destructive behavior, feeling guilty or irritable, and re-experiencing trauma.

54. B: Palliative care refers to care provided to patients with a life-long or life-limiting disease that centers around comfort for the patient and maximizing quality of life. Choice *A* is incorrect because curative care focuses on restoring a patient's health back to their baseline after an illness or injury. Choice *C* is incorrect because urgent care focuses on conditions that are not life threatening but still need immediate attention such as sprains, stomachaches, and minor cuts or burns. Choice *D* is incorrect because long-term care is for when patients can no longer complete their regular activities of daily living and often need to stay in specific long-term care facilities.

55. A: The correct order for the five stages of grief in the Kubler-Ross grieving model are denial, bargaining, depression, anger, and acceptance. This is a general outline for how patients may grieve; however, it is possible that a person may experience these out of order or may not go through each stage. The remaining choices are incorrect because they do not put the stages of grief in the anticipated order.

56. B: Asking an open-ended question to a patient about their feelings is an example of correct therapeutic communication. This puts the patient at the focus of the conversation and helps open an honest dialogue for the patient to work through their feelings. These conversations may feel uncomfortable to have, but they are important for patients' care and healing. Choice *A* is incorrect because it may invalidate what a patient is feeling and give false reassurance. Choice *C* is incorrect because grief is inevitable and should not be ignored or dismissed. Instead, the nursing assistant should try to assist the patient through their grief. Choice *D* is incorrect because this gives the patient false reassurance and may invalidate their feelings. While it is important to remain optimistic for patients, encouragement should still be realistic.

57. C: In certain cultures, such as Hinduism, it is part of their customs for the family members of the deceased to wash the body and complete post-mortem care. As long as there are no safety concerns, the nursing assistant should respect the family's culture and provide them with supplies to complete this care. The remaining choices are not correct because they do not allow the family to provide care that is respectful of their culture. The nursing assistant should be aware that different religions and cultures have different customs surrounding death, and they should be respectful of those customs.

58. A: Patients who are in the process of dying may appear to be asleep, but they can still be aware of their surroundings and hear what is going on around them. It is important for the nursing assistant to still speak with the patient, identify who they are, and explain any tasks they are completing. Choice *B* is incorrect because this patient may still be aware of their surroundings and be confused or scared if the

nursing assistant begins performing perineal care unannounced. Choice *C* is incorrect because this patient may not be able to awaken fully, and they could become startled by bright lights and louder noises. Choice *D* is incorrect because the nursing assistant should understand that the patient may still be sleeping later, and perineal care should not be postponed because this can cause discomfort for the patient and lead to skin breakdown.

59. D: After a patient is declared dead, it is possible and common for changes to still occur with the body. This may make it appear as though the patient gasps, cries, has muscle twitches or slight movement, and may urinate or have a bowel movement. It can be distressing to provide post-mortem care and see these signs in a patient, but the nursing assistant should understand that these tasks provide compassionate and respectful care for the patient. If the patient has already been pronounced dead by a doctor or nurse, then there is no cause for alarm and the nursing assistant can continue regular post-mortem care; therefore, the remaining choices are incorrect.

60. D: If available, the nursing assistant should use a cool air humidifier to help reduce secretions, not a dehumidifier. Increased secretions may be common in a patient who is dying. The remaining choices are incorrect because they are all appropriate actions to take to help reduce the discomfort caused by secretions.

Index

Dear CNA Test Taker,

We would like to start by thanking you for purchasing this study guide for your CNA exam. We hope that we exceeded your expectations.

Our goal in creating this study guide was to cover all of the topics that you will see on the test. We also strove to make our practice questions as similar as possible to what you will encounter on test day. With that being said, if you found something that you feel was not up to your standards, please send us an email and let us know.

We would also like to let you know about other books in our catalog that may interest you.

ATI TEAS

This can be found on Amazon: amazon.com/dp/1637759886

CEN

amazon.com/dp/1637752229

DTR

amazon.com/dp/1628458232

We have study guides in a wide variety of fields. If the one you are looking for isn't listed above, then try searching for it on Amazon or send us an email.

Thanks Again and Happy Testing!
Product Development Team
info@studyguideteam.com

FREE Test Taking Tips Video/DVD Offer

To better serve you, we created videos covering test taking tips that we want to give you for FREE. **These videos cover world-class tips that will help you succeed on your test.**

We just ask that you send us feedback about this product. Please let us know what you thought about it—whether good, bad, or indifferent.

To get your **FREE videos**, you can use the QR code below or email freevideos@studyguideteam.com with "Free Videos" in the subject line and the following information in the body of the email:

      a. The title of your product
      b. Your product rating on a scale of 1-5, with 5 being the highest
      c. Your feedback about the product

If you have any questions or concerns, please don't hesitate to contact us at info@studyguideteam.com.

Thank you!

Made in the USA
Monee, IL
01 May 2023

32788491R00122